BASEBALL HISTORY 4

An Annual of Original Baseball Research

Baseball and American Society
Series ISBN 0-88736-566-3

BASEBALL HISTORY 4

An Annual of Original Baseball Research

Edited by
Peter Levine

Meckler

BASEBALL HISTORY
An Annual of Original Baseball Research

ISSN 1047-3521
ISBN 0-88736-578-7

Meckler Publishing, 11 Ferry Lane West, Westport, CT 06880.
Meckler Ltd., 247-249 Vauxhall Bridge Road, London SW1V 1HQ, U.K.

Printed on acid free paper.
Printed in the United States of America.

Contents

EDITOR'S NOTE

This year's edition of *Baseball History* focuses both on individuals and on larger developments within baseball guaranteed to broaden the knowledge of even our most knowledgeable readers. John Holway and James Overmyer enlarge our understanding of the talent of African-American ballplayers and the discrimination they faced by, respectively, exploring the exploits of Piper Davis and Frank Grant. Robert Cole's essay on baseball barnstorming, Jesse Berrett's story of how organized baseball sought to stay alive financially during the Great Depression, and Joel Franks' original discussion of the early days of professional baseball in California offer a variety of connections between baseball and American culture.

On an international note, Stephen Thompson's special story of an American baseballer's adventures in Japan provides insights into that culture, which, among other things, will make you think differently every time you pass a Kentucky Fried Chicken outlet. Once again, Bill Kinsella offers us a baseball fantasy, joined this time by Bill Meissner, another award-winning writer with a timeless tale about fathers, sons, and baseball. Thanks to the good work of Fred Roberts, our review of last year's baseball books includes the efforts of a number of prominent authors and scholars such as Larry Ritter, Larry Gerlach, and Bruce Kuklick. And back by popular demand is a bibliography of all baseball books published over the last year, ably compiled by Richard Arpi. Enjoy!

Peter Levine
East Lansing, Michigan

Organizing California Baseball, 1859–1893*

JOEL FRANKS

Post-gold rush California was a region of startling paradoxes. It promised a glorious escape from the Puritan work ethic and just as glorious a manifestation of what industry, business acumen, thrift, and ruthlessness could bring to the individual of little means. The mines in the mother lode and the faro tables in San Francisco offered a gilded promise of instant wealth for the very lucky, very shrewd, and very dishonest. Yet there were also shoes to make, goods to sell, livestock to raise, and land to harvest for those who considered California one of America's last sanctuaries; a place where hard work and the vote would save the common man from the concentration of power that was in the hands of a few businessmen in the North and slave masters in the South.[1]

Sports, as well, became precious as many Californians learned there was good money to be made in a climate that encouraged year-round sporting events. Sports became just as precious to others, who simply looked upon them as one of many ways to develop a sense of community in a state where so many people were newcomers. This essay describes the manner in which the organization of professional baseball in late-nineteenth-century California contributed to community development and reinforcement.

California professional baseball in the nineteenth century did more than provide a form of community and foster the Golden State's rampant boosterism; it also illuminates a significant social and economic process—what Alan Trachtenberg calls "the incorporation of America." For Trachtenberg, the last quarter of the nineteenth century witnessed "the emergence of a changed, more tightly structured society with new *hierarchies of control,* and also changed conceptions of that society." Moreover, this process generated regional as well as class conflict, because "[t]he corporate mode inscribed itself in a continental system. Its principle was coordination, and its method subordination of individ-

---

*I would like to thank Peter Levine for his editorial help.

ual units (factories, offices, retail counters—and whole cities) to *metropolitan headquarters.* Not rationalization alone, not the production–distribution nexus, but the principle of hierarchy governed the development." (emphasis mine)[2]

The nationalization of professional baseball, the effort to link the West Coast to the capitals of the professional baseball establishment in the industrialized/ urbanized East and Midwest, reproduced this incorporation process.[3] By the end of the 1880s, it was just not enough that professional baseball appeared to capture the hearts of many Californians. Rather, "the principle of hierarchy" manifested in organized baseball east of the Rockies had to impose its control over professional baseball in California, meeting a mixed bag of resistance and consent from Californians.

Although California's first club was organized in San Francisco in 1859, it was not until after the Civil War that anything resembling baseball fever infected Californians. During 1866 and 1867, several nines were assembled in the San Francisco Bay area, prompting San Francisco's *Daily Alta California* to remark that "[b]aseball clubs are now the rage, and, as nearly every Engine Company in the city has organized one, the hose boys of Old California Engine Co. No. 4 have followed suit and organized one to be known as the Lone Star Base Ball Club."[4]

Convinced of the rapid, undisciplined growth of baseball in their midst, several clubs from the San Francisco Bay area launched the Pacific Coast Base Ball Convention in the hopes of attracting membership from nines throughout California and imposing order on the way the youthful sport was played in the Golden State. According to convention rules, members were asked to comport themselves as gentlemen amateurs. Indeed, proper behavior at convention meetings was deemed nearly as important as proper behavior on the playing field. Fines of one dollar and fifty cents were levied for boisterous conduct, smoking, and leaving meetings before adjournment. The convention denied players permission to argue with umpires. Nor was player involvement in betting on the outcome of games countenanced. Most important, the convention banned professional ballplayers and expelled and blacklisted clubs that knowingly used professionals.[5]

The Pacific Baseball Convention's stress upon propriety no doubt reflected the social background of its membership. San Francisco's best-publicized ballplayers in the 1860s were, as in other American communities, a mixture of professional men, clerks, and skilled craftsmen. In 1860, the most important baseball club in San Francisco was the Eagles. The club's president and catcher was M.E. Gelston, who clerked for his family's real estate firm. Vice President Michael Kennedy worked as a waiter, and one of the team's stars was a smelter, John M. Fisher. Ten years later, the Eagles' delegate to the Pacific Baseball Convention was fire marshall John M. Durkee. A law clerk named Marcus Wiggin represented the Pacifics. J.G. Carson, a notary public, served on behalf of the Bradericks, while C.A. Carpenter, a bookkeeper, was a Bay City player. The one worker delegate was machinist T.J. Cashmen of the Atlantics.[6]

Despite the Pacific Coast Base Ball Convention's concern for propriety, the sport drew a very demonstrative gambling element. Undoubtedly some participants earned money for playing exceedingly well or poorly. As a consequence of local baseball's inability, or unwillingness, to isolate itself from the seamier aspects of San Francisco society, the San Francisco *Chronicle* grumbled that "baseball, when played for exercise by the flaccid-muscled clerk or as an agreeable recreation by the hard-working mechanic, will always have a good word from the press and be regarded with favor from the people." However, it insisted that the public would no longer tolerate baseball's existence if gambling continued to shadow the sport.[7]

Perhaps the *Chronicle*'s admonishment was not out of place, since the fervor displayed for baseball in 1867 waned considerably in 1868. However, the fall of 1869 witnessed a turning point in the development of baseball as a spectator sport in California. At that time, baseball enthusiasts were presented with the convergence of two events—the opening of the transcontinental railroad and the willingness of the famed Cincinnati Red Stockings to exhibit their skills anywhere in the country for, of course, the right price. The Red Stockings, in touring the United States in 1869, had beaten all of their opponents, frequently quite handily. The clubs they encountered in San Francisco and Sacramento were woefully inept in comparison to the pioneering professionals. Still, baseball fans and players in California were enthralled by the Red Stockings' peerless mastery of the game. The professionals, and not the ostensibly gentlemen amateurs, pointed the way toward progress.

A reporter for the *Daily Alta California* was amazed at the backwardness of California baseball. Red Stocking pitchers, for example, actually propelled the ball by advancing their legs with their arms, whereas pitchers in San Francisco stood stiffly while flipping the ball forward to the understandably optimistic batter. But historian Robert Barney may have exaggerated when he claims that the Red Stockings "charmed multitudes, whetted the supporting appetite of all who paid witness to their playing prowess, and most certainly developed in California the germ of the idea that baseball was an important entertainment."[8] The Red Stockings' visit amply demonstrated that professional baseball could cultivate an audience in California. Reportedly, good crowds of 2,000 watched their local heroes dismantled by the professionals. Still, it wasn't until 1878 that anything resembling professional baseball on a significant basis surfaced in California.

It is not clear why it took so long. For most of the 1870s, Californians, especially in the Bay area and Sacramento, played and watched the game with varying levels of enthusiasm. Certainly, San Francisco had the makings of a fine baseball town. Regardless of its obvious geographical isolation from the communities represented in the Eastern and Midwestern professional leagues, San Francisco was about as "big league" as most American cities claiming major league status at this time, if not more so. It had a large working population eager for entertainment, and an ambitious cadre of entrepreneurs willing to provide that entertainment for a profit. Since its gold rush birth, San Francisco had supported a variety of theatrical ventures, as well as such spectator sports as horse racing, pedestrianism, and prize fighting.[9]

Perhaps the visit of the Red Stockings to California set back the development of baseball as a commercialized amusement in San Francisco; perhaps it whet

These photographs of school boy baseball clubs in Santa Clara, California, (c. 1895) suggest the pervasiveness of the national pastime during the late 19th century. (Photo: Santa Clara University Archives)

appetites for baseball, but not the kind of baseball played by the home-grown boys of San Francisco, Oakland, and Sacramento. Newspaper accounts of games in the early and mid-1870s typically praised the enthusiasm of California players, but not necessarily their prowess. In 1874, a relatively large, fashionable crowd reportedly showed up in Oakland to watch a game between the Oakland and Grand Central nines. Sadly, according to the San Francisco *Chronicle,* "from the fourth inning to the end of the game, the playing on both sides was simply execrable and not worthy of note."[10]

Nevertheless, by the spring of 1878, it was decided that San Francisco was ready for weekly professional games. An organization called the Pacific Baseball League staged Sunday ball games and featured Eastern professionals such as Ferguson Malone, as well as up-and-coming local stars and future major leaguers such as Jerry Denny, Sandy Nava, Bob Blakiston, and Andy Piercy.

Certainly, the fact that the professional version of the national pastime had achieved some success in Eastern and Midwestern cities undoubtedly influenced the decision to initiate an earnest venture into the business of professional baseball. The effort of the infant National League to restrict contract-jumping and discipline those players deemed miscreants made California baseball more appealing to Eastern professionals. At the same time, the skills of some youthful California ballplayers were maturing to a point where they could be presented unashamedly to a critical audience.

But politics also might have played a consequential role. It was a curious time for San Franciscans and other Californians, who found themselves in the midst of a serious national social, economic, and political crisis that nurtured unemployment, class conflict, and ethnic antagonism. Many of them responded by forming and supporting the potent Workingmen's Party of California (WPC), which organized Sunday rallies on a site near what is now San Francisco's civic center. Decrying monopoly and Chinese immigration, the WPC's greatest threat to the established order was seen in its ability to undermine the two-party system, in particular the Democratic Party whose constituency of Irish and other white immigrant workers and tradesmen had scattered to the WPC.[11]

Interestingly, the primary venue for professional baseball in San Francisco was the Recreation Grounds in the Mission District. Its owners and operators were Democratic politicians, among whose number was Captain Al Fritz, a man who once threatened to train the guns of the militia battery he led on the WPC. As Steven Riess points out, the relationship between politics and professional baseball in urban America was extensive. In San Francisco, particularly, the ability of Democrats to withstand and eventually smash the WPC threat was based largely upon their success at identifying working-class recreation and leisure pursuits with the party of Jefferson and Jackson. Democrats like saloon-owner Fritz might well have believed that professional baseball diverted people from WPC rallies, demonstrated to voters that Democrats were good fellows, and put some money in Democratic party coffers.[12]

The Pacific Baseball League, according to the *Chronicle,* had its problems in 1878. Foremost was the instability of its clubs, resulting in constant personnel changes, accompanied by sloppy play. Also, players manifested a slovenly attitude toward what the *Chronicle* considered proper decorum. The newspaper complained that "it is clear that when ballplayers go upon the field with cigars or cigarettes in their mouths, their effectiveness is not increased . . . nor does it add to the beauties of the national pastime."[13]

Yet professional baseball held its own in San Francisco during the late 1870s. Not only did the Pacific Baseball League survive its inaugural season, but in 1879 it was joined by the California Baseball League. The two leagues were helped by well-known professionals seeking greener pastures in California. For example, an exceptional crowd of 4,000 people attended a Pacific League game in June, 1879. What made this game special was that a club called the Knicker-bockers had attracted the services of pitcher Edward "The Only" Nolan and catcher William Barnie, both of whom were noted Eastern veterans.[14]

Within a year, Barnie and Nolan were joined by Cal McVey, a long-time Red Stocking standout. On a barnstorming tour of California, the heavy-hitting, versatile McVey had taken a liking to the climate and decided to make San Francisco his home. His skills were, of course, well in demand among those promoting professional baseball in the Bay area, and he signed for the 1880 season with the Bay City club.[15]

The 1880 season dimmed the promise of professional baseball in the Bay area. Organizational confusion reigned even though few cities outside the National League could have boasted of better players. Two organizations, the Pacific Baseball and California Baseball Leagues, began the spring with a presumably stable number of clubs and set schedules. Within a few months, however, both leagues were in disarray. The California Baseball League, for example, started with four clubs: Bay City, the Athletics, the Knickerbockers, and San Francisco. The latter club dropped out when it refused to play Bay City, which in turned jumped to the Pacific Baseball League in July. Replacing the Bay City club in the California Baseball League was the Californian Club. At the outset, the Californian club fielded locals; but as Pacific Baseball League nines, such as Bay City, folded, "advantage was taken of the presence of several unemployed professionals, who were engaged with the understanding that the club's propor-tion of the gate receipts should be divided among them."[16]

It soon became apparent that the Californian club's Eastern professionals wanted just enough money to book comfortable passage back home, thus abandoning what remained of the California Baseball League. Sensing the Californian club's instability, the Knickerbocker and Athletic clubs arranged its expulsion. This prompted the *Chronicle* to grumble in October that "[t]he defection of the other clubs" in the California Baseball League "is due to a variety of causes, the principal being mismanagement and cupidity on the part of the club directors."[17]

Still, large, appreciative crowds often saw some good, even great, ballplayers in 1880. Aside from Nolan, Barnie, and McVey, formidable professionals such as William Sweeney, Bobby Mathews, James Devlin, Jim Whitney, and "Pud" Galvin appeared in San Francisco in 1880. The latter embarrassed the California League by jumping his nine month, $1200 contract to pitch for Buffalo. Of course, the California Baseball League was upset, and league directors took the laughably needless step of expelling Galvin "for decamp[ing] in a surreptitious and unprofessional manner for Buffalo." Moreover, the California League resolved to "caution the public and the upright and honorable men connected with the baseball profession to beware of said Galvin, and brand him as unworthy to be associated with honorable players."[18]

All in all, the bittersweet 1880 season apparently had turned a substantial portion of San Francisco's sporting public away from professional baseball, and the sport would suffer for nearly half a decade. Moreover, the narrow demographic foundations of California professional baseball in the early 1880s blended with a falling-off in the quality of the game to precipitate a decline in the national pastime's financial fortunes in the Golden State.

In California during the early 1880s, professional, commercialized baseball was limited nearly exclusively to San Francisco and Oakland. (A typical league may have consisted of three or four clubs from San Francisco and one from Oakland.) And the various San Francisco nines apparently were not distinguished from one another by politics, neighborhood, class, or ethnicity. Consequently, the kind of intense partisanship that helped to fill empty seats was largely missing. However, the development of keenly felt community rivalries that found expression on the baseball diamond generated profits for professional baseball promoters in the East and the Midwest.[19]

Less grave, but still important, was the fact that the opportunities for California's professional leagues to avail themselves of talented Easterners or to hold on to skilled locals dissipated in light of the proliferation of professional leagues throughout America during the early and mid-1880s. For instance, on the major league level, the National League was joined by the American Association in 1883, while the Union Association entered, and left, the scene in 1884. Accordingly, the quality of play displayed by professionals in California suffered significantly during these years as the market for good ballplayers expanded nationally.

Because of its narrow demographic base and its inability to lure and keep topflight talent, commercialized baseball in California was in a comparatively weak position to overcome the prevalent charges regarding the sobriety and honesty of professional ballplayers in the Golden State and elsewhere. The directors of the California League in 1883 demanded that no player consume liquor on the ball grounds and warned that drunkenness or any other form of indecorous behavior would result in the expulsion of the guilty parties, Yet, the California League soon had other things to worry about than whether its performers would show up sober at the ball grounds. For instance, the league was attacked by an epidemic of dishonest play during the early months of the 1883 season. By May, the California League had expelled seven players, including the famous Charley Sweeney, for trying to throw games.[20]

Even when its players were honest and sober, professional baseball in California presented neither much diligence nor skill during the early to mid-1880s. Too typical was a *Chronicle* commentary on the poor state of professional baseball in San Francisco early in 1884:

> This is the result of a falling-off of public patronage and interest in the game, owing to the many disappointments that have occurred through the failure of some of the best men of the different organizations to appear at various times; and until the

players themselves recognize the necessity of enforcing the strictest discipline in this respect, and also of playing in their best style, it will not be possible to revive the general interest in the game.[21]

Fortunately, the passion for baseball in San Francisco was kept alive in the winter. Indeed, during the early and mid-1880s, winter ball proffered a lifeline for the sport as a commercial enterprise in the Bay area during its dark days and a source of continued support when things started to look brighter after 1885. For winter ball in California provided an opportunity for some of the better ballplayers in the country to congregate, typically in San Francisco, and even in the growing southern California metropolis of Los Angeles, hitherto ignored by promoters of professionalism.

The perennial migration of "Easterners" back to their California homes was cause for celebration by local fans, who saw in the feats of Jerry Denny, Charley Sweeney, Jim Fogarty, Ed Morris, Fred Carroll, and Henry Moore, among others, proof of the worthiness of California baseball. Hence, a *Sporting Life* correspondent's rapturous description of various "Easterners" practicing at Central Park in San Francisco during the late fall of 1885:

> Charley Sweeney was pitching to San Francisco's favorite ballplayer, Jim McDonald, and Jim was receiving him in grand shape. "Silent" Bob Blakiston whom to know is to love and honor was on the field with the wonder, Jim Fogarty, the heavy-hitting, Hen Moore, the erratic Patsy Cahill, the cynical Live Taylor, steady Pete Meegan, gentleman George Fisher, genial Cal McVey, the brilliant "Daddy" Hayes and jovial Gagus.[22]

Winter baseball built on and reinforced community pride in San Francisco, while in Sacramento, the national pastime amassed fervent support in the spring and summer of 1885. Two teams, the Altas and Unions, were locked in a fierce rivalry for the community championship. On July 4, 1885, an enormous crowd of 10,000 people jammed Sacramento's Agricultural Park to watch the Altas and Unions play. By the end of the summer, however, the Altas had clearly surfaced as the better team. The dispirited Unions disbanded and, subsequently, Sacramento baseball fever subsided for a while.[23]

Yet, the emergence of the Altas as Sacramento's champion baseball team contributed enormously toward renewing interest in the national pastime as a commercial venture in San Francisco. With the rise of a presumably powerful Sacramento nine, baseball promoters cultivated an intercity rivalry between the Altas and San Francisco's best nine, the Haverlys. During the fall of 1885, a best-of-five-game series was staged between the Altas and the Haverlys. This series evoked a great deal of passion in San Francisco, and when the Haverlys took the deciding third game in San Francisco's Central Park, baseball took on a new, marketable life in San Francisco.[24]

By the end of 1885, a *Sporting Life* correspondent reported that in San Francisco "a great boom is raging here, 5,000 being the average attendance."[25] Other California regions also caught the baseball fever. Apparently, between San Francisco, Oakland, and Sacramento, was a strong enough fan base to encourage the reformation of the California League, and even a new organization, the California State League in 1886. Neither was truly a state league. Of the four clubs starting the season in the California League, only one hailed from outside of San Francisco—the Altas of Sacramento. And the Greenhood and Morans of Oakland competed against three San Francisco clubs in the California State League (CSL) until the East Bay contingent jumped leagues, thus strengthening the California League considerably.

With the fabrication of what was called the "baseball boom," there was considerable talk of looking to the East for models of how baseball should be organized on the West Coast. Before the 1886 season began, the *Chronicle* commended the California State League's objective of introducing "sound business practices" to the game by copying as much as possible the organizational structure of Eastern leagues. Recognizing that there was something called "Organized Baseball" taking hold east of the Rockies, and wishing to bring the two coasts closer together on the matter of professional baseball, the CSL applied for membership in the National Association. In so doing, it agreed to abide by the terms of organized baseball's National Agreement, which restricted player mobility between clubs and leagues by means of the reserve clause and the blacklist.[26]

After the season got under way successfully, the San Francisco correspondent for the *Sporting Life* claimed that applying the practices of eastern "organized baseball" to financial matters and player discipline had proven a boon to California baseball. He wrote that "the businesslike way in which baseball is now conducted here is largely responsible for the great boom. . . . The players are under control and the games are played regularly and on their merits."[27]

In actuality, professional baseball in California was still a long way from endearing itself to men like A.G. Spalding, who sought to bring some order to the sport at the expense of player freedom and the so-called "outlaw" league's ambition. For example, in California, players retained a significant amount of independence until 1889. They split the gate, and stars such as pitcher William Incell and catcher Lou Hardie could take home an impressive one hundred dollars each for a single game—well over a month's wage for a skilled shoe worker in one of San Francisco's factories. Moreover, they didn't always acknowledge the power of their contracts with their California clubs. In the spring of 1886, California League pitcher Jim Mullee ostensibly took the box in a state of intoxication. Scandalized, the California League suspended the pitcher, only to discover that he had found employment in the California State League, thus arousing suspicion that Mullee had put on an act to get out of his contractual arrangements with his former club.[28]

Although it is not mentioned in the contemporary paeans to the baseball boom in California, commercial baseball's promoters were wise enough to take advantage of the community rivalries that were becoming increasingly vociferous in the dawning of the state's age of boosterism. It was evident that community pride was inspired by the success of the community's ball club. Fans in Oakland and Sacramento took particular pleasure in seeing their teams defeat nines from San Francisco, as well as each other. The Oakland *Morning Times* credited the Greenhood and Morans with spurring on great sporting interest in the East Bay city. "The beauty of the sports that are given in this city," according to the *Morning Times,* "are given by amateurs who play to win and have not a money consideration in view. Whenever you find professionals on this coast, you will find hippodroming." But somehow the G & M's were different, and somehow their home grounds had become "the best athletic grounds in the state."[29]

Stirred by the popularity of the professionals, baseball fever swept much of the Golden State. The national press took notice of what was happening. In late June 1886, the *Sporting News* announced that "the two California leagues now have all they can do to handle the vast throngs of spectators that weekly assemble to witness the spirited contests between the competing clubs. Five thousand is no longer a myth, and ballparks are always adding to their seating capacities."[30]

The California League became one of America's most formidable minor leagues during the late 1880s. By 1887, it had vanquished the California State League and generally reigned unrivaled by competing organizations. The California State League's death was fostered early in the 1886 season when the formidable G & Ms switched allegiance to the California League. Although various promoters, notably former professional Andy Piercy, tried to take on the California League, such pretensions were quickly swept aside by what San Francisco sports scribes called "the league."[31]

The California League built an impressive baseball field on Haight Street near Golden Gate Park. The grounds were leased from the Market Street Railroad Company, which was, in turn, all too happy to take thousands of fans to and from the Haight Street Park every week during the season. Aside from making money for an urban transit system operated by Charles Crocker of the Southern Pacific Railroad, these grounds provided the showcase for California League baseball. Other communities with representatives in the California League built their own fields. But the Haight Street Park, which seated over 10,000 and often uncomfortably held more for key games, was the most remunerative.[32]

Over the years, California League fans were attracted by tight pennant races and well-known ballplayers such as George Van Haltren, Charley Sweeney, Ed "Live" Taylor, Hen Moore, George Stallings, Jerry Denny, Fred Carroll, Phil Knell, Heinie Reitz, Bill Lange, and Clark Griffith. Even the managers were colorful, controversial characters, who garnered followers and critics, but, most important, nurtured public interest in professional baseball in California.

Interestingly, the most popular California Leaguer was a man who, unlike George Van Haltren and Charley Sweeney, gained no renown in the East. Rather, he was a San Francisco-born, Jewish shoe cutter, who became a California League institution. Rube Levy was often pronounced the king of California League outfielders: a sure fly catcher, a deadly thrower, and a dangerous hitter. He performed consistently for San Francisco professional nines throughout the 1880s and into the 1890s, while other Californians moved on from town to town, league to league. Accordingly, the Haight Street fans were his for the asking. Those especially enamored with Levy were the unaccompanied boys exiled to an area beyond the left field foul line. Left fielder Levy was a hero to these "kindergarten" denizens, who, when they weren't trying to burn the stands down with their cigarettes, hooted with delight when he made his frequent running one-handed catches.[33]

Aside from Levy, California League players, always looking for opportunities in the East, rarely lasted long in a city. Voluntarily or through release and trades, a Charley Sweeney wound up in Stockton, San Francisco, and Oakland after returning to California for good after his curious major league career. The instability of team rosters from year to year consequently lent greater importance to the trio of managers dominating the California League from the Bay area.[34]

Each of these three men expressed different components of baseball entrepreneurship in the Gilded Age and after.[35] Thomas P. Robinson was the promoter and self-promoter. Henry Harris was the reserved, community-minded businessman. And Mike Finn was the baseball man. All three were fairly young when they took over California League clubs. Robinson, for example, was twenty-six when he became manager of the Greenhood and Morans. None of the three descended from Nob Hill or rose from Skid Row to become baseball magnates. Robinson was the son fo a Dutch ship ballaster; Harris was a clerk of German descent; and Finn was an Irish-born bootmaker/professional ballplayer.[36]

Robinson was a fixture in Oakland baseball from 1886 through 1893. Though some doubted his baseball acumen, no one doubted his capacity to generate publicity for himself, his team, and the league. None of his peers spent as much on opening day parades and brass bands as Robinson, and none shoved money at unemployed eastern ballplayers so gratuitously. "Robinson," the San Jose *Daily Herald* maintained in 1891, "is a hustling manager and he has a good team; and if it is not good enough he will hustle about until he makes it pretty nearly good enough."[37] The bottom line for Robinson and other baseball entrepreneurs down through the years was not how much money they spent, but how much money they stood to make through effective promotion and fielding a winning team.

Harris expressed a far more conservative approach to baseball management. Less flamboyant than Robinson, "Uncle" Henry began his managing career with the Haverlys. Although he possessed significant insight into how the game should be played, Harris tried to put the best men he could in uniform and leave them alone. Baseball played well was a good enough product for Harris to merchandise. Moreover, he made more of a concerted effort than his peers to sign local ballplayers. Whether Harris was motivated by a desire to keep his payroll down or by a real pride in San Francisco and California is not clear. Still, Harris's San Francisco nines were constant favorites of Haight Street fans, not just because they represented the city, but because they truly consisted of many San Franciscans.[38]

More colorful than Harris and more cautious with a dollar than Robinson, "Duke" Finn more effectively assumed the duties of a modern-day field manager than his contemporaries. He was once a fine California professional, and his judgment of baseball talent was exceptional. For example, his San Jose club of 1891 and 1892 had such outstanding players as Heinie Reitz, George Stallings, William Everett, and Jerry Denny. At the same time, he assiduously monitored the practice time of his players and demanded intelligent, disciplined play.[39]

Thanks to its magnates and players, the achievements of the California

George Van Haltren, in a photo presented to him with the compliments of the Oakland Baseball Club. (Photo: National Baseball Library, Cooperstown, N.Y.)

League inspired "Organized Baseball" to cut the wings of this outlaw aggregation by the late 1880s. Yet, the Eastern baseball establishment gave little thought to what was happening on the Pacific Coast until one of its architects, A.G. Spalding, discovered Californians blocking his design to sign George Van Haltren in 1887. Taking the box for the G & M's of Oakland in 1886, Van Haltren, now known as one of the finest outfielders never selected for the Hall of Fame, was one of the California League's premier pitchers. By the end of the 1886 season, it looked like Van Haltren would inevitably wind up with a major league club. Spalding's Chicago franchise reportedly was seeking to sign Van Haltren as early as November, 1886. But it was Pittsburgh's boss, Al Nimick, who finally signed Van Haltren early in 1887 at a bar near the Haight Street Grounds.[40]

However, Nimick was unable to put Van Haltren in a Pittsburgh uniform and wound up trading to Spalding his rights to the Californian. Despite the fact that now he was dealing with organized baseball's most powerful figure, Van Haltren balked at going East. He contended that he was always willing to consider Eastern engagements; however, his very ill mother was comforted by his continued presence in Oakland. At the same time, Van Haltren claimed Nimick had insulted him by selling his services to Spalding. In his judgment, the Eastern baseball establishment had treated him as "a piece of merchandise."[41]

Spalding, however, was unconvinced by Van Haltren's explanations, although the young man's mother did soon die. The Chicago magnate believed that the "outlaws" running the California League stood behind Van Haltren's reluctance to accept the challenge and the glory of big league ball. If the California League didn't want to confront the hostile power of "Organized Baseball," Spalding advised, then it had better stop urging Van Haltren to stay on the West Coast. The Oakland pitcher flirted with a blacklist, Spalding insisted, and California League bigwigs should recognize that any player competing against someone blacklisted, under the National Agreement, could also risk blacklisting. Not only would this jeopardize the future of California League players, but, just as important, California League profits. It would ruin winter ball in California by deterring the Jerry Dennys and Ed Morrises from playing in their home state, as well as alienating touring major league clubs which might otherwise pursue engagements in San Francisco and Sacramento.[42]

After his mother died, in June 1887 Van Haltren agreed to a contract with Chicago for $300 in advance and $300 a month.[43] However, the relationship between the California League and organized baseball remained troubled. California League owners, on the one hand, enjoyed the privilege of signing anyone they chose regardless of whether the player was blacklisted by the National Association or under contract to clubs bound by the National Agreement. On the other hand, as long as they were outside of organized baseball, their teams faced plundering without protection. This latter situation prompted the *Chronicle,* in November 1888, to call for the California League's acceptance of the National Agreement:

> As soon as a player here amounts to anything he is wanted in the east, and he is free to get up and just leave his manager in the lurch without protection; where, if this agreement was signed, he could not do this without being blacklisted and his release would have to be purchased.[44]

Still, the *Sporting Life* signaled concern that the California League was perhaps getting too powerful to control. According to *Sporting Life,* the California League's employment of players who were blacklisted under the National Agreement had become a significant problem. It stated:

> The California League surely needs looking after. It is a prosperous institution, pays good salaries and is apparently permanently established. Under the circumstances, no strong efforts should be spared to make the league an ally instead of a menace to National Agreement interests.[45]

Into the spring of 1889, baseball people inside and outside of the Golden State pressured the California League to surrender its outlaw status. However, league magnates moved slowly. The San Francisco correspondent to the *Sporting News* expressed some of the thinking going on in California baseball circles. The writer complained, "the big clubs have never hesitated to go out to California and steal a pitcher or two when they were needed."[46] Generally, this was not a dominant view; although the impatient *Sporting Life* wondered why Californians lingered so long outside of organized baseball. "If the California League can afford to go without protection well and good," it said. "But in case of future raids it should hold its peace."[47]

A few weeks later, the *Sporting Life* advised that joining the National Agreement would improve player behavior in the California League, which had signed a number of eastern players for the 1889 season. Many of these men reportedly were "addicted to drunkenness." However, they were immune to discipline, because a California League suspension went unrecognized throughout the country; thus, once kicked off a team, they could readily find employment elsewhere.[48]

Eventually, the *Sporting Life* triumphantly proclaimed that the California League was swayed by the arguments that it was in its interest to enlist in the ranks of organized baseball. "This will be a good thing," the weekly explained, "for the national game in general and the California League in particular, as the latter will now be excused from the invasion of outside influences and will have a chance to develop her own players and profit thereby accordingly."[49]

However, into the early 1890s, California League top brass and supporters remained somewhat unappreciative of organized baseball, a sentiment among Californians which endured well into the twentieth century. One writer for the *Sporting News* contended in 1891 that since joining the National Agreement, the California League was no longer a "mecca" for contract-jumpers.[50] But the *Chronicle* asserted that the California League had wasted $800 in trying to gain the benefits of the National Agreement. The league clubs were no safer from contract-jumpers than before, and "not withstanding the claims made by the board of control, the country is full of contract-jumpers from various clubs under the National Agreement."[51] While admitting to hiring players under contract elsewhere, the California League challenged organized baseball in 1891 to take it on. Its magnates had seen other clubs under the National Agreement raid their rosters, and they would only consider "giv[ing] up players received from [Eastern] clubs when [their] own stolen players were returned and not before."[52]

While not ardent in its embrace of organized baseball, the California League experienced nationalization, and the incorporation of professional baseball in other respects, during the late 1880s. For example, by 1890, California League teams no longer bore typical California social clubs' names such as the Altas or Pioneers, on the one hand, or those of theatrical or commercial sponsors such as the Haverlys or the Greenhood & Morans. Rather, the team names represented various large and medium-sized communities such as Sacramento, Stockton, and Oakland, as well as, of course, San Francisco.

By this time, the role of management visibly expanded as well. Consequently, California League players lost considerable control over their share of a team's earnings. Upon returning to Boston from a few years in the California League, catcher Jerry Hurley told a *Sporting Life* correspondent that during his sojourn in the Golden State, players split the receipts from California League games cooperatively. Each side got a third of the gate, while the owners of the ballpark pocketed the remaining third. Accordingly, California League players earned $100 to $200 a game as late as the 1888 season. However, Hurley remarked, a new order took over the California League in time for the 1889 season, an ambitious order determined to separate players from major financial decisions as well as limiting salaries.[53] Moreover, the California League sought to crack down on contract-jumpers and discipline problems. Such means as suspensions, fines, and, ultimately, the blacklist were used by California League magnates to keep players in line.

But the incorporation process here, as elsewhere in American life, faced conscious opposition and residual cultural practices. California League players didn't suffer their employers' growing command of financial decisions silently. Many California Leaguers and California League alumni were sympathetic to the cause of the Players' League in 1890; not a surprising turn of events considering the Golden State's (in particular San Francisco's) strong support for labor and populist movements.[54] At times, furthermore, league teams collectively went public with their salary grievances. In 1890, Sacramento players refused to participate in a play-off game against San Francisco unless promised half the gate receipts or a month's salary. Rather than give in, Sacramento's management allowed San Francisco to claim the league pennant.[55]

Some California League players did not get the league's or organized baseball's message regarding contract-jumping or good behavior. Sacramento-born George Borchers, who pitched a bit for Chicago, was caught sneaking out of the state capital in 1889 for a more financially rewarding engagement elsewhere. Borchers and other "culprits" not only flirted with a blacklist, but also courted legal action instituted by league magnates.[56] Player behavior, moreover, had always proved difficult to maintain in the California League, which gave employment to feisty lads who regarded the authority of incorporation with suspicion. Even after the California League became covered by the National Agreement, player drunkenness and rowdiness remained a problem. The tremendously talented, but erratic, George Borchers, according to the San Francisco *Evening Post*, "could not hold out long against his arch enemy, John Barleycorn."[57] In 1890, the Oakland club became infamous for the rudeness and obscenity showcased by star players, Joe Cantillon and "Tip" O'Neill. A weakness for the bottle infected not only the playing ranks, but the umpires as well. Also in 1890, the troubled Charley Sweeney was, for some unexplained reason, selected to umpire league games and was soon discharged for a not surprising inability to stay sober.[58]

The problem in the Golden State, and wherever organized baseball sought hegemony over the national pastime, was that not only were leagues and clubs trying to cope with the incorporation process, but the players were as well. Many of these players honored residual, preindustrial cultural practices, which mandated working and playing hard. Often second- and even first-generation immigrants from rural Ireland and Germany, they tended to resist acceptance of the more modern forms of work discipline and hierarchical control favored by their bosses.[59]

Controversy related to the honesty of California League games also dogged the circuit. The eastern baseball establishment was vitally and understandably concerned with the integrity of professional baseball. Organized baseball attempted to guarantee the purity of its product through more modern, hierarchical control of players' on- and off-field behavior. Fixes and "hippodroming" were not frequent occurrences in California professional circles. Yet, a troubling blemish surfaced on the California League's record. In the fall of 1890, San Francisco and Sacramento were locked in a heated pennant race. In order to gain at least a tie, Sacramento had to beat Stockton on the last day of the regular season. The Capital City nine succeeded; but within a day, rumors were flying that the Stockton club had let Sacramento win. Substantiating these rumors was the claim by the game's umpire and former major leaguer, Pete Meegan, that the Stockton ballplayers displayed a suspiciously keen interest in abetting Sacramento's pennant chances.[60]

But if the California League proved less than the ideal organized baseball league, much of the responsibility fell on management. The *Chronicle* perfectly summed up the 1890 season and management's onerous contribution to it:

> There has been poor management and bitter quarrels, petty spite work, breaking of contracts and agreements. A total disregard for league rules, miserable work by the umpires, of whom we have had a dozen or more; scandals and drunkenness among the players, charges of "fake" and "sell-outs" and everything else that tends to make baseball rank and disagreeable.[61]

Moreover, league affairs were so confused that no official records were kept. It was bad enough that no one knew who had the highest batting average. Much worse was that the California League proposed a San Francisco–Sacramento play-off for the pennant, because it could not officially declare the league champion.[62]

Until 1892, the California League did not venture into the state's southern region. Just as southern California remained undeveloped economically and politically in comparison to the metropolitan north in the late nineteenth century, the region's effort to establish a commercial base for professional baseball was overshadowed by the national pastime in the Bay area. In spite of southern California's impressive population and economic growth in the 1880s, few seriously entertained the notion that a growing Los Angeles could sustain professional baseball for more than a handful of winter exhibition games. The demographic factors making professional baseball potentially profitable were still missing in Los Angeles, which did not readily shed its rural character and transform itself into a city of lower-middle and working class people eager for diversions such as spectator sports. Northern California cities could brag about their big league stars such as Charley Sweeney, Jerry Denny, and Ed Morris; they could, in fact, claim something of a tradition of top-flight baseball. Southern California had not sent a flock of residents to the major leagues and could claim, at best, a modest interest in baseball as a recreational pursuit. Moreover, the region's generally dry weather seriously damaged potential playing surfaces except during the winter.[63]

Nevertheless, promoters of winter ball in southern California during the late 1880s optimistically and tirelessly associated the sport's commercial possibilities with the region's burgeoning boosterism. The southern California correspondent to the *Sporting Life* boasted, in November 1886, that the area was "the best winter home for baseball in the United States." He called upon readers of the famed sporting publication to spread the word about southern California and when ". . . speaking of California also to remember that the southern part of the state offers almost as many advantages and even greater attractions than the vicinity of San Francisco."[64]

Even so, professional baseball sunk few roots in southern California's consciousness during the late 1880s, and some speculated that it was for want of a stable league or a good baseball park in downtown Los Angeles. Certainly, some Angelenos struggled to at least make winter ball a thriving enterprise in Los Angeles and among its neighbors. For instance, southern California baseball promoters and fans looked forward to the 1880–89 winter season, and the region's correspondent to the *Sporting News* foresaw a new day for baseball in Los Angeles. "Never in the history of Los Angeles was there such a stirring of baseball matters as at present," he wrote. "Commercial nines are forming and everything points to the establishment in this city and surrounding towns of baseball on a sound footing for years to come."[65]

A group called the Southern California Baseball Association was organized late in 1888 to start a winter league in Los Angeles, as well as in towns such as San Bernardino, Pasadena, and Colton. New grounds were built in Pasadena, and on Washington and Main Street in Los Angeles. A handful of worthy professionals and future professionals played. The leading light of the Colton nine was Frank Graves, who was southern California's most notable contribution to the eastern leagues. Brought in to captain the San Bernardino club was one of the most famous Afro-American ballplayers of his time, Bud Fowler. Others competing that winter were future major leaguers Pete Lohman and Sam Dungan.[66] Still, within a few months, the Los Angeles *Tribune* complained that "[b]aseball was never so dead since Los Angeles could be termed a city." The lack of good management capable of constructing a substantial, centrally located ballpark in Los Angeles was to blame, according to the *Tribune,* which asked, "Why can't Los Angeles have a baseball park?"[67]

A saviour seemed on hand a few years later in the person of Marco Hellman, scion to one of the wealthiest families in California. In the fall of 1890, young Hellman set about establishing a strong winter league in southern California. Like many baseball entrepreneurs, he understood the importance of seeking the help of a transit company capable of moving fans to and from the ballpark. He reportedly agreed to pay the Temple Street Cable Co. $5,000 to carry Angeleno baseball fans. At the same time, he headed East to sign on eastern talent and convinced the *Sporting News* that the success of his enterprise was inevitable. The *Sporting News* claimed that estimable California League and eastern players such as Phil Knell, Jim Fogarty, and George Van Haltren were going to winter in southern California. It appeared that "Hellman . . . has shown a great deal of pluck in his enterprises of organizing the [winter] California League. He went about it in the right way and showed good business sense when he secured the leading members of the Philadelphia club, and such other leading clubs of the Brotherhood and National Leagues as he could, to take a team to the coast with him."[68]

A month later, the *Sporting News'* warmth for Hellman's entrepreneurial abilities decidedly cooled. The prospects for a southern California winter league had soured and Hellman was to blame. "Had Mr. Hellman kept his numerous promises," the *Sporting News* contended, "and put up the necessary cash, all would have been serene, but baseball leagues, even if they do consist of but four clubs, cannot possibly be run on wind and broken promises."[69]

By the early 1890s, Los Angeles sought entry into the California League and finally succeeded in 1892. However, the state circuit demonstrated an inconsistent response to community and regional pride, while recognizing the economic importance of local boosterism. From the fans' perspective, California League teams ideally should have been good, and local. A magnate such as San Francisco's Henry Harris sought nines that were both, with the result that his teams usually were competent but scarcely dominant. Club managers in the "interior" towns, such as Stockton, Sacramento, San Jose, and Los Angeles, had other problems. With relatively small population bases from which to draw, they had to rely more upon imports than Harris did. These easterners stretched budgets and didn't always inspire confidence among community-minded fans. However, the best teams in the California League from 1891 to 1893 were Los Angeles and San Jose, teams substantially consisting of expensive non-Californians.[70]

Adding to the California League's woes was the issue of community and league expansion. Professional baseball in California took an important step in moving beyond the confines of the Bay area so as to take advantage of community rivalries that pervaded the state in the late nineteenth century. However, boosterism in California revealed two of the league's most troublesome weaknesses: the centrality of the San Francisco market and the circuit's inability to expand beyond the Bay area without overextending itself. The result was the glutting of places like Stockton, San Jose, and Los Angeles with numerous professional games when they were incapable of supporting more than just a handful of such events, as well as sparking controversy and jealousy within the ranks of increasingly peevish California League executives.

In the 1880s and 1890s, community leaders throughout California generally took for granted a zero-sum approach to economic development and population growth that corresponded with postbellum America's romance with social Darwinism. Some residents of Sacramento, Stockton, San Jose, and Los Angeles believed that getting a professional baseball team would "put their towns on the map," which, in turn, would aid local business. Each year California League directors faced pleas for franchise placement or retention in the state's larger communities. And the losers in the competition for California League clubs did not always resign themselves quietly to their fate. In February 1888, a group of Sacramentans expressed indignation at seeing their franchise switched to Stockton by heading to San Francisco and marching upon the offices of the Market Street Railroad Company, which, to put it mildly, held considerable influence on California League directors and had reportedly reaped the biggest profit of anyone durng the previous season.[71]

Sacramento lost its franchise for the 1888 season only to pick one up again in 1890. But the experience of Sacramento and the other "interior towns" points out that the Bay area-based California League leadership took an almost sadistic delight in playing one supplicant town against another. Since the late 1880s, San Jose had expected that the California League eventually would see its way to granting a franchise in what was then one of the garden spots of the state. Business and community leaders displayed their town's wares until it looked like the California League would transfer the Stockton franchise to San Jose for the 1890 season. A manager for the San Jose nine was selected, a ballpark chosen, and players signed for the coming 1890 season. However, at the last minute, Stockton convinced the California League it was still viable by coming up with a $2,000 bond. Poor gate receipts did in the Stockton franchise in 1890, and San Jose replaced it in 1891. But the Santa Clara County club also failed to attract local interest despite possessing an outstanding team that fielded, at one time or another, Jerry Denny, Heinie Reitz, Bill Everett, and George Stallings. In 1893, Stockton was back in the California League and San Jose was out.[72]

This California League merry-go-round was aggravated by the league magnates' wanting their organization to be a typical professional baseball league, with franchises representing various cities and exploiting intercity rivalries. However, the only guaranteed money-making venue for the California League was its San Francisco Haight Street Grounds. As many games as possible were scheduled in San Francisco, but sometimes San Jose, Stockton, or Los Angeles would have to play a few home games, where they and the visiting club might luckily break even. And the addition of Los Angeles in 1892 to the California League made for long and expensive train rides, which resulted in little profit and many frayed nerves.

These nerves reached a breaking point in 1893, when Bay area arrogance and the demographic problems facing non-Bay area franchises combined with a depression that lashed out at Californians as fiercely as at other Americans. The California League's economic vulnerability was divulged when first Oakland, and then Stockton, franchises fell behind in paying its players, and the spendthrift Tom Robinson was forced out of the league and the Stockton franchise switched to Sacramento. Apparently tired of the "metropolitan headquarters" in San Francisco dominating league affairs, club executives from Sacramento, Oakland, and Los Angeles staged a rebellion against the San Francisco resident and league president, John Mone, as well as his constant ally, Henry Harris. Mone was deposed from office and Harris was stripped of his league office.[73] Nevertheless, by midsummer, receipts had fallen drastically in the Bay area, and in August, the *Chronicle* complained that "Los Angeles is dead as a baseball town."[74] The rural/urban division, which was growing more significant in the state's economic and political affairs, had spilled over into professional baseball and helped vanquish the California League in mid-August.[75]

The incorporation process had succeeded in subordinating California professional baseball to the needs of organized baseball. But the Golden State still lacked the kind of broad economic and demographic base that nurtured organized baseball in the populous regions east of the Rockies. After the fall of the California League, professional baseball was, until the late 1890s, limited to match games and barnstorming Eastern professional clubs, although short-lived efforts to revive the California League continued. Presumably, the California League debacle in 1893 could not easily overcome the California sporting public's suspicion, nor the rising popularity of prizefighting, bicycling, and college football in San Francisco, San Jose, Sacramento, and Los Angeles.[76]

Those involved in nineteenth-century professional baseball most likely did not consider themselves on the cutting edge of any transforming cultural development in American sports. Professional baseball as a commercial enterprise had been successful elsewhere in America, and its proponents in California reasonably assumed that, despite baseball's relatively short history in the Golden State, at least San Franciscans might pay good money to see grown men play a child's game. Moreover, as the game developed in the 1880s, it was apparent that little out of the ordinary was happening. If professional baseball found it sometimes difficult to thrive in California, such was often the case in significantly agrarian regions. If the ranks of magnates and players in California were not filled with "role models," this was hardly unique to the Golden State. If labor and management disputes found their way into the California version of the national pastime, they were unwelcome, but scarcely unique, signs, from organized baseball's standpoint, that things were not going smoothly for the Spaldings of the sport. If, at times, Californians took an enthusiastic shine to professional baseball, then, of course, they were far from alone. And if they, often irrationally, identified their community and regional welfare with the fate of their baseball teams, they were merely typical American sports fans.

But in trying to demonstrate that California could be just as American as anyplace else, despite its geographic isolation from the nation's centers of Gilded Age social, economic, political, and cultural power, the early pioneers of professional baseball in California were helping to lay the foundation for a rather extraordinary twentieth-century development in the social history of American sports and recreation. They did not resist the incorporation of sports so much as they wanted a hand in it. For although the connection between boosterism and sports remained viable throughout the country, one could reasonably argue that no group of Americans has proven as adept at seeing so clearly how sports and recreation contribute economically and demographically to a community, region, and state as have Californians.[77] In other words, in realizing that professional baseball had to take advantage of community rivalries and California's somewhat histrionic regional pride, California's nineteenth-century baseball promoters nurtured a future in which Californians, in all their cultural diversity, would stalk better health, and better baseball, football, and basketball teams with blood and dollar signs in their eyes.

NOTES

1. Carey McWilliams, *California: The Great Exception,* (Santa Barbara: Perregine Publishers, 1976); Alexander Saxton, *The Indispensable Enemy: Labor and the Anti-Chinese Movement in California,* (Berkeley: University of California Press, 1971); Michael Kazin, *Barons of Labor: The San Francisco Building Trades and Union Power in the Progressive Era,* (Urbana, Illinois: University of Illinois Press, 1987); James J. Rawls, (ed), *New Directions in California History,* (New York: McGraw-Hill Company, 1988).

2. Alan Trachtenberg, *The Incorporation of America: Culture and Society in the Gilded Age,* (New York: McGraw-Hill, 1982), pp. 3–4, 116–117.

3. *Ibid.*

4. Fred Lange, *History of Baseball in California and the Pacific Coast Leagues, 1847–1938,* (San Francisco, 1938), 6; Harold Petersen, *The Man Who Invented Baseball,* (New York: Charles Scribner's and Sons, 1963), 168–169; Brian McGinty, "The Old Ball Game," *Pacific Historian,* XXV, (Spring, 1981), p. 14; *Daily Alta California,* February 6, 1867, p. 1.

5. Pacific Baseball Convention, *Pacific Baseball Guide for 1867,* (San Francisco: A. Roman & Company, 1867).

6. San Francisco City Directories, 1860 and 1870; George B. Kirsch, *The Creation of American Team Sports: Baseball and Cricket, 1838–1872,* (Urbana: University of Illinois Press, 1989); Warren Goldstein, *Playing for Keeps: A History of Early Baseball,* (Ithaca, NY: Cornell University Press, 1989).

7. Seymour Church, *Baseball,* (San Francisco, 1902), 39; San Francisco *Chronicle,* June 24, 1867, p. 3.

8. Robert Barney, "Of Rails and Red Stockings: Episodes in the Expansion of the National Pastime in the American West," *Journal of the West,* 17 (July, 1978), 64; *Alta,* September 26, 1869, p. 1.

9. Harold Seymour, *Baseball,* Vol. 1. (New York: Oxford University Press, 1966), 76; Joel Franks, "The Rise of Spectator Sports in California, 1850–1900," *Southern California Quarterly* (Winter, 1989); Roberta J. Park, "San Franciscans at Work and at Play, 1846–1869," *Journal of the West,* 22, (January, 1983), 44–51.

10. San Francisco *Chronicle,* October 4, 1874, p. 4. Another instance of the comparative ineptness of California ballplayers occurred in the fall of the same year. In a game in San Francisco, the Californians used an easterner named Waterman as pitcher. Possibly, this Waterman was the Fred of Red Stocking fame. In any event, he threw so hard that his California catcher couldn't handle him and suffered a couple of dislocated fingers for his trouble. Consequently, Waterman had to be removed to second base and his teammates kept out of harm's way. San Francisco *Chronicle,* November 27, 1874, p. 3.

11. For published information on the Workingmen's Party of California, see Neil L. Shumsky, "San Francisco's Workingmen Respond to the Modern City," *California Historical Review,* LIV (Spring, 1976), 46–58; Saxton, *Indispensable;* Ira Cross, *A History of the Labor Movement in California,* (Berkeley: University of California Press, 1935); Frank Roney, *Frank Roney, Irish Rebel and California Labor Leader,* edited by Ira Cross, (Berkeley: University of California Press, 1931).

12. Steven A. Riess, *Touching Base: Professional and American Culture in the Progressive Era,* (Westport, CT: Greenwood Press, 1980), 66–68; William A. Bullough, *The Blind Boss and His City: Christopher Augustine Buckley and Nineteenth Century San Francisco,* (Berkeley: University of California Press, 1979), 64–66, Roney, *Irish Rebel,* 302.

13. San Francisco *Chronicle,* September 16, 1878, p. 3.

14. *Ibid.,* June 2, 1879, p. 2.

15. *Ibid.,* January 5, 1880, p. 3.

16. *Ibid.,* April 10, 1880, p. 3; July 9, 1880, p. 5; September 18, 1880, p. 3.

17. *Ibid.,* October 18, 1880, p. 3.

18. *Ibid.,* March 3, 1880, p. 2; June 27, 1880, p. 5; June 21, 1880, p. 3.

19. I suspect that some clubs were organized to conform at least to neighborhood and political distinctions. However, more research involving city directories and manuscript census schedules will have to be undertaken to bear this suspicion out.

20. San Francisco *Chronicle,* March 17, 1883, p. 1; May 19, 1883, p. 4; *Sporting Life,* June 3, 1883, p. 4. For Charley Sweeney, see Joel Franks, "Sweeney of San Francisco: A Local Boy Makes Good, Then Not So Good," *Baseball History,* II, (Winter, 1987), 52–63.

21. *Ibid.,* February 19, 1884, p. 2.

22. *Sporting Life,* December 2, 1885, p. 2.

23. *Sacramento* Bee, July 13, 1885, p. 3; *Sporting Life,* October 28, 1885, p. 2; December 2, 1885, p. 2.

24. *Sporting Life,* December 2, 1885, p. 2.

25. *Ibid.,* December 9, 1885, p. 3.

26. San Francisco *Chronicle,* March 9, 1886, p. 3.

27. *Sporting Life,* Juy 21, 1886, p. 6.

28. Peter Levine, *A.G. Spaldng and the Rise of Baseball,* (New York: Oxford University Press, 1985), 65; San Francisco *Chronicle,* July 13, 1886, p. 3; Joel S. Franks, "Boot and Shoemakers in Nineteenth Century San Francisco, 1860–1892: A Study in Class, Culture, and Popular Protest in an Industrializing Community," (unpublished dissertation: 1983), chapter three; San Francisco *Chronicle,* May 10, 1886, p. 3; May 11, 1886, p. 3.

29. Carey McWilliams, *Southern California Country,* (New York: Dell, Sloan and Pearce, 1946), chapters six and seven; Oakland *Morning Times,* April 12, 1886, p. 1.

30. *Sporting News,* June 28, 1886, p. 1.

31. San Francisco *Chronicle,* May 9, 1887, p. 5; April 30, 1888, p. 5.

32. *Ibid.,* October 3, 1887, p. 5; November 25, 1889, p. 5.

33. Joel Franks, "Rube Levy: A Jewish Shoecutter and Baseball in Nineteenth Century San Francisco," unpublished ms.

34. Joel Franks, "Sweeney."

35. For an entrepreneur who successfully combined all three components, see Peter Levine, *Spalding.*

36. Oakland City Directories, 1878–1900; San Francisco City Directories, 1878–1900.

37. San Jose *Daily Herald,* April 13, 1891, p. 3; San Francisco *Chronicle,* April 13, 1892, p. 7; Oakland *Tribune,* May 10, 1893, p. 8.

38. San Francisco *Chronicle,* April 6, 1891, p. 3; November 16, 1891, p. 3; February 18, 1893, p. 5.

39. San Francisco *Chronicle,* March 9, 1891, p. 5; July 13, 1891, p. 3; San Jose *Mercury,* March 15, 1891, p. 3; July 24, 1892, p. 5.

40. *Sporting Life,* November 24, 1886, p. 5; February 23, 1887, p. 1.

41. *Ibid.,* May 4, 1887, p. 1.

42. *Ibid.,* May 11, 1887, p. 1; Levine, *Spalding,* 39.

43. Sacramento *Bee,* June 11, 1887, p. 5; San Francisco *Chronicle,* June 13, 1887, p. 5.

44. San Francisco *Chronicle,* November 26, 1888, p. 8.

45. Cited in *ibid.,* January 7, 1889, p. 5.

46. *Sporting News,* February 9, 1889, p. 1.

47. *Sporting Life,* April 24, 1889, p. 4.

48. *Ibid.,* May 6, 1889, p. 4.

49. *Ibid.,* May 22, 1889, p. 1.

50. *Sporting News,* January 10, 1891, p. 2.

51. *San Francisco Chronicle,* August 3, 1891, p. 3.

52. *Ibid.,*August 17, 1891, p. 3.

53. *Sporting Life,* February 9, 1889, p. 1.

54. For a seminal critique of modernization's relationship to culture, see Herbert Gutman, "Work, Culture, and Society in Industrializing America: 1815–1919," *American Historical Review,* 78 (June, 1973), 531–587; McWilliams, *Exception,* chapter eight; Saxton, *Indispensable,* passim; Kazin, *Barons;* Oakland *Tribune,* September 14, 1887, p. 3; San Francisco *Chronicle,* September 26, 1887, p. 2.

55. Sacramento *Bee,* November 24, 1890, p. 3.

56. San Francisco *Chronicle,* July 10, 1889, p. 7.

57. San Francisco *Evening Post,* October 28, 1890, p. 3.

58. *Ibid.,* October 20, 1890, p. 3; October 23, 1890, p. 1; October 27, 1890, p. 3.

59. Gutman, "Work, Culture, and Society"; Bruce Laurie, *Working People of Philadelphia,* (Philadelphia: Temple University Press, 1980); Paul Faler, "Cultural Aspects of the Industrial Revolution: Lynn, Massachusetts Shoemakers and Industrial Morality, 1826–1860," *Labor History,* (Summer, 1974) 381, 383, 393–394.

60. Sacramento *Bee,* November 25, 1890, p. 1.

61. San Francisco *Chronicle,* November 24, 1890, p. 5.

62. *Ibid.,* November 26, 1890, p. 2.

63. Two good introductions to southern California history and culture are Williams, *Southern California,* and Kevin Starr, *Inventing the Dream: California Through the Progressive Era,* (New York: Oxford University Press, 1985); *Sporting Life,* November 24, 1886, p. 2.

64. McWilliams, *Southern California,* chapters five and six; *Sporting Life,* November 24, 1886, p. 2.

65. *Sporting News,* September 8, 1888, p. 1.

66. Los Angeles *Tribune,* October 21, 1888, p. 3; November 3, 1888, p. 6; November 12, 1888, p. 6.

67. *Ibid.,* January 14, 1889, p. 3.

68. Ted Vincent, *Mudville's Revenge: The Rise and Fall of American Sport,* (New York: Seaview Books, 1981), 175–178; *Sporting News,* November 15, 1890, p. 1.

69. *Sporting News,* December 20, 1890, p. 1.

70. San Francisco *Chronicle,* March 25, 1889, p. 5; July 24, 1889, p. 5; October 21, 1889, p. 5; August 24, 1891, p. 2; May 13, 1893, p. 5; October 7, 1893, p. 7; San Jose *Daily Herald,* June 4, 1891, p. 3; *Sporting Life,* April 24, 1889, p. 6.

71. California *Alta,* February 17, 1888, p. 8; San Francisco *Chronicle,* November 14, 1887, p. 5.

72. San Francisco *Chronicle,* September 30, 1889, p. 5; December 23, 1889, p. 8; January 13, 1890, p. 5; June 28, 1890, p. 3; July 11, 1892, p. 5; October 17, 1892, p. 5; October 31, 1892, p. 5.

73. *Ibid.,* May 27, 1893, p. 5; August 31, 1893, p. 5.

74. *Ibid.,* August 12, 1893, p. 6; August 15, 1893, p. 6.

75. William A. Bullough, *The Blind Boss;* San Francisco *Chronicle,* August 15, 1893, p. 6; August 17, 1893, p. 4.

76. Joel Franks, "The Rise . . ." By 1900, a new and increasingly strong outlaw California League had been established in the Golden State. Aided by an economic upturn in the state's economic fortunes and a willingness to build on local talent and a few well-known imports such as Jay Hughes and Rube Waddell, this California League gave birth in 1903 to the venerable Pacific Coast League.

77. Steven Riess, "Power Without Authority: Los Angeles Elites and the Construction of the Coliseum," *Journal of Sports History,* 8 (Spring, 1981), 50–65; Cary S. Henderson, "Los Angeles and the Dodger War, 1957–62," *Southern California Quarterly,* LXII (Fall, 1980), pp. 261–289; Neil J. Sullivan, *The Dodgers Move West* (New York: Oxford University Press, 1987).

Frank Grant

JAMES E. OVERMYER

By the spring of 1889, Frank Grant had been an important part of the Buffalo Bisons International League team for three years straight. He had hit well over .300 with surprising power in an era when homers were rare, he drew raves from fans and sportswriters for his acrobatic fielding, and he was a good base runner.

Still only 23 years old and a standout just one step below the major leagues, he appeared to be a man on his way up.

Instead, Grant was on his way out, for talent was not an issue in determining his baseball future. Grant was a black man, and by that spring, Jim Crow had a reserved season box seat in nearly all major and minor league parks.

The commonly held view of black progress after the Civil War is that of a river, its current often moving sluggishly, but always flowing toward equality for the race. In the late 1800s, however, that current slowed to a stop and in some parts of society, began to run backwards.

So it was with baseball, the "National Pastime." Ability did not matter, as blacks were systematically squeezed out of organized ball. Tolerance of the handful of blacks who had broken into early organized baseball in its formative years wore thin, and Grant was one of the last to perform in a league as fast as the International.

While not the only black ballplayer in the organized leagues at that time, he was one of the best. Given his youth, he was one of the few who would have had the chance to make a long career in the majors or high minors. And, he was in his prime just at the moment in baseball history when there was an unprecedented growth in demand for major leaguers.

The 1890 founding of the Players' League as a challenger to the two existing majors increased the demand for big leaguers by 50 percent. But none of these newly minted big leaguers was to be black.

Instead of eventually earning his own statistical entry in the Baseball Encyclopedia, Grant spun out a long career first in second-rate minor leagues, and then on the other side of the color line, albeit with the best barnstorming black teams of his day. For Frank Grant, life after baseball was marked by anonymity and ended in an unmarked pauper's grave.

Grant's story, while not unique to its times, comes from a cruel chapter of baseball, when people in the sport were all too ready to conform to the prejudices of society around them. Almost everyone knows how Jackie Robinson heroically broke the color line in 1946; but Frank Grant was there when that line was first drawn, bisecting his career nearly at its apex.

If it had not been for baseball, relative anonymity would have been the story of Grant's entire life. He was born August 1, 1865, in Pittsfield, Massachusetts, the central town in a rural agricultural region at the westernmost end of the state.[1] The Grant family's primary occupation was farming, either as land owners or as hired hands.

Frank was the youngest of seven children, and his birth just after the end of the Civil War seems to have inspired his being named after one of the greatest Northern heroes, since his full name was Ulysses F. Grant.[2] But it was not long before his family jettisoned that cumbersome first name and he became known as Frank.[3] One reason for the change may have been to honor his father, Franklin, who died of an internal infection at age 48, just four months to the day after young Frank's birth.[4]

By 1871, young Frank's mother, Frances Hoose Grant, and her children had moved about 25 miles north to Williamstown, in the extreme northwest corner of the state.[5] Mrs. Grant died in 1883, but her children settled in that town, except for Frank. By the time he was 20, he was living the nomadic life that nineteenth-century baseball demanded of its players, especially its black ones.

He had already made a name for himself locally on the diamond with the Greylocks, a South Williamstown amateur team which played its home games in the shadow of Mount Greylock, Massachusetts' highest mountain. He pitched for the team in the summer of 1884, and won three of the four games for which box scores appeared in the local newspaper.[6]

A short biographical sketch contributed anonymously to the local historical society's files recalls that Grant "could do more tricks with a baseball than anyone I ever saw." The contributor remembered that Grant could "catch [the] ball behind [his] back before Rabbit Maranville was born."[7]

A year later, Frank Grant had moved north to Plattsburgh, N.Y., on Lake Champlain near Canada. He showed up in mid-season as a replacement, or "change" catcher, on the local semipro team, the "Nameless."

Grant may have been in the area working at one of the Lake Champlain resort hotels, which offered seasonal employment to blacks as waiters, porters, and other staff. He could not have been there to make money in baseball. A big payday for the Nameless was a winner-take-all match at the nearby Franklin County fair, where the team earned $100 for destroying the Ogdensburg, N.Y., Stars 24 to 1.[8]

Plattsburgh was a hotbed for baseball and other sports, and seemed to appreciate black and other minority ballplayers. (Harry Cato, a sometimes Cuban Giant, played in the town in 1895, and Louis "Chief" Sockalexis, the Native American outfielder, was on the team for the summer of 1896, between Holy Cross University and the majors.)[9]

Frank Grant was the regular second baseman for the Buffalo Bisons in 1887. The only black on the team, he was one of seven blacks in the International League. (Photo: from the author)

The Plattsburgh daily, the *Morning Telegraph,* reported that in an August 23 game, "Grant played a very strong game throughout" and that his catches of four pop-ups "were among the game's best plays."[10] That last compliment mirrors a presumably exaggerated claim made later by Sol White, the black player and manager of that time, that Grant climbed eight feet up a telegraph pole behind the Plattsburgh diamond to snag one foul pop-up.[11]

The *Morning Telegraph*'s baseball writer, while generally an early Frank Grant enthusiast, was also willing to criticize him. As whites continued to write about black ballplayers, there were many echoes of his observation that "there is one great fault with Grant's work and that is he is too much of a grandstand player. While this delights the audience, it is fatal to the success of the team."[12]

The argument that the black participant was too flashy and undisciplined to be a truly good player was a common crutch for whites, at least until Jackie Robinson led blacks back into organized baseball. Although there is substantial evidence that Grant was, indeed, a flashy player, the *Telegraph*'s man may also have found it easy to rely on a not-yet-old saw to justify a touch of white superiority.

The next time Grant's name showed up in a box score was the following spring. He had joined Meriden, Connecticut, in the Eastern League, and was heralded as "a young colored catcher and general player, who is expected by his friends to do great work in the ball field the coming season."[13]

And he did, opening in center field in the team's first exhibition game April 21 and contributing a home run and a single to a 22–0 rout of Trinity College.[14] Early in the regular season, he established himself as Meriden's regular second baseman. He also pitched occasionally and was leading the team in hitting when, in mid-July, the club suffered a fate all too common in the early days of pro ball. It went out of business.[15]

A lot of minor league teams (and some in the majors) in baseball's early days existed on a thin line between profit and financial disaster. While new money usually could be found to bail out a suffering major league franchise, the disappearance of minor league teams, sometimes whole leagues, in the middle of a season was not uncommon.

Although 1886 was a relatively stable year for the minors, with only five of 47 teams folding, three were in the Eastern League, where, according to *Spalding's Official Base Ball Guide,* "bad management, and an entire lack of harmony among the clubs . . . made its season of 1886 a decided failure, financially and otherwise."[16]

But Meriden's disaster was good fortune for Grant, who was hitting .325, nearly 100 points above the league average, and was second in fielding among second sackers.[17]

Although organized baseball had already evolved its reserve lists and several rules designed to prevent teams from raiding other clubs for their best talent, no restrictions applied to signing players from defunct organizations. So Grant, along with two other Meriden starters—outfielder and manager Jack Remsen and first baseman Steve Dunn—signed with Buffalo.[18] There, Grant became an immediate, if too short-lived, success.

The Buffalo team had started the 1886 season at a distinct disadvantage. The city had been in the big leagues, but had lost its National League team to Detroit at the close of the 1885 season. By the time entry in the International League could be negotiated, the club was far behind in putting together a competitive group of players.[19]

As a result, the Bisons were not playing well, having lost well over half their games. They were stuck in sixth place in an eight-team league, with a .383 winning percentage when Grant and his two teammates, management's latest improvement project, arrived in town.[20]

Buffalo's morning daily, the *Express,* noted that there had been competition for Grant's services when Meriden folded, and described him as "the strong player" of the defunct Connecticut squad. But the paper also acknowledged, in a curious fashion common to the era, that Grant was a marked man in another respect. It referred to the new second baseman, clearly a Negro to the most casual observer, as a "Spaniard."[21]

One of the informal rules of organized ball in the late nineteenth century encouraged references to America's black ballplayers as something other than American Negroes, so as to give them a measure of acceptability they would otherwise lack in a society that was recoiling from the black progress that had come out of the Civil War.

This odd convention went back at least to the first fully professional black team, organized from among waiters at the Argyle Hotel on Long Island, N.Y., in 1885. The men on the squad, famous for their early barnstorming success, often took the field chattering gibberish that was supposed to pass for Spanish, and called themselves the "Cuban Giants."[22]

White fans could thus appease their racial sensitivities during a barnstorming team's brief stay in town, but such blatant denial would hardly do when the black player was in their park for every home game. In Grant's case, the charade didn't last two weeks, by which time the *Express* was describing him as the "colored second baseman."[23]

And the paper had a lot to say about him. In his first game on July 14, he cracked a triple and drove in a run in an 8–3 pasting of Toronto.[24] On August 8, the *Express* praised him for his play in the previous day's win over Utica: "Too much cannot be said in praise of Grant's phenomenal work at second. He was the favorite with the audience yesterday, and was heavily cheered for every good play he made."[25]

Grant ended the season with a .340 batting average, third highest in the league.[26] In addition to starring at second, he also pitched in four games, winning two of them.[27] With the help of Grant and the other mid-season acquisitions, Buffalo won two-thirds of its games from July 14 on, and finished with a .526 winning percentage, although it could only improve its league standing to fifth place.[28]

David Q. Voigt, a leading baseball historian, calls the 1880s major league baseball's first "Golden Age," when the professional game began to evolve into a stable sport with a successful present and future. For example, the decade saw the emergence of the familiar format of two major leagues with a postseason series between them to establish an overall champion (although the other league besides the National League was the American Association, which lasted as a major circuit only from 1883 through 1891).

In 1889, both leagues drew a total of well over two million fans. The hot dog had become a common snack at ballparks, although you could get a beer to go with it only in the American Association. Not only was the National League dry, it also refused to play games on Sundays.

By 1888, playing rules in organized leagues had evolved to three strikes, you're out; and by 1889, four pitches outside the strike zone meant a walk in any league.[29]

Yet, one of the few significant features of today's baseball not to take shape in the 1880s was the acceptance of the skilled black player. Frank Grant's next season, 1887, was the watershed year for the squeezing out of blacks.

The season started out well enough for Grant and Buffalo, which had the nucleus of its fast-finishing 1886 team intact. When the Bisons won their opening home game at Olympic Park on May 14, 7–3 over Toronto, the *Express* noted that "Grant, as usual, was the favorite with the on-lookers."[30] On May 18, the paper observed, in a linguistic feat that rivaled the athletic one it described, that the nimble Grant "made a double back-action-compound-reversible-reflex slide" into second base on a play the day before.[31] One hopes he was safe.

Buffalo chased the pennant all season long, in the end finishing a bare two victories behind Toronto. But for Grant and the other blacks in the International League, it was not a good year. Including Grant, there were seven of them in the International at the beginning of 1887: George Stovey and Moses Fleetwood Walker with Newark, second baseman John "Bud" Fowler and a pitcher named Renfroe with Binghamton, pitcher Bob Higgins with Syracuse, and second baseman Randolph Jackson with Oswego.

The best of the group, along with Grant, were Stovey and Higgins, the pitchers; Fowler, the first known black in professional baseball, and "Fleet" Walker, who actually held the distinction 63 years before Robinson of being the first black in the majors. He had been with Toledo in 1884 when the club entered the American Association.

Before the season ended, all five were to be personally involved in unpleasant incidents that, when looked at together, show how strongly the tide was running against all blacks in what was fast becoming the white man's side of the game.

On June 5, two white members of the Syracuse Stars refused to sit for the team's official photograph if Higgins was going to be in it. An ensuing argument led to a brief fist fight between one of the players, pitcher Doug Crothers, and manager Charlie Simmons.[32]

On July 7, Fowler (and Renfroe, too) was released by Binghamton, even though Fowler was hitting .350 at the time and the Bingos, in eighth place in a 10-team league, were weak enough to have needed all the help they could get. To make matters worse, Fowler was forbidden to sign with another International League team, in effect locking him out of the league. Certainly it was no coincidence that at the beginning of the month, the white Binghamton players had been fined for refusing to take the field with Fowler.[33]

But the big blowup was reserved for Stovey. On July 14, his Newark club had a financially lucrative exhibition game scheduled with Chicago of the National League, a powerhouse club in baseball's strongest league. Its playing manager, Adrian "Cap" Anson, a future Hall of Famer, was one of the best-known figures in the game.

Stovey, a 35-game winner that season and Newark's star pitcher, was to start against Chicago, a fact that was part of the pre-game publicity. But Anson, whose antipathy to blacks was known inside baseball circles, if not publicly, refused to allow Chicago to play if Stovey pitched. With revenues from a crowd of 3,000 at stake, the Newark management caved in and substituted a white pitcher. This move also took Walker, Stovey's regular catcher, out of the game before it began.[34]

The lack of club support for Stovey should not be surprising, for that very day, the league's directors met in a Buffalo hotel, primarily to work out the transfer of the financially moribund Utica, N.Y., franchise to Wilkes-Barre, Pa. But the directors also discussed the question of retaining black players in light of the rumor that many good white players would leave the league if the blacks did not. In the end, the four teams with black players—Buffalo, Syracuse, Newark, and Oswego—were outvoted by the other six, and league secretary C.D. White was told "to approve of no more contracts with colored men."[35]

It is impossible to say precisely what effect these events had on Frank Grant, but it is a fact that in July and August of 1887, he played poorly. He had two

Grant during his barnstorming years, after leaving organized baseball. He played with the Cuban Giants and the Philadelphia Giants, among the best black teams of the 1890s. (Photo: from the author)

extremely cold streaks at bat, going 9 for 42 (.214) from July 1 through 13, and 12 for 73 (.164) from Aug. 1 through 20, and was dropped from cleanup to as low as seventh in the batting order during the August swoon. (He did, however, slug .421 in the 13 games between those slumps.)[36]

He came in for criticism for his fielding, also. On July 19, he had his fourth three-error game of the month in a 5–1 loss to Newark in which the Bisons made several miscues. The *Express* said that Grant, "who started out in Buffalo with such brilliant prospects, is fast losing the confidence of his friends. His work both at the bat and in the field is by far not what ought justly to be expected of him."[37]

He was having his own racial trouble, too. Bad blood existed between Buffalo and Toronto during this pennant race, and the Toronto *Dispatch* reported that when the teams played in that city September 1, the crowd was spoiling for trouble. Since Toronto easily smashed the Bisons, 12–4, the home fans calmed down and apparently confined themselves to picking on the easiest Buffalo target, yelling "Kill the nigger" when Grant came to bat.[38]

Grant hit .366 in 1887, but sank in the league standings from 3rd to 29th, this being the year that organized baseball experimented with counting bases on balls as hits. The league average was .324, and eight players hit (or walked) to better than .400 averages.[39]

The league failed to follow through on its July 14 decision to ban blacks absolutely, probably because of its preoccupation with continuing money troubles. The biggest decision at the November 16 winter meeting in Toronto was to reorganize the 10-team league as the eight-team "International Association," thus excluding Newark and Jersey City, which were proving an expensive drag on the upper New York State and Ontario-based league because of travel costs.[40]

The ban on blacks was not rigorously enforced, but neither was it rescinded. The trend was obvious by now, and while the Buffalo *Express* praised Frank Grant in its season-ending wrap-up, it felt the need to hope that "colored players will not be barred from the International League next season."[41]

Grant hit .346 in 1888, and with the "walk as a hit" rule abolished, that was good enough for fifth in the league.[42] He also hit 11 home runs.[43] But Buffalo faded badly in the standings, dropping to seventh. In addition, Grant was hurt and missed nearly a month of play in July and August. When he returned to the lineup he played the outfield, his usual second base job having gone to an International League journeyman, Red Bittman.[44]

Grant's arm and leg injuries and fielding lapses at second base may have been the result of another unfortunate convention of that era's baseball—the black infielder as target for runner's spikes.

In 1889, an International League player told *The Sporting News* that both Grant and Bud Fowler had been singled out for rough treatment by runners sliding into second. Of Grant, the anonymous player said that "the runners chased him off second base. They went down so often trying to break his legs or injure them that he gave up his infield position the latter part of last season and played right field."[45]

In 1891, Charlie Cushman, the Toronto manager during Grant's years with

Buffalo, gave *Sporting Life,* the east coast sports weekly, an inside look at how white players treated their black rivals. Cushman said that during an 1887 game with Buffalo, Gus Alberts of his team was tagged particularly hard by Grant on a steal attempt, and had the wind knocked out of him. When Alberts limped back to the bench, pitcher Ed Crane, looking out at the infield, asked the team, "Well boys, what'll we do with him?"

"Put him out of the game," was the chorused reply; so later, when Crane got a chance to steal second, "he ducked his head after measuring the distance and caught Grant fairly in the pit of the stomach with his shoulder. The son of Ham went up in the air and when he came down he looked as if he had been in a threshing machine. They took him home on a stretcher, and he didn't recover for three weeks."[46]

There are some factual problems with Cushman's story. First of all, Grant missed only one game in 1887, and his long hiatus in 1888 came after a game with Hamilton, Ontario, not Toronto. But even if it is partly myth, Cushman's tale gets right to the heart of the way prejudice translated into violence and intimidation against blacks, even on the field of fair play that the baseball diamond is thought to represent.

By 1888, the league was down to three blacks: Grant, Higgins, and Walker, and Higgins quit near the end of the season rather than put up with any more abuse.[47] On November 21, the league again voted to bar future contracts with blacks. Grant and Walker were excepted, although they, like Fowler in 1887, were forbidden to sign with any other International team when their services were no longer required by Buffalo and Syracuse.[48]

Grant's prospects with Buffalo for 1889 were uncertain, a situation not helped by his spending the winter barnstorming in the south with the Cuban Giants, the original black professional team, which made him unavailable to Buffalo management and the northern sporting press.

The press worried, on Buffalo's behalf, that Grant's sore arm had not healed (although he was playing all winter for the Giants), and a report surfaced that he was holding out for a higher salary.[49] But a writer for the Buffalo *Courier* got to the heart of the situation. On April 14, the paper reported that "it is very doubtful if the present members of the Buffalo team would play ball if the colored player, Grant, of last year's team was to sign."

A returning player from the 1888 team told the *Courier* that Grant, like Bob Higgins with Syracuse the previous year, had been the reason for the lack of a Bisons team photo. He said that "the only reason why we didn't have our picture taken last year was on account of that nigger. [Manager Jack] Chapman wanted us to come around and be photographed, but one of the boys said: 'Not if the nig is in the picture, and we all backed him up.' "

"The feeling is pretty general among professional ballplayers that colored men should not play with white men," the *Courier* reported.[50]

So although Grant might have returned to Buffalo, instead he made what was a wise personal choice under the circumstances by staying with the Cuban Giants. After all, Jackie Robinson may have met terrible resistance in 1947, but at least he had Branch Rickey, the Brooklyn organization, and most of his teammates on his side.

Ironically, although he was now with the all-black Cuban Giants in 1889, Grant played again in a white man's league. The Giants, based in Trenton, N.J., signed up in their entirety to represent the city in the Middle States League, a lower-level minor league. Grant hit .313, and the team nearly won the pennant.[51]

In 1890, Grant jumped teams, signing with the integrated Harrisburg, Pennsylvania, squad which had finished first the year before in the Middle States League, and now was a member of its successor, the Eastern Interstate League. This move made him the object of a lawsuit by the Cuban Giants, now representing York, Pennsylvania, in the same league.[52]

The Giants' attempt to bar Grant from taking the field for Harrisburg was denied by the local court, and final resolution of the dispute came from baseball's own ruling body. The three-man arbitration board set up by the National Agreement governing organized baseball ruled that Grant could play with Harrisburg, since his contract with the Giants had been signed before they entered the Interstate. Grant received a stiff reprimand for his move, though.[53]

Then the Harrisburg club succumbed to an invitation to join the better Atlantic Association and jumped, en masse, in July 1890. This ended the season for the wobbly Interstate, which had already been reduced to four teams before the defection.[54]

Grant went along, and found, if he needed to be reminded, that while the black player's lot was no longer very good in the north, it was considerably worse the farther south one ventured. When the team arrived in Wilmington, Delaware, in early August he was refused service at the team's hotel, whereupon the entire squad refused to register there and found lodgings elsewhere. In the new hotel, however, Grant was still obliged to eat with the black help in the kitchen—he wasn't allowed into the dining room.[55]

Throughout the year, with court cases, reprimands, and Jim Crowing, Grant continued to do what he always did: put the bat on the ball. He hit a reported .325 in the Eastern Interstate League and .328 in the Atlantic Association, good enough to finish fifth in its batting race.[56]

In 1891, Grant signed with a black team out of New York City called the Big Gorhams. The team began the season representing Ansonia in the Connecticut State League, but went barnstorming when the league, short on money and organization from the start, folded in June.[57]

The Gorhams, playing all sorts of teams, most of them white, amassed about 100 wins and suffered only four defeats. However, they, too, lost money and went out of business, allowing Grant to return to the Cuban Giants.[58]

So far as current baseball historians can discern, he barnstormed with the Giants for most of the 1890s. In 1902, Grant was recruited for the Philadelphia Giants, another of the best black teams of that period. But after the 1903 season, at the fairly advanced (for baseball) age of 38, he was dropped by Philadelphia, and apparently never played again with a top flight club.[59]

The descending color line aside, was Frank Grant good enough to have been a major leaguer? The critical years to examine are those in Buffalo, when he was in his early 20s and playing just a step below the big leagues. Fans and baseball writers in Buffalo clearly thought Grant was special—they called him "the colored Dunlap," a highly flattering comparison to Fred Dunlap, then considered the best fielding second baseman in the majors, and a career .292 hitter to boot.[60]

And the Buffalo fans should have been good judges of talent. Until the year before Grant came there, the city had been in the National League, and the squads from 1884 and 1885 had included Dan Brouthers, Jim "Pud" Galvin, and Jim O'Rourke, all eventually to make the Hall of Fame.

Comparing Grant statistically to his International League peers shows that he shone among them. His three-year batting average of .354 is 26.4 percent better than the league average for 1886 through 1888. In his two best years, his first and third, he was, respectively, 38.8 and 35.7 percent ahead of the league.

For the sake of comparison, New York Yankee star Don Mattingly, current Boston Red Sox batting star Wade Boggs, and ex-Red Sox great Carl Yastremzski all played very well in their last minor league seasons before making the majors, but only ranked 26, 30, and 28 percent ahead of their peers, respectively.

Ted Williams hit .366 for Minneapolis in the American Association in 1938 before going up to the Red Sox, and was 32 percent ahead of the league average.

Grant's 11 home runs in 1888 came in 347 at bats, giving him a better home run-per-at-bat ratio than either Jim Ryan, who led the National League with 16, or Long John Reilly, whose 13 topped the American Association.

Grant's fielding statistics seem to give the lie to the fans' and writers' adulation of his defensive skills. He never led the International League in fielding percentage at second, nor came anywhere near to doing it, for that matter. But, significantly, he always had more chances per game than the league leader, nearly one fifth more in 1887.

His low fielding percentage probably can be attributed to two things: his ability to get his hands on hard chances that other infielders wouldn't have reached, and errors that resulted from being targeted by base runners down at second.

But perhaps the best gauge of Frank Grant's ability is the roll of his white teammates who passed him by and went to the majors. John McGlone from the 1886 club played part-time in the American Association during the next two years. Mike Lehane from the 1887 roster went on to play two full, undistinguished seasons in the American Association in 1890 and 1891. Charlie Hamburg also played in the Association in 1890. Even Bittman, Grant's replacement at second base, got a cup of coffee in the same league in 1889. All these men were position players, but, except during Grant's subpar 1887 season when Lehane and Bittman topped him, none of them ever outhit him in the International.

With the possible exception of Stovey, who won 35 games for Newark in 1887, Grant was in the best position of any of the International League blacks to be promoted to the majors, being both young and a consistently good hitter. Fowler, in his mid-30s, would no longer have had the likelihood of a long career, and Walker's best batting average in the International League was .264 in 1887, when the "walk's a hit" rule inflated most averages.

Sol White, in his *Official Base Ball Guide,* the best contemporary chronicle of black baseball before the turn of the century, claims that the New York Giants were indeed interested in Stovey, but that the indefatigable Anson used his immense influence in the National League to kill the deal.[61]

Although organized baseball was far from developing the minor league "farm system" concept that more or less guarantees the worthiest young players a chance to rise toward the majors, the major and minor league strata in the late 1800s were not without avenues of advancement. When Grant was with Buffalo, he was always on the Bisons' reserve list, meaning that other teams tampered with him at their peril. But Buffalo could have sold his contract to a National League or an American Association club at any tme.

By 1892, had he still been in the International League, the revised National Agreement governing organized ball would have allowed a major league team to draft him for a $1,000 payment to Buffalo.[62]

In 1890, there was a massive talent search on when the Brotherhood of Professional Base Ball Players, the major league players' labor organization, broke with the major league owners and organized their own eight-team league. Although the Players' League lasted only one season, it drew about 120 defectors from the other two leagues, creating for some young men opportunities that turned into long major league careers. Cy Young broke in during 1890, for example.

Sol White, who played alongside Frank Grant in the Philadelphia Giants' infield and lived to see Jackie Robinson play in the majors, said that despite the lack of opportunity in his time, baseball "should be taken seriously by the colored player, as honest efforts with his great ability will open an avenue in the near future wherein he may walk hand in hand with the opposite race in the greatest of all American games—base ball."[63]

Undoubtedly, Frank Grant had the ability at least to play, if not to star, in the majors; but for him, the future Sol White saw was not anywhere near enough.

Who set up the main roadblocks to progress for Grant and his fellow black players? Among the fans, there did not seem to be strenuous opposition to black players. Witness the plaudits Grant received from the Buffalo faithful, and the newspaper account of his dramatic arrival for his first game with Harrisburg in 1890: The crowd at the ballpark was waiting in anxious expectation for the arrival of the "most famous colored ball player in the business," and when a carriage drawn by a locally famous trotter approached from the direction of the railroad station, Grant was recognized as its passenger. " 'Here he comes,' went through the crowd like magnetism and three cheers went up." Grant soon emerged from the players' dressing room in a Harrisburg uniform and "a great shout went up from the immense crowd to receive him, in recognition of which he politely raised his cap."[64]

But clearly there was opposition to the blacks from the white players, who may have feared their competition for roster spots in addition to more visceral racial feelings. Club owners, apparently, were ready to interpret incidents such as the team photo boycotts in Syracuse and Buffalo and the reluctance of the Binghamton players to take the field with Fowler as serious threats to the stability of their business. So they did away with the most expendable part of the problem, the black minority.

In 1988, Grant was elected to the Buffalo Bisons' Hall of Fame, receiving belated recognition for his three fine seasons there. But his life had been lost to the public almost as long as he had been gone from Olympic Park. For a time after the turn of the century, at least until 1904, he kept his official address in Williamstown with his older unmarried sisters, Amelia and Harriet, and a bachelor brother, Willis.[65] But shortly after that, a family dispute, the reason for which no one in current generations can now recall, led him to sever connections with his family, and they eventually lost track of him.[66]

He appears to have spent much of his last three decades in or around New York City. The New York *Age,* a black weekly, listed him among the old-timers lined up to play a benefit game in New Jersey for the ailing Bud Fowler in 1909 but the game never came to pass, and Grant sank out of sight again, as least as far as the sporting press was concerned.[67]

A New York City directory shows him living in Manhattan in 1932, at the same West 17th Street address listed on his death certificate.[68]

He died of arteriosclerosis in Bellevue Hospital in Manhattan on May 27, 1937.[69] At least in the end he was properly mourned. Sol White, legendary black pitcher Smokey Joe Williams, and Nux James, who had played black ball in Philadelphia and New York City, were among his pallbearers from a Harlem funeral home.[70] But burial was in a grave with no stone, across the Hudson River in the East Ridgelawn Cemetery in Clifton, New Jersey, under an arrangement in which the cemetery took "charity cases" from New York City.[71]

Grant's death certificate states only that he had been a waiter for the past 36 years, and mentions nothing about baseball.[72]

NOTES

1. Vital Records, City of Pittsfield, MA.
2. Vital Records, City of Pittsfield, MA.
3. Berkshire County, MA, Probate Court, appointment of guardian for Grant children, April 7, 1871.
4. Berkshire *Eagle,* Dec. 2, 1865.
5. Berkshire County, MA, Probate Court, appointment of guardian for Grant children, April 7, 1871.
6. North Adams, MA, *Transcript,* Aug. 7, 21, and 28 and Oct. 2, 1884.
7. Files of the Williamstown, MA, House of History.
8. Plattsburgh, NY, *Morning Telegraph,* Oct. 2, 1885.
9. Plattsburgh, NY, *Press,* Aug. 12, 1896.
10. *Morning Telegraph,* Aug. 24, 1885.
11. *Sol White's Official Base Ball Guide,* p. 127.
12. *Morning Telegraph,* Aug. 20, 1885.
13. *Sporting Life,* March 24, 1886.
14. *Sporting Life,* April 21, 1886.
15. *Sporting Life,* July 21, 1886.
16. *Spalding's Official Base Ball Guide,* 1887, p. 80.
17. *Sporting Life,* Nov. 10, 1886.
18. Buffalo, NY, *Express,* July 13, 1886.
19. *Express,* May 16 and Oct. 3, 1886.
20. The weekly league standings in the *Express* on July 18, 1886, had Buffalo 21–29, but they had played, and won, three games since Grant, Remsen, and Dunn had joined the team (*Express* of July 15, July 16, and July 18).
21. *Express,* July 13, 1886.

22. *Only the Ball Was White,* by Robert Peterson, p. 36.

23. *Express,* July 27, 1886.

24. *Express,* July 15, 1886.

25. *Express,* Aug. 8, 1886.

26. *Sporting Life,* Nov. 17, 1886.

27. *Sporting Life,* Jan. 12, 1887.

28. *Express,* Sept. 21, 1886, carried final standings, from which the difference was computed.

29. "The History of Major League Baseball," by David Q. Voigt, in *Total Baseball,* p. 11.

30. *Express,* May 15, 1887.

31. *Express,* May 18, 1887.

32. "Out at Home," by Jerry Malloy, in *The National Pastime,* 1983, p. 23.

33. "Out at Home," pp. 23–24.

34. "Out at Home," p. 25.

35. "Out at Home," p. 25, and *Sporting Life,* July 20, 1887.

36. Author's analysis of International League box scores in *Sporting Life,* summer of 1887.

37. *Express,* July 20, 1887.

38. Quoted in the *Express,* Sept. 4, 1887.

39. *Sporting Life,* Nov. 9, 1887.

40. *Sporting Life,* Nov. 23, 1887.

41. *Express,* Oct. 2, 1887.

42. *Sporting Life,* Oct. 24, 1888.

43. *Sporting Life,* Oct. 17, 1888.

44. *Sporting Life,* July 25, 1888.

45. *Only the Ball Was White,* p. 41.

46. *Sporting Life,* April 11, 1891.

47. *Only the Ball Was White,* p. 43.

48. *Sporting Life,* Nov. 28, 1888.

49. *Express,* March 6, 1889, and *Only the Ball Was White,* p. 44.

50. Buffalo, NY, *Courier,* April 14, 1889.

51. *Nineteenth Century Stars,* published by the Society for American Baseball Research, 1989, p. 54.

52. *Sporting Life,* May 10, 1890.

53. *Sporting Life,* May 24, 1890.

54. *Sporting Life,* July 26, 1890.

55. *Sporting Life,* Aug. 9, 1890.

56. *Nineteenth Century Stars,* p. 54, and *Sporting Life,* Nov. 1, 1890.

57. *Sporting Life,* May 2, May 23, and June 20, 1891.

58. *Sol White's Official Base Ball Guide,* p. 25.

59. Research by Merl Kleinknecht of the SABR Negro Leagues Committee, supplemented by the author.

60. *Sporting Life,* March 14, 1888; *Express,* April 14, 1888.

61. *Sol White's Official Base Ball Guide,* p. 83.

62. National Agreement of 1892, reprinted in *Reach's Official Base Ball Guide,* 1892, pp. 99–105.

63. *Sol White's Official Base Ball Guide,* p. 71.

64. Harrisburg, PA, *Patriot,* May 6, 1890.

65. Williamstown, MA, Town Directory, 1903–04, p. 40.

66. Interview with Virginia Grant Royston, North Adams, MA, January 1989.

67. New York *Age,* Feb. 25, 1909.

68. *Polk's New York City Directory,* 1933–34.

69. Death certificate 13454, Bureau of Records, Department of Health, Borough of Manhattan, New York City.

70. Pittsburgh *Courier,* July 3, 1937. (The writer, Cumberland Posey, refers to the funeral as having been that of Charles Grant, a famous black player who was a contemporary of Frank

Grant's. But since Charles Grant died in Cincinnati in 1932, Posey is undoubtedly referring to Frank Grant's funeral.)

71. Interview with staff at East Ridgelawn Cemetery, Clifton, NJ, April 1989.

72. Death certificate 13454, Bureau of Records, Department of Health, Borough of Manhattan, New York City.

Baseball and the Heart and Mind of Japan: The Randy Bass Case*

STEPHEN I. THOMPSON

It is widely believed that there is an intimate relationship between baseball and the American way of life. In spite of recent inroads from football and basketball—the latter arguably the most truly American of all sports, at least in terms of its origins—the summer game remains, to millions of Americans, our national pastime. It is indeed our "field of dreams"—although it is interesting that Bill Kinsella, author of that novel, is not American, but Canadian. For many of us, time does, in fact, as Tom Boswell says, begin on opening day; and life really does imitate the World Series. There is no epic poem about football or basketball of the stature of "Casey at the Bat"; the mighty Casey's failure to deliver in the clutch is a classic American tragedy.

The durability of the Abner Doubleday myth, in the face of conclusive debunking by Robert Henderson, Harold Seymour,[1] and many others, is further testimony to the depth of these feelings. There is something positively unpatriotic about the proposition that baseball derived from the British schoolyard game of rounders and was eventually codified by the immigrant Englishman Alexander Cartwright, rather than springing from the brow of an obscure Civil War general at Cooperstown, and no amount of compelling evidence will persuade most of us otherwise. In the oft-quoted words of Jacques Barzun, "Whoever wants to know the heart and mind of America had better learn baseball."[2]

Numerous authors—e.g., Joseph Durso in *Baseball and the American Dream*,[3] Richard Crepeau in *America's Diamond Mind*,[4] Tristram Coffin in *The Old Ball Game*[5]—have attempted, in various ways and with varying degrees of success, to elucidate the nature of the relationship between baseball and Amer-

*ACKNOWLEDGEMENTS: I am grateful to Rev. John R. Terry of Nara, Japan, for providing me with Japanese press reaction to the Bass case. An earlier version of this chapter was presented at the 1990 annual meeting of the Central States Anthropological Society.

ican culture and/or American ideology. Recently, there have been two perceptive historical studies of the reasons for the ascendancy of baseball over cricket in nineteenth-century United States.[6] What all these writers fail to come to grips with, however, and what is also ignored by the conventional wisdom cited above is the fact that baseball is no longer solely an American game. It is not enough merely to trace some hypothetical connection between baseball and the American psyche; a thoroughgoing analysis of the sport's emotional appeal in the world today must explain why it is the national game of Venezuela but not of Colombia, of the Dominican Republic but not of Haiti, on the opposite end of the same island, of Japan but not of Korea.[7] Or why it has apparently surged in popularity in recent years in Australia but not in New Zealand, in the Netherlands but not in Belgium, in Italy but not in Greece. Can it be that there is some element of national ethos that is shared by Americans, Venezuelans, Dominicans, Japanese, Australians, Dutch, and Italians but which is absent among Colombians, Haitians, Koreans, New Zealanders, Belgians, and Greeks? That proposition seems inherently unlikely, but it would take several books, rather than a brief chapter, to explore it fully. A much more plausible possibility is that the game of baseball may have a somewhat different appeal in each of the countries where it has become popular, and that, indeed, it becomes a very different game; that is, that the game played by Japanese schoolboys in the annual national high school tournament at Koshien Stadium in Osaka is not the same game as that played by Dominican peasant kids on the sandlots of San Pedro de Macorís, or in, say, the Nebraska state American Legion finals. I will explore that contention more fully with respect to Japanese baseball in a moment, but first I must undertake a brief digression into the history of my own academic discipline, anthropology. More specifically, I want to examine a rather murky episode in the recent past of American anthropology: the emergence, and then the virtual disappearance, of national character studies.

From the mid-1930s until the early fifties, many American anthropologists became almost obsessed with the issue of the relationship between culture and personality.[8] This research was heavily influenced by Freudian psychoanalytic theory, at a time when that approach was already obsolescent in psychology, and much of it stemmed, directly or indirectly, from an annual seminar conducted in the anthropology department at Columbia University by the psychoanalyst Abram Kardiner. Columbia, at the time, was the preeminent department in American anthropology; and among the participants in Kardiner's seminars, either as faculty members or graduate students, were such influential figures as Ralph Linton, Cora DuBois, Ruth Benedict, and Margaret Mead. The underlying premise of the approach was the notion that human nature is almost infinitely malleable, and that different cultures, through their own distinctive child-rearing practices, mold this flexible raw material in different ways to produce standardized adult personality types. The task of the anthropologist then became that of identifying the "typical" personality of the society under study and, if possible, specifying the mechanisms by which this personality was formed. Because of their orthodox Freudianism, most proponents paid particular attention to such topics as toilet training and weaning practices in pursuit of the latter goal. For example, Geoffrey Gorer, in a famous paper, attempted to explain the docility of the Russian people and their acceptance of authoritarian government by the practice of swaddling Russian infants, which supposedly rendered them incapable of questioning authority as adults.[9]

Culture and personality studies of this sort, when carried out on small-scale societies, usually were framed in terms of "basic personality" or "modal personality"; when they were conducted on nation-states, the standard term was "national character." During the 1940s, a plethora of monographs appeared on the national character of Americans, Russians, Germans, English, and Japanese, among others. With the benefit of almost fifty years of hindsight, many of these works seem shockingly naive, particularly in terms of their use of statistics. Researchers thought nothing of going into a society of a hundred million people, interviewing and administering projective psychological tests to a sample of a hundred, and making confident statements on that basis about "the national character" of the so and so. There is an old academic adage to the effect that the difference between sociologists and anthropologists is that anthropologists flunked elementary algebra in high school. It is a fact that, while some of us may have scraped through that course with Cs and Ds, my colleagues and I are not generally noted for our mathematical sophistication.

In 1952, however, Anthony Wallace, an anthropologist who had undergraduate training in engineering and who was, therefore, much more competent in statistics than the majority of his fellows, published his Ph.D. dissertation, "The Modal Personality of the Tuscorora Indians as Revealed by the Rorschach Test."[10] Concerned about sampling problems, Wallace had deliberately chosen to work with a small-scale society (approximately six hundred people), and was able to interview and test almost every Tuscorora. He employed what had by then become the standard technique in such studies, the administration of the Rorschach, or ink blot, test. Subjects' responses to the Rorschach cards were quantified, and "modal personality" was then defined in terms of the statistical mode of these responses—at least, it was in theory. To oversimplify a bit, the problem Wallace encountered was that there was no genuine mode in the Tuscorora case; no matter how he manipulated his data, he was forced to conclude that at least 40% of the Tuscorora population was nontypical and deviant.

This perplexing finding led Wallace to reassess the prevailing view of the relationship between culture and personality. He characterized the traditional approach with the phrase "replication of uniformity"; that is, culture is a mold that stamps out identical, or at least similar, personality types from the raw material of human nature. A more accurate depiction of reality, however, is provided by the notion of "organization of diversity"; culture provides a set of patterned behaviors through which individuals may satisfy very different motivations.[11] For example, suppose you and I encounter each other on the sidewalk. Since we're Americans rather than Japanese, we shake hands rather than bowing—that's the standard greeting behavior provided by our shared culture. But on the individual level, your reason for shaking my hand may be very different from my reason for shaking yours. You may want to impress your companion with the fact that you know the eminent anthropologist Thompson well enough to shake his hand on the street, while I may be a kinky skin fetishist who gets off on shaking hands. The point is that this culturally specific behavioral act enables each of us to satisfy quite different motivations.

By this time you are undoubtedly wondering what all of this has to do with baseball. The answer, I would argue, is that Barzun was indeed on to something when he advocated the study of baseball as a way to understand the hearts and minds of Americans, but that the same study also will provide insight into the hearts and minds of Venezuelans and Dominicans and Japanese, different as those hearts and minds may be from ours. The key lies in understanding the way the game is played in these other baseball-loving nations, and, even more important, the way it is perceived and understood.

The purpose here is to describe and analyze a recent series of events in Japanese baseball—events involving an American player, Randy Bass—in an attempt to elucidate some significant differences between Japanese and American behavior and ideology. I say "behavior and ideology" rather than "national character" because I have serious reservations concerning the validity and utility of the latter concept. On the other hand, no one could seriously argue that there are not major differences in the ways Japanese and Americans act and in their views of the world; nor could anyone who has ever watched even one Japanese baseball game, at any level, fail to detect striking differences in the game itself.

Baseball in Japan dates back more than a century, although it did not become a professional sport until 1935.[12] It was originally introduced by returning students from American universities, and quickly gained wide acceptance. Donald Roden attributes its early popularity to a growing sense of national identity—in his words, the "quest for national dignity"—characteristic of Japan in the Meiji Era (1868–1912).[13] The Japanese penchant for borrowing from other cultures has often been exaggerated, but, like most such stereotypes, it contains a grain of truth. What is often forgotten, however, is that such cultural loans are invariably reinterpreted and modified until they become uniquely Japanese.

A case in point: two indications of recent American influence in Japan are the growing significance of Christmas, and the ubiquity of fast-food restaurants. Christmas, barely celebrated at all two decades ago, is now perhaps the third most important holiday on the Japanese calendar, surpassed only by New Year's and by O-bon, the Buddhist festival of the dead in August. In a country where less than one per cent of the population is Christian, however, it is a purely secular occasion, without even the vestigial religious connotations that still attach to it in the United States. American fast-food outlets are everywhere, particularly in the larger cities; one can barely walk a block without encountering a McDonald's,[14] a Wendy's, a Shakey's Pizza emporium, or a Kentucky Fried Chicken place. But in Japan, these two manifestations of American culture have merged in a specifically Japanese amalgam. In front of every sizable Kentucky Fried Chicken store in Tokyo there stands a life-sized statue of Colonel Sanders. A couple of weeks before Christmas each year, the colonel is bedecked in a Santa Claus costume. Somehow—either as a result of a brilliant marketing ploy or by sheer happenstance—millions of Japanese have gotten the notion that the traditional American Christmas dinner consists of Kentucky Fried Chicken. Every Christmas morning at 7:30 or so, long lines begin to form outside each neighborhood chicken emporium, waiting to pick up a bucket or a box for the family's American-style holiday meal.

One more non-baseball example: Eri Chiemi, a popular Japanese female vocalist, had a major hit record in the late fifties with a Japanese rendition of "Rock Around the Clock." After one quick swing through the English lyrics—although she specialized in American songs at the time, Eri spoke no English and memorized the words phonetically[15]—the singer switches to her native language. This creates a difficulty, however, since the English expression "around the clock," in the sense of the twelve- or twenty-four-hour period it takes the hour hand to traverse the dial, is an idiom, and has no equivalent in Japanese. Therefore, the Japanese version, a literal translation of the English, conveys the image of a large clock standing in the middle of a dance floor with a group of people rocking around it in a circle. The song can still be heard occasionally in Japan, some thirty-five years or so after the original recording, and to a whole new generation of Japanese listeners, that remains its meaning.

I do not propose to analyze in detail here the various ways in which baseball has similarly been modified and reinterpreted to fit into the overall context of Japanese culture; much of that task has already been accomplished by Robert Whiting in two excellent books, one of them reviewed in this volume.[16] Instead, I will focus on one aspect of traditional Japanese ideology—the conflict between *giri* and *ninjō* and examine the relevance of that conflict to the Japanese baseball career of Randy Bass.

"Giri" in Japanese refers to duty, and *"ninjō"* to human feelings; and the conflict between them is a recurrent theme in drama, literature, and culture in general. When the demands of *giri* clash with ties to family and loved ones, there are only two acceptable resolutions—to ignore human feelings altogether and fulfill one's obligation to the Emperor, the feudal lord, or, in modern times, one's employer, or to escape from an impossible situation through an honorable suicide.

This classic Japanese ethical dilemma is exhaustively discussed in Ruth Benedict's famous wartime book on Japanese national character, *The Chrysanthemum and the Sword*. In Benedict's view, the *giri–ninjō* conflict is best epitomized by what she calls "the true national epic of Japan,"[17] *Chūshingura,* or "The Treasury of Loyal Retainers."[18] Originally a puppet play first staged in 1748, it was adapted to the Kabuki theater a century later, and more recently has appeared in innumerable film and television versions. The co-author of a standard history of Japanese cinema recounts that he once attempted to enumerate the various film treatments but stopped counting when he reached two hundred and twenty.[19] As Donald Keene points out in the introduction to his translation of the puppet play, "Its popularity in Japan has always been such that managers of Kabuki or puppet theaters have traditionally staged it whenever in financial straits, and film companies today have followed their example."[20]

Chūshingura is based on an actual historical incident of 1703; but with the passage of time—even the forty-five years between the historical event and the first puppet play—fact and legend became so intertwined that they are now all but inseparable. In 1701, Asano Noganori, feudal lord of the Akō domain in western Japan, had been assigned the important task of organizing the cere-

Randy Bass as a Hanshin Tiger. (Photo: courtesy of Robet Klevens, Sports Card Heaven, Davie, Florida)

monial reception of an imperial envoy to the Shogun's court at Edo (now Tokyo). The Tokugawa Shogunate was, by that time, a century old. It had been a period of internal peace, and, in the eyes of many Japanese traditionalists, then and later, the result had been decay in the warrior virtues of an earlier era and growing dilettantism and degeneracy. Asano is depicted as the living embodiment of the much-lamented bygone martial characteristics. As a result, he was uncomfortable in the effete atmosphere of the Shogunal court, and sought instruction from Kira Yoshinaka, the chief of protocol. In his naiveté, he failed to offer Kira the customary bribe for this help, and Kira taunted him for his social ineptitude. Angered, Asano drew his sword to attack his tormentor and, before controlling himself, inflicted a superficial wound. For the crime of unsheathing his weapon in the Shogun's palace he was sentenced to commit suicide. His estates were confiscated and his retainers set adrift as *rōnin,* masterless samurai.

The general expectation was that Asano's former followers would seek to avenge their dead lord, and most of the play concerns their successful attempts over the next twenty-one months to lull Kira's suspicions. Under the leadership of Oishi Kuranosuke, Asano's chief retainer, forty-seven of his samurai embarked on lives of dissipation and debauchery to mask their real intentions. Oishi divorced his wife—a precaution designed to protect his family from sharing in his ultimate punishment—and consorted with prostitutes. Another of the *rōnin,* needing money to finance his façade, sold his wife into prostitution. A third had his sister installed as one of Kira's concubines to act as a spy within the enemy's entourage. All forty-seven became the objects of public scorn and reprisal for their apparent disloyalty.

On the night of January 30, 1703, as a blizzard raged outside, the retainers burst into Kira's mansion, overcoming his complacent guards. After searching the house, they found their prey cowering in a storage closet. Using the same sword that Asano had employed to disembowel himself, they cut off Kira's head, washed it, and triumphantly carried it through the streets of Edo to the grave of their dead lord.

In Keene's words, "The boldness of the vendetta caught the imagination of men of every class. At a time when the samurai ideals of loyalty and resolute action seemed to have been forgotten, thanks to the peace of almost a hundred years, this sudden dramatic gesture came as a heartening reminder of what being a samurai had once meant."[21]

The government was confronted with a major dilemma. The forty-seven were popular heroes, hailed as exemplars of traditional virtue, yet they had assassinated one of the Shogun's chief courtiers. The official response was quintessentially Japanese; the *rōnin* were honored by the court, and then condemned to commit mass suicide. Their immolation took place in front of Asano's grave, and they were buried at his side at Sengaku-ji temple. The cemetery where they are interred remains, almost three centuries later, a magnet for pious pilgrims, and their graves are never without fresh flowers.

Chūshingura is a classic example of the virtuous resolution of a *giri–ninjō* conflict. Whatever the relationship between Oishi and his wife may have been in real life, in the fictional versions, it is depicted as a loving one; yet he unhesitatingly casts her aside for the sake of his duty to his dead lord. Each of the forty-seven, in fact, similarly subordinated his personal feelings toward his family and loved ones to his feudal obligations.

Benedict's book, with its six-page synopsis of *Chūshingura,* was translated into Japanese after the war and became a major best-seller in Japan. The initial Japanese response was somewhat ambivalent, but several writers criticized her mildly for depicting as current a national ethos which had, in their view, expired with the Meiji Restoration of 1868.[22] Today, four decades later, Japanese seldom speak of *giri,* and on the rare occasions that they do, it is invariably the older generation disparaging what is perceived as the improper behavior of the young. Yet a case can be made that these traditional values still survive, in the improbable milieu of the baseball stadium.

A modern day counterpart of *Chūshingura,* with a very different outcome, is the saga of Randy Bass. Bass, a farm boy from Lawton, Oklahoma, capped a spectacular minor league career with back-to-back banner seasons with Denver of the American Association in 1979 and 1980—consecutive .333 batting averages, 36 and 37 home runs, and 105 and 143 RBIs, respectively. He never came close to matching those statistics in the American majors, however; in six partial seasons with five different teams between 1977 and 1982, his career major league totals were 325 at bats in 130 games, with nine home runs, 42 runs batted in, and a meager lifetime batting average of .212.

In 1983, following in the footsteps of many marginal and over-the-hill American ballplayers, Bass signed with the Hanshin Tigers of the Japanese Central League. Hanshin is the second oldest Japanese professional baseball team, and the second most popular. The Yomiuri Giants of Tokyo, the New York Yankees of Japan, are the favorites of at least seventy-five per cent of Japanese baseball fans, and the recipients of obsessive media attention and consistent favoritism from umpires.[23] But the Tigers, from Osaka, have a strong regional following in the Kansai area and appeal to a small national minority of Giants-haters, this writer among them. Modest success at the box office has seldom been matched on the field, however. Founded in 1935, Hanshin had claimed only six pennants at the time of Bass's arrival, the most recent coming in 1964. Meanwhile, the hated Giants had dominated the league, winning nine straight titles from 1965 through 1973, and thirty-one altogether.

From the outset of his Japanese career, Bass began to duplicate his impressive American minor league power figures. In 1983, helped to some extent by the generally smaller ballparks in Japan—but handicapped by the shorter 130 game season—he hit 35 home runs, drove in 83 runs, and batted .288. The following year his batting average rose to .326, although his home run and RBI productivity fell off to 27 and 73. Some of that decline in power totals came about because he missed several weeks of the season to sit by his father's deathbed and then attend the funeral. A few mumblings of discontent were heard from diehard Tiger fans over the length of that absence, but filial piety is a trait much admired in Japan, and Hanshin was already out of the pennant race in any case.

I talked with Bass during that 1984 season. He admitted to a bit of difficulty in adapting to some aspects of Japanese life, especially the diet—I was living two blocks from the Giants' stadium in Tokyo, and he and my twelve-year-old son regularly ate lunch together at McDonald's whenever the Tigers were in town—but he expressed admiration for the national work ethic and the Japanese player's dedication to his team.

Whatever his initial problems may have been, Bass's adjustment was clearly complete by 1985. His batting average soared to .350, his home runs to 54, and his RBIs to 134—all league-leading totals. He also led the league in hits, doubles, game-winning hits, slugging percentage, on-base percentage, and total bases. More important for Hanshin fans, the Tigers' long pennant drought was ended with a Central League title and a victory over the Seibu Lions in the

Japan Series. Bass was the Most Valuable Player in the regular season, and, after stroking three homers in six games, in the Series as well—the first player to achieve that double honor since his fellow Oklahoman, Joe Stanka, had done it as a pitcher with the Nankai Hawks in 1964.

The only negative event in that spectacular year occurred in the final series of the regular season aganst the Giants. Bass had already accumulated his 54 homers, and was one behind the all-time Japanese single-season record of 55, set in 1964 by the legendary Sadaharu Oh. The same Oh was, in 1985, the Giants' manager. Bass batted nine times in that two-game series and drew six walks; on the other three occasions, he swung at balls far out of the strike zone, singling twice, and popping up once. Keith Comstock, an American pitcher with the Giants, later revealed that Oh had threatened a heavy fine to any pitcher who threw Bass a strike.[24]

The Tigers failed to repeat in 1986—Okada and Kakefu, their other two sluggers, were clearly over the hill—but Bass racked up his second consecutive triple crown, with 47 homers, 109 RBIs, and, after flirting with .400 for much of the year, a .389 batting average. By now, he was definitely the most popular, as well as the most successful, American ever to play in Japan, and was hailed as the honorary mayor of Kobe, the port city near Osaka where he lived during the season.

His numbers declined somewhat in 1987—.320, 37 homers, 109 RBIs—but were still more than respectable by any standard. The team as a whole, however, had a horrendous year, winning fewer than a third of its games and falling to last place, 37½ games behind the arch-rival Giants. The pitching staff had collapsed completely, and several aging stars reached the end of the line simultaneously, with no young replacements ready to step into their shoes.

The Hanshin Company, a railroad and department store conglomerate, responded by firing the field manager and shaking up the front office. Shingo Furuya, previously an executive with Hanshin Railways, was appointed managing director. The team's performance was not much better in the first month of the 1988 season, however, even though Bass, who hit .321 in the first 22 games, got off to a fairly good start. Then, in May of that year, Bass's eight-year-old son Zachary was found to have a brain tumor, and his father was granted a "compassionate leave" to accompany the boy to San Francisco for surgery. Complications developed—the initial surgery was unsuccessful, a drainage tube was inserted into Zachary's skull, and radiation treatments were begun. When, a month later, Bass had not yet returned to Japan, the team unceremoniously released him.

According to Robert Whiting, whose excellent account of the Bass case I am following closely here, a major factor in this seemingly heartless decision was the team's reluctance to pay Zachary's medical expenses, a contractual obligation so long as his father remained with the club.[25] An acrimonious dispute ensued, Bass claiming that Hanshin owed him a million and a half dollars in unpaid salary as well as medical costs, and the team replying that he had violated a written agreement to return by mid-June. Bass then produced a tape recording of a telephone conversation with a Hanshin executive granting him permission to remain in the U.S. until his son's condition stabilized.

As this controversy intensified in the press and in the courts, the Tigers sank deeper into the cellar. Ruppert Jones, the American journeyman signed as Bass's successor and hailed as Hanshin's saviour, was to finish the year with an anemic .254 batting average and a mere eight home runs. On July 19, Furuya, the hapless railroad man trying unsuccessfully to run a baseball team, atoned for his failure by jumping to his death from an eighth-floor balcony of the Hotel New Otani in Tokyo.

Giri and *ninjō* loom large in this tragedy. Randy Bass, the foreigner,[26] placed his feelings for his son above his loyalty to his team and by doing so, literally rendered himself ineligible, despite his spectacular statistics, to play again in Japan. In 1989, the Yakult Swallows, another perennial also-ran, indicated an interest in signing Bass and were informed by the Japanese Baseball Commissioner's office that such a transaction would not be approved.[27] Furuya, the organization man, had failed in his duty to his employer by mishandling the Bass case and could only atone, both for that and for the team's dismal performance, by taking his own life. Some segments of the highly sensationalistic Japanese sporting press have blamed Bass for that suicide.

Epic dramas seldom have happy endings, but this is not an unrelieved tragedy. Zachary Bass seems on his way to a complete recovery. Randy Bass has purchased a large cattle ranch near his home town of Lawton, and in a *Japan Times* interview late in the 1989 season, professed to be enjoying his retirement.[28] During the winter of 1989–90, however, apparently he felt the itch. At the age of 35, he joined the fledgling Senior Professional Baseball Association, where he hit a resounding .393. That performance earned him an invitation to training camp with the Baltimore Orioles as a prospective designated hitter, but a muscle pull and the owners' lockout combined to deprive him of any real chance of making the team. Thus, he remains a victim of what we might call the Kipling syndrome—the failure of the twain to meet.

In the halcyon days before free agency, American ballplayers were presumed to be loyal to their teams, even if that purported loyalty was sometimes more apparent than real and was seldom reciprocated by management. Not even John McGraw or Miller Huggins, however, would have expected a player to ignore the plight of a critically ill child for the sake of an already hopeless pennant race. Clearly, things are different in Japan. All disclaimers to the contrary notwithstanding, the importance of *giri* is a concept still internalized at an early age by every well-socialized Japanese. The older generation may lament that youngsters nowadays actually want to go home right after work and spend time with their families,[29] but the primary loyalty of the overwhelming majority of Japanese workers is still to their employer. Most labor unions are enterprise unions, enrolling everyone in the company, from the shoproom floor to the president's office, but not crossing corporate boundaries. As a result, strikes are virtually nonexistent, since they would place the employer at a competitive disadvantage. A growing labor shortage has begun to erode slightly the traditional system of lifetime employment, but workers who shift jobs in mid-career almost never join a competitor. Most Japanese simply do not understand how a Lee Iacocca could move from Ford to Chrysler and be accepted by his corporate colleagues.[30] These attitudes pervade Japanese baseball as they do the rest of Japanese life. To foreigners in Japan, including American baseball players, they will forever remain utterly alien.

NOTES

1. Robert Henderson, *Ball, Bat, and Bishop: The Origin of Ball Games.* (New York: Rockport Press, 1947); Harold Seymour, *Baseball: The Early Years.* (New York: Oxford University Press, 1960).

2. I have been unable to track down the original source of this famous Barzun aphorism, but it is quoted in Seymour, *Baseball: The Early Years,* p. 3.

3. Joseph Durso, *Baseball and the American Dream.* (St. Louis: *The Sporting News,* 1985).

4. Richard C. Crepeau, *Baseball: America's Diamond Mind, 1919–1951* (Orlando: University Press of Central Florida, 1980).

5. Tristram Coffin, *The Old Ball Game: Baseball in Folklore and Fiction* (New York: Herder and Herder, 1971).

6. Melvin L. Adelman, *A Sporting Time: New York City and the Rise of Modern Athletics, 1820–70* (Urbana: University of Illinois Press, 1986); George B. Kirsch, *The Creation of American Team Sports: Baseball and Cricket, 1838–72* (Urbana: University of Illinois, 1989).

7. Two excellent studies of Dominican baseball have appeared recently: Alan M. Klein, *Sugarball: The American Game, the Dominican Dream* (New Haven: Yale University Press, 1991); and Rob Ruck, *The Tropic of Baseball: Baseball in the Dominican Republic* (Westport, CT: Meckler, 1991). Both analyze the appeal of the game to Dominicans, but neither addresses the Haitian contrast.

8. The following historical discussion is based primarily on Milton Singer, "A Survey of Culture and Personality Theory and Research" in Bert Kaplan, ed., *Studying Personality Cross-Culturally* (Evanston, IL: Row, Peterson, 1961), pp. 9–90.

9. Geoffrey Gorer, "Some Aspects of the Psychology of the People of Great Russia." *American Slavic and East European Review* 8, No. 3 (1949): 155–66.

10. Anthony F.C. Wallace, "The Modal Personality Structure of the Tuscorora Indians as Revealed by the Rorschach Test," *Bureau of American Ethnology, Bulletin No. 150* (1952).

11. Anthony F.C. Wallace, *Culture and Personality* (New York: Random House, 1961).

12. The origins of professional baseball in Japan are summarized briefly in Stephen I. Thompson and Masaru Ikei, "Victor Starfin: The Blue-eyed Japanese," *Baseball History* 2(4) (1987): 4–19.

13. Donald F. Roden, "Baseball and the Quest for National Dignity in Meiji Japan," *American Historical Review* 85 (1980): 511–534.

14. When, in 1984, a berserk gunman massacred several customers in a California McDonald's, a Japanese TV newsman reporting the story felt it necessary to inform his audience that "There are McDonald's in the United States, too."

15. The results of this memorization were sometimes bizarre; in Eri's version of "Dance with me, Henry" the line "It's intermission in a minute" is transposed to "It's in a intermission minute" no fewer than four times on the record. Evidently, no one noticed. A contemporary Japanese country singer, who likewise speaks no English, specializes in Willie Nelson songs; his two biggest hits are "An za Wo Agen" (as in "Just can't wait to get an za wo agen") and "Whiskey Liver."

16. Robert Whiting, *The Chrysanthemum and the Bat: Baseball Samurai Style* (New York: Dodd, Mead, 1977); *You Gotta Have Wa: When Two Cultures Collide on the Baseball Diamond* (New York: Macmillan, 1989).

17. Ruth Benedict, *The Chrysanthemum and the Sword: Patterns of Japanese Culture* (Boston: Houghton Mifflin, 1946).

18. Izumo Takeda, Shōraku Miyoshi, and Senryū Namiki, *Chūshingura (The Treasury of Loyal Retainers)* (New York: Columbia University Press, 1971), Donald Keene, translator.

19. Joseph L. Anderson, "Second and Third Thoughts about the Japanese Film," in Joseph

L. Anderson and Donald Richie, *The Japanese Film: Art and Industry* (Princeton, NJ: Princeton University Press, 1982), p. 446.

20. *Chūshingura*, p. 25.

21. *Chūshingura*, p. 2.

22. For a survey of Japanese reactions, *see* John W. Bennett and Michio Nagai, "The Japanese Critique of Benedict's *Chrysanthemum and the Sword*," *American Anthropologist* 55 (1953): 401–411.

23. Whiting dissects this phenomenon in chapter 11 (pp. 210–220) of *The Chrysanthemum and the Bat*.

24. Whiting, *You Gotta Have Wa*, p. 294.

25. Ibid., 303–304.

26. *Gaijin*, the Japanese word for "foreigner," literally means "outside person." The term is fraught with symbolism; in Japan the foreigner is perhaps more thoroughly and completely an outsider than anywhere else in the world.

27. *Japan Times*, August 22, 1989, p. 12.

28. Ibid.

29. Jared Taylor, *Shadows of the Rising Sun: A Critical View of the Japanese Miracle* (New York: William Morrow, 1983), p. 184.

30. Iacocca is a much hated figure in Japan, and not merely because of his inveterate Japan bashing; *see* the depiction of the Iacocca-like character "Ironcoke" in Shōtarō Ishinomori, *Japan Inc.: An Introduction to Japanese Economics (The Comic Book)* (Berkeley: University of California Press, 1988), Betsey Scheiner, translator.

Diamonds for Sale: Promoting Baseball During the Great Depression*

In 1930, baseball teams advertised games with only an announcement of the opponent and game time in that day's paper. "In covering baseball," the *Sporting News* noted in 1932, "papers are only satisfying a demand on the part of their readers, and such coverage, from a strictly news standpoint, helps a newspaper to retain and develop circulation." Newspapers, in other words, needed baseball much more than the game needed them. By the next year, the paper had changed its tune, however, arguing that "any attraction that is worthwhile is worth advertising." Or, as Giants' first baseman and manager Bill Terry confessed in 1936, "up to now I have believed in being quiet, doing the sporting thing and taking things as they are handed out. But I have found that doesn't go in baseball. The fans don't like it . . . [and] the quiet fellow invariably comes out on the short end." Indeed, by the end of the depression, "color" had become almost as important as skill in the evaluation of a player.[1]

This shift in opinion reflected both major league baseball's changing attitude toward self-promotion and larger trends within the mass culture. Promotion of baseball began in the late nineteenth century under Albert G. Spalding, whose tactics enacted his progressive ideology. As part of the nation's "search for order," Spalding organized baseball rationally into a respectable, healthful industry that would revitalize America both individually and en masse. Baseball, in his eyes, developed moral and physical fitness that made possible renewed national commitment and growth. Its success, and that of the progressive movement—as well as of the nation as a whole—were ultimately

*I would like to thank everyone at the National Baseball Library for their help. Thanks also to Susan Etlinger, Beth Haiken, Professors John Fine and Gerald Linderman, and especially to Professor Sidney Fine.

synonymous. When Spalding called baseball "America's national game" he meant the term literally.[2]

By the dawn of the thirties, baseball men had forgotten this past. Although the decade began with almost no advertising, in the early depression years a few "innovators" returned to methods that Spalding had begun. By decade's end, promotion and spectacle had swept the game, mirroring a cultural transition from "idols of production" to "idols of consumption," in the words of Leo Lowenthal. The idol of production provided a "model for individual imitation" and advancement, as in Spalding's contention that baseball built the character and discipline necessary for continued American greatness. The idol of consumption simply showed one how to enjoy one's leisure time, usually by consuming. In this sense, the idol of consumption, such as the "colorful" player of the depression, was often reduced to a commodity and sold as one. Team owners were, therefore, neither the capitalist entrepreneurs of Spalding's time nor the civic-minded gentlemen-sportsmen of the 1920s. Rather, they conceived of themselves as competitors for the entertainment dollar. The depression induced them to turn to new media and more effectively utilize old media to peddle their game and its players to the public.[3]

No one needed to compete for the entertainment dollar in the 1920s. During this Golden Age, barely three of the sixteen teams lost money in any given year. The average team made a profit of more than $115,000.[4] Only the Boston Red Sox, seriously weakened by the loss of players whom owner Harry Frazee had sold to finance a run of unsuccessful Broadway shows, ran into serious financial trouble. The game roared into the new decade: since 1930 marked the most profitable year in baseball's history until 1950, the onset of the depression's effects in the next year proved even more shocking. Just four franchises showed a profit in 1932, a mere two the following year. For the decade, profits fell off by more than 90%. Although the game's losses stabilized by 1936, not until World War II and the adoption of night baseball did true stabililty return. In the meantime, the National League had directed the Braves' operations for several months, and the poverty-stricken Athletics, Braves, and Browns had become chronic losers. Yet only two teams actually failed because the owners and league heads responded so effectively. Baseball executives followed the lead of other businessmen by cutting expenses, firing employees, and working together to contain problems before they got out of hand.[5] So, too, did they return to promotion, hoping to entice poverty-stricken fans to ease their woes and rest their feet with an idyllic afternoon at the ballpark.

This rediscovery of advertising proved so popular that "by the end of the thirties," according to one author, "the 'sideshow accessories' of 1930 had become sound business technique." As early as 1933, calls for excitement, color, and showmanship resounded from all quarters. "More showmanship," demanded respected New York sportswriter Dan Daniel, "more innovation, in place of mental static and physical inertia which are now found in so many high places in the game." The *Sporting News* jumped on the bandwagon in 1933 by envisioning an NRA-style insignia to symbolize and promote the game. After St. Louis's Dizzy Dean captured the nation's imagination in 1934 by winning thirty games and mangling the English language, his consequent appearance on sweatshirts, toothbrushes, caps, booklets, and a comic strip advertising food products led to a contract in 1935 which included promotional activities to be arranged by the team. New National League commissioner Ford Frick emphasized the league's good fortune in 1935 because it sported "probably the most colorful as well as competent assemblage of players in its long history." *Baseball* magazine described the season—like the circus—as "the greatest show on earth," then ran articles with such titles as "Wanted—Up-to-Date Showmanship" and "Selling Baseball to the Public."[6]

Team newspapers such as *Giants Jottings, Cubs News,* and *Dodger Doings* appeared. They previewed future opponents, printed letters from fans, and offered such interesting bits of trivia as the fact that the Wrigley Field concessionaires had sold sixty thousand hot dogs over the July 4th weekend. By 1937, ballplayers regularly spoke at banquets, talked to boys' clubs, appeared at charity drives, and frequently endorsed commercial products. Baseball had begun to promote itself as a corporation, with the players as both its spokesmen and its products. In keeping with this corporate ethic, maintenance of baseball's "dignity" remained paramount. As Washington owner Clark Griffith put it, the national pastime would never "go in for any Hippodrome stuff." That is, spectacle would never distort the game's essence. Yet spectacle did become a central part of the game. Unlike Spalding, who railed against the "spectacular," baseball men of the thirties accepted spectacle if it would help their industry survive.[7]

The ascendancy of Ford Frick clearly symbolized baseball's new ethic. He rose meteorically through the official hierarchy: Beginning as a sportswriter, he moved to radio, then ran the National League Service Bureau (an official promotional organization) for nine months before becoming league president in November 1934. As the most dynamic and influential of the game's executives, Frick promoted flexibility, cooperation, and attention to detail in the selling of baseball. He saw Spalding as "ruthless," "arrogant," "no paragon of sportsmanlike virtues," and, worst of all, "selfish" because he entwined his fortunes with those of the game. Frick, in contrast, saw baseball as a commodity, not an agent of moral reconstruction. "Baseball is not, nor does it profess to be," he wrote in his autobiography, "a builder of human character or a champion of moral uplift. It is a game—and a good one! . . . Whatever may be its impact as a social or moral influence is incidental." With a reporter's eye for detail, he pushed for more polite stadium help, convenient drinking fountains, better-quality seating, and exciting and attractive play.[8]

Frick extended a plan begun by his predecessor, John Heydler. Before the 1933 season, Heydler proposed an unprecedented five-point plan that exhorted the players to "build up and maintain the interest in our game by a display of the heads-up, winning spirit which does not surrender." To emphasize this spirit, Heydler laid down the following restrictions:

1. Do not mingle on the field with players of the opposing club.
2. Do not enter the clubhouse or dressing rooms of the other team.
3. Do not take it for granted that with a lopsided score against you the game is lost. The man who pays is still entitled to your best effort.

4. Action and hustle, and still more action and hustle, are needed in our game. Be enthusiastic and cheerful.
5. Be alert and interested every moment of the game.

In essence, Heydler attempted to codify what was known as "color," a quality increasingly divorced from the ability to play baseball well. Color could derive from a player's general appearance, such as Pepper Martin's lean, grizzled face and hard-nosed play, both evocative of the national will to persevere in the face of overwhelming odds; or it might reside in outrageous behavior, such as Dizzy Dean's country bragging. If a player was not particularly colorful, the proclamation encouraged him to excite fan interest by at least simulating a degree of color. Thus Heydler's proposition was significant in that he was one of the first to posit organized self-promotion as a cure for baseball's financial crisis.

But Heydler did not share Frick's promotional genius. Horrified by a widely-publicized 1931 photograph of Cub catcher Gabby Hartnett smilingly autographing a ball for twelve-year-old Sonny Capone while his father Al and bodyguards looked on, Heydler banned all contact between fans and players. The ensuing storm of criticism caused him to rescind the ban halfway through the season. He spent the next three years glumly cataloguing the depression's ravages. To Frick, who traced a legacy of fandom back to Abraham Lincoln and Ulysses Grant, the photo would not have posed a problem. After all, it made good copy.[9]

If baseball were to remain good copy in the depression, it required a mythologized history free of objectionable facts. Frick labored to create an edited version of baseball's past that deleted its less savory aspects. The Service Bureau carried out most of Frick's rewriting. Originally created by the major leagues in 1922 to respond to sportswriters' requests for information, by 1934 the bureau had become aggressive. It sent information to more than 250 newspapers, wrote radio dramatizations of players' lives, and published record books. Its publications determinedly sanitized the game's history: a 1937 publication entitled *Major League Baseball: Facts and Figures,* for example, not only smoothed over baseball's repeated brushes with gambling and thrown games in the 1915–1919 period but glossed over the entire Black Sox scandal as well. The bureau tried to mitigate the depression's effects on baseball by ignoring them. Although Connie Mack clearly explained that he had traded his stars because he could no longer afford their salaries, a release discussing the trade of Philadelphia's Al Simmons, Jimmy Dykes, and Mule Haas to the White Sox emphasized their superiority to the players they were replacing and concluded that they would strengthen the team both offensively and defensively. The release did not explain why Chicago had been able to acquire three such excellent players in exchange for clearly lesser(-paid) talents.[10]

On the slim pretext that it was the sixtieth anniversary of the founding of the National League, Frick made the entire 1936 season into a gala birthday party. The league's fiftieth anniversary had passed without a murmur, *Baseball* magazine remembered, adding that "the Frick idea is a big step in advance." Beginning with a dinner at the Waldorf in February, continuing with a reenactment of an 1876-style game in June, and spreading to every league park, the season-long celebration made baseball seem comfortable and familial: the game never forgot its past and welcomed players after their careers ended.[11]

This mythology culminated in the Hall of Fame, which opened in 1939 and ratified the legend of Alexander Doubleday. Originally, a baseball museum had been proposed in 1934 by a civic group from Cooperstown. Of baseball's three major officials, Frick involved himself the most with the hall's founding. Rather than merely collecting historical memorabilia, Frick suggested that baseball promotion itself be institutionalized in an actual Hall of Fame. After the announcement of the hall in 1935, the Cooperstown group began a national advertising campaign that included movies, radio announcements, newspaper and magazine articles, even ashtrays and an official postage stamp. Frick took little part in this campaign. He intervened to ensure that Cooperstown would remain only a part of baseball's centennial celebration. When disputes arose over the Doubleday legend, Frick emphasized baseball's image rather than the search for the truth, then endorsed Doubleday after the controversy died down. The entire process erased baseball's British ancestry and firmly cemented the Doubleday legend in the public mind. Its official proclamation of baseball's distinctly American heritage resonated strongly in an era so devoted to rediscovering the "real" American past. And Frick's determination to make the game as attractive a product as possible, even at the cost of distorting history, resonated equally strongly.[12]

Spurred by Frick's example, others undertook to sell the game. Almost every team installed a public address system to bring the fans closer to the action. Many teams courted the female fan with the institution of a weekly Ladies' Day

The Centennial Parade, Cooperstown, New York, 1939. (Photo: Homer Osterhoudt; from the National Baseball Library, Cooperstown, N.Y.)

The National Baseball Hall of Fame Dedication Ceremonies, Cooperstown, 1939. Front row (left to right): Eddie Collins, Babe Ruth, Connie Mack, Cy Young; back row: Honus Wagner, Grover Alexander, Tris Speaker, Nap Lajoie, George Sisler, and Walter Johnson. (Photo: National Baseball Library, Cooperstown, N.Y.)

(depending on the team, free admission for either all women or all escorted women). Twenty-two thousand women attended one such day in St. Louis.[13] In 1933, the Boston clubs began an annual series of games enlivened by vaudeville and athletic contests to benefit the city's Unemployment Fund. These games drew huge crowds of 15,000 which greatly exceeded the typical attendance for either team.[14]

Lew Fonseca took a more systematic approach. His movies elevated a base-ball game to high drama and cast players as actors. Horsehide and celluloid first converged when Fonseca worked as an extra in several films while playing winter ball in Los Angeles in 1927. As manager of the White Sox, he decided to use film to study Ted Lyons's pitching form and Al Simmons's famous "bucket-foot" batting stance. When the club fired Fonseca in 1934, he tried his hand at directing. After securing the approval of the American League owners, he approached league president William Harridge. Harridge paid Fonseca $500 for a one-month trial period in which he screened the film, free of charge, at high schools, colleges, banquets, businessmen's clubs, luncheons, and anywhere else that a large number of fans might be expected to congregate. At year's end, he had received so many requests to show the film that the league hired him on a full-time basis.[15]

More than three million people had seen Fonseca's first two movies, *Play Ball* and *Take Me Out to the Ball Game,* by 1936. The American League garnered comparatively little revenue from these showings, but they maintained the league's control of its image and helped spread baseball's popularity in the face of growth by other spectator sports.[16] The National League entered the movie business within two years, and more than fifteen million flocked to the resulting films. By 1938 the major leagues' director of promotion, Fonseca was booked six months in advance to show *The National Game,* which compared the youth of Europe and Asia marching off to war to the young men of America playing baseball.[17]

For Fonseca the medium was the message: He proved that baseball could be repackaged and sold as effectively as could any other consumer good. Chicago Cub owner Philip Wrigley, already adept at mass marketing, shared Fonseca's insight. Wrigley sold his team just as he sold his gum. Because Wrigley had found that constant repetition of a theme in advertising built a desire for the product in the public consciousness, in the winter of 1934, he announced an intensive advertising campaign for the Cubs based on the themes of "sunshine, recreation, and pleasure." He made his product (the Cubs) more pleasant by removing sidewalk vendors, newspaper boys, and panhandlers from the stadium, and more convenient by stationing ushers out front to guide people to their sections. He insisted that ticket sellers be polite and courteous. His announcers constantly repeated the phrase "beautiful Wrigley Field" on the air, describing it as "so great an attraction that it would be thought of as a place to take the whole family for a delightful day." Wrigley ran two-column display ads every other day in the Chicago newspapers. Bill Veeck edited a magazine entitled *Fan and Family* for him. All of these approaches drummed into the fans' heads the notion that one attended a baseball game for much more than the quality of play. An afternoon at the ballpark was healthful, relaxing, and pleasant. Perhaps the *Cubs News* best enumerated the team's platform:

1. A World Championship
2. Comfort for the fans
3. Convenient ticket offices
4. To make Wrigley Field America's finest recreation center

This platform positioned the Chicago Cubs as perhaps the finest product available to the discerning consumer, combining safety (the second and fourth points), high quality (the first point), and availability (the third). Chicagoans got the message: the Cubs had the largest total attendance in the National League between 1931 and 1940.[18]

Lacking Wrigley's financial resources, the Cardinals' Gene Karst served as a one-man promotion department. The young reporter talked his way into St. Louis general manager Branch Rickey's office in 1932, proposing to spread the Cardinals' name throughout the surrounding areas by working closely with newspapermen. Intrigued, Rickey hired Karst as "Director of Information." Karst immediately began to supply all media outlets within three hundred miles of St. Louis with photographs, interviews with players, and radio dramatizations of their lives. He published a weekly newspaper highlighting the Cardinals' next opponents to generate enthusiasm further. Vendors gave out as many as fifty thousand copies at a game. Karst sent off regular dispatches to country editors, gave out numerous free passes, distributed railroad and bus handbills and the *Cardinal News,* placed cards in hotel lobbies, and produced radio programs. By 1937, the Cardinal players and logo so saturated the midwest that most midwesterners identified baseball with the Cardinals until the Braves moved to Milwaukee in 1952.[19]

Larry MacPhail tried a profusion of sideshows to excite the fans. Too redolent of "hippodroming," many of them failed. In Brooklyn, he paid $30,000 to have Ebbets Field painted turquoise, proposed yellow balls for better visibility, began to fly the team to games, outfitted the Dodgers in kelly-green caps for one year, and introduced such extra attractions as cigarette girls wearing colorful satin pants. Most important, in Cincinnati, MacPhail and Reds' owner Power Crosley introduced night baseball to the majors. Their continued agitation throughout the early thirties for baseball after nightfall finally induced the other owners to allow them six games on a trial basis in 1935. The first game, against the Phillies on May 24, drew 20,422 curious fans; in all, more than 120,000 fans attended six games. Cincinnati's other seventy-one home games drew a total of 328,000 fans. Nevertheless, most owners refused to be convinced, grumbling that night baseball would never work. Detroit's Frank Navin called it "purely a spectacle," while Gerry Nugent of Philadelphia predicted that interest and attendance would fall off markedly if more than six night games took place.[20]

The conventional wisdom held that night baseball would fail both on the field and in the stands. MacPhail ignored it. The minors had begun night baseball in 1930, but minor leaguers had complained about poor visibility. MacPhail discovered that higher-quality lighting would solve the problem. Attendance at night games increased in 1936—primarily due to a new audience, employed fans and their families—and confounded MacPhail's critics. In 1937, the Browns' new owner stipulated as a condition for purchasing the team that he be allowed to schedule night games. By the time that MacPhail brought night baseball to Brooklyn in 1938, many teams were considering the issue. After Cincinnati's increased profits enabled the team to reach the World Series in 1939 and 1940, however, other owners began to experiment with night baseball in earnest. All but five teams took part in night games by 1940.[21]

If parents wanted to provide the family with a convenient and inexpensive dinner while at a night game, they could purchase food from the concession stand. In a literal manifestation of the change from an ideology of production to one of consumption, concessions too became a part of successful promotion during this period.[22] "Your refreshment concession," a 1935 Jacobs Brothers ad promised, "properly operated, can build good will . . . your scorecard can perform an appreciated service—for both advertiser and fan. . . . [I]n general, your concessions can increase your attendance as well as your revenue. . . . It is our business to accomplish these results. It is our record that we do accomplish them." By 1938, the brothers had spread their operation to nine cities, but competitors had also taken the field. Southwest Concessions, the Dixie Concession Company ("We deliver the goods!"), and National Concessions ("the finest in food concession operations") also competed for the baseball fan's refreshment dollar. The majority of major league clubs received a flat fee from a concessionaire, who exercised complete control; others drew a share of the profits. The Cubs and Cardinals, in keeping with their emphasis on courtesy, ran their concessions themselves.[23]

Of all the period's innovations, night baseball proved the most significant. It both altered the game and symbolized changing popular attitudes. Baseball players began to compete at night, not because nocturnal air was assumed to provide respiratory benefits, not because children's morals would improve were they in the bleachers rather than on the streets, but because night baseball opened up a new market. As Ford Frick explained in 1936, studies of the demographics of crowds at night games revealed that "whole families are likely to go to the game. If the man of the house can afford it, he may even hire a box. . . . Night crowds are essentially different from day crowds. Night games reach a different type of people, a type that the daytime game has failed to attract, a type that we should attract." Baseball had become a corporation that organized self-promotion by commodifying the players and the game itself. Such commodification inaugurated a revision of standards in which Cobb was better than Speaker, Ruth better than Gehrig, and Dean better than Hubbell because they did more good for baseball. They received more newspaper coverage—Ruth's annual battles over his weight and salary generated reams of newspaper copy—made more quotable remarks, and attracted more fans. Men like Wrigley, Fonseca, and most of all, Frick, had triggered this revision: Wrigley by selling baseball as if it were gum, Fonseca by conflating baseball games and feature films, and Frick by legitimating promotion of any kind, anything that would increase baseball's appeal.[24]

American families cheerfully accepted baseball promotion in an era that habitually detested such tactics. Advertising, Will Rogers explained, "makes you spend money you don't have for something you don't want." In 1933, F.J. Schlink published *100,000,000 Guinea Pigs,* which charged that every day the hapless American consumer unwittingly tested a variety of dangerous products. It sold a quarter of a million copies in the next six years. Yet baseball never came in for such criticism. The ultimate triumph of men like Frick came in their ability simultaneously to market the game and to mask this process under the rubric of tradition. Their version of "history," like others that saturated mass culture, had much more to do with the depression itself than with any actual past. Just as Scarlett O'Hara's optimism in 1939's *Gone with the Wind* offered hope for the day, the opening of the Hall of Fame, allegedly devoted to the history of baseball, actually cast in stone Ford Frick's vision of baseball-as-consumer-good.[25]

NOTES

1. *Sporting News,* September 22, 1932; Richard Crepeau, *Baseball: America's Diamond Mind 1919–1941* (Orlando: University of Central Florida, 1980), 111; *New York Times,* January 11, 1936.

2. Peter Levine, *A.G. Spalding and the Rise of Baseball* (New York: Oxford, 1985), 25–26, 67, 95, 98, 119; Robert Wiebe, *The Search for Order 1877–1920* (New York: Hill and Wang, 1967).

3. Leo Lowenthal, "The Triumph of Mass Idols" in *Literature, Popular Culture and Society* (Palo Alto, Ca.: Pacific Books, 1968), 114–15; Levine, *A.G. Spalding,* 99; letter from Richard Crepeau to the author, June 19, 1987; David Voigt, *Baseball: An Illustrated History* (University Park: Pennsylvania State Univ., 1987), 171.

4.

	Teams Showing:	
Year	Profit	Loss
1920	14	1*
1921	15	0*
1922	13	2*
1923	12	4
1924	13	3
1925	14	2
1926	14	2
1927	11	5
1928	10	6
1929	13	3
1930	14	2

*No figures are given for the Red Sox, but presumably they lost money in each year. U.S. Congress, House Committee on the Judiciary, *Monopoly Power: Hearings on . . . ,* 82d Cong., 2d sess., 1952, 1599–1600.

5. *Ibid.; New York Times,* February 5, 1934; Voigt, *Illustrated History,* 172. The major leagues cut team rosters from 25 to 23 players in 1931; the owners fired coaches and umpires, hired more player-managers, and paid everyone less. The total payroll dropped by 25% between 1930 and 1933. Even Commissioner Landis voluntarily cut his own salary by $25,000. The owners shortened the season, cut back on spring training, stopped paying for players' breakfasts, and even fined players who threw the game's last ball into the stands. For the National League's collective action in the Braves' case, see the following 1935 issues of the *New York Times:* Jan. 29, Jan. 31, Feb. 6, May 7, May 9, June 3, June 5, Aug. 1, Aug. 7, Aug. 8, Sep. 19, Nov. 22, Nov. 27, Nov. 28, Dec. 7, Dec. 10, Dec. 11. To my knowledge, no one has covered this subject adequately. Even David Voigt's excellent new book, one of the few sources to note the Braves' problems, casually dismisses the league's actions.

6. *Baseball* (February 1930): 388; Crepeau, *Diamond Mind,* 111–12, 139; *New York Times,* February 3, 1935, April 14, 1935; *Baseball* (May 1935): 543, 530; *ibid.* (December 1936): 213.

7. Anton Grobani, *Guide to Baseball Literature* (Detroit: Gale Research Co., 1975), 131; *Chicago Cubs News* (1936): 1–4; "Big-League Baseball," *Fortune* (August 1937): 112; Crepeau letter; *New York Times,* August 23, 1933; Levine, *A.G. Spalding,* 66.

8. Harold Johnson, *Who's Who in the Major Leagues* (Chicago: B.C. Callahan, 1938), 3; Ford Frick, *Games, Asterisks, and People* (New York: Crown, 1973), 11–12, 152; *Spalding's Guide* (1937): 311; *Baseball* (December 1936): 293; Gerald Holland, "Baseball and Ballyhoo," *American Mercury* (May 1937): 82.

9. *New York Times,* April 11, 1933; John Kobler, *Capone* (New York: Putnam, 1971), photo insert; *Sporting News,* May 26, 1932; *New York Times,* May 20, 1932; Frick, *Games, Asterisks, and People,* 54. In 1932, the International League had offered an even more effective incentive by awarding $1000 to the team displaying the most "hustle and spirit on the ball field." (*New York Times,* February 3, 1932.)

10. Gene Karst and Martin Jones, *Who's Who in Professional Baseball* (New Rochelle, NY: Arlington House, 1973), 130; Johnson, *Who's Who in the Major Leagues* (Chicago: B.C. Callahan, 1936), 5; *Major-League Baseball: Facts and Figures and Official Rules* (1937); Henry Edwards, American League Service Bureau press release about Simmons, Dykes, and Haas, February 12, 1933, Simmons file, Baseball Hall of Fame, Cooperstown, New York.

11. *Spalding's Guide* (1937): 311; *Baseball* (December 1936): 293; *ibid.* (June 1936): 296; Holland, "Ballyhoo," 82; *New York Times,* April 24, 1936.

12. James Vlasich, *A Legend for the Legendary: the Origin of the Baseball Hall of Fame*

(Bowling Green: Popular Press, 1990), 31–38, 74, 76–78, 82, 89–90, 92, 109, 132–34, 140–41, 145, 171, 214. Near the end of his life, Frick claimed to have come up with the entire idea. For a discussion of the era's determination to find the "real America," see Warren Susman, *Culture as History* (New York: Pantheon, 1984), 153–58. This was not the first time that baseball had rewritten its history; for one of the earliest examples, see Warren Goldstein's fascinating *Playing for Keeps: a History of Early Baseball* (Ithaca: Cornell University Press, 1989).

13. I have found several different accounts of the history of Ladies' Day. Hy Turkin attributes the first Ladies' Day to the Giants in 1883 and the first regularly-scheduled Day to the Browns in 1912. A.H. Tarvin dated it to 1889 in Cincinnati. Several writers attribute it to Philip Wrigley, and one to Branch Rickey. See Hy Turkin and S.C. Thompson, *The Official Encyclopedia of Baseball* (New York: A.S. Barnes & Co., 1968), 618; *Baseball* (November 1930): 561; *ibid.* (July 1934); *ibid.* (December 1934): 295; *Spalding's Guide* (1933): 13. The Braves' owner, Judge Emil Fuchs, offered women free tickets on Friday and half-price tickets on every other weekday in 1932. (*Sporting News,* May 12, 1932.)

14. Bill Rabinowitz, "Baseball and the Great Depression," *Baseball History* (Premier Edition, 1989): 55; *Sporting News,* May 12, 1932; *Baseball* (September 1930): 480; *ibid.* (November 1930): 56; *ibid.* (December 1934): 295; *New York Times,* September 28, 1933, September 1, 1934. A series of charity games in 1931 netted approximately $250,000 for the unemployed. See Rabinowitz, "Baseball and the Great Depression," 55.

15. *Sporting News,* March 6, 1965; *New York Times,* June 27, 1934.

16. Although baseball admissions struggled back to their 1929 level in 1936, football admissions tripled in the same period, and horse/dog admissions increased fourfold. U.S. Congress, *Organized Baseball,* 12.

17. *New York World-Telegram,* February 2, 1937; *New York World-Telegram,* December 16, 1938; Announcement of premiere of new American League movie, December 1938, Fonseca file, Baseball Hall of Fame, Cooperstown, New York; "Baseball Picture Assured Success," AP report, December 23, 1936, Fonseca file; *New York World-Telegram,* January 14, 1938; *New York World-Telegram,* October 25, 1938.

18. Crepeau, *Diamond Mind,* 108–112; Bill Veeck with Ed Linn, *Veeck—As In Wreck* (New York: Putnam, 1962), 40; *Cubs News* (1936): 2; see *Official Baseball Dope Book* (St. Louis: Sporting News, 1981), 24, 38, 60, 96. The Yankees had the largest total attendance in the major leagues.

19. Gene Karst resume, Karst file, Baseball Hall of Fame, Cooperstown, New York; *Heilbroner's Yearbook* (1935): 76; Karst and Jones, *Who's Who In Professional Baseball,* 504; Holland, "Baseball and Ballyhoo," 85.

20. "Gimmicks Were MacPhail's Business," Larry MacPhail file, Baseball Hall of Fame, Cooperstown, New York; "Hats Off To Caps," *Los Angeles Times,* August 25, 1987; Crepeau, *Diamond Mind,* 112; *Baseball* (November 1932): 535; Holland, "Ballyhoo," 84; *Baseball* (July 1935): 351; *ibid.* (October 1935): 489, 522; *Official Baseball Dope Book,* 64. Although seven night games were scheduled, Giant manager Bill Terry refused to allow his team to play at night because he believed that the lights would damage his players' batting eyes.

21. *Baseball* (October 1935): 523; *ibid.* (August 1936): 386; *Spalding's Guide* (1937): 7; Crepeau, *Diamond Mind,* 188.

22. Concessions' share of major league revenue increased by more than 25% between 1929 and 1939. In 1929, concessions brought in $582,800 in revenue, accounting for 5.5% of the total; in 1939, they brought in $850,300, 7% of the total. U.S. Congress, *Organized Baseball,* 6.

23. *Baseball Blue Book* (1935): 1; *ibid.* (1938): 2; ibid. (1937): 1–4; Peter Craig, "Organized Baseball" (BA thesis, Oberlin, 1950), 201–202.

24. *Baseball* (December 1936): 332; *ibid.* (January 1935): 375.

25. Stephen Fox, *The Mirror Makers* (New York: Vintage, 1985), 123; Susman, *Culture as History,* 154–58, 164; for a discussion of "Gone with the Wind," see Lawrence Levine, "American Culture and the Great Depression," *Yale Review* 74 (Winter 1985), 208–09.

Piper Davis

JOHN B. HOLWAY

Tall and skinny, shortstop Lorenzo "Piper" Davis was called "the black Marty Marion" back in 1943, when he cavorted for the Birmingham Black Barons. After the Cincinnati Reds general manager, Warren Giles, watched him and second baseman Tommy Sampson turn five double plays in the Reds' park, Crosley Field, he called the two over to talk to them. First Giles shook their hands, then he shook his head.

"Too bad," he muttered softly. "It's just too bad."

There was one big difference between Davis and Marion, however. Marion hit .268 lifetime; Davis .309.

Seven years later, the 33-year-old Davis almost broke the Boston Red Sox color line before he was abruptly cut from their Scranton farm club under circumstances that still have never been fully explained.

But if Piper couldn't enter the Promised Land himself, he could send his protege up to enjoy it, a teenaged shortstop by the name of Willie Mays.

Today the gangling Davis still bubbles with the rich sense of humor that made him a hit with the Harlem Globe Trotters in the off-season.

Davis was born July 17, 1917, in the little coal mining town of Piper, Alabama. The mine is closed now, but the town, he insists, "is still on some maps."

The Birmingham coal mines and steel mills sent more players to the Negro leagues than any other city, Davis says. Home run king George "Mule" Suttles was one. Two others were pitchers Sam Streeter and Harry Salmon, who taught another Birmingham rookie, Satchel Paige, his fabled control back in 1927. The last of the line, of course, was Mays.

Like many Alabama black kids before him, Piper worked for the Tennessee Coal and Iron Company and played on their kids' team, while mascoting for the men's team. When the men's first baseman got hurt, someone told the coach to "put in that little ol' boy over there." Piper was wearing overalls and street shoes with spikes bradded to the soles. He hastily tucked his overalls under his socks, put a uniform shirt on, and trotted out to first base. "The first baseman never did get back," Piper says with a smile.

In 1936, Piper's fame began to spread to Birmingham's Fourth Avenue and 16th Street, which he calls "the main drag" of the city. The Omaha Tigers, barnstorming through the south, heard of the 19-year-old boy and signed him up. The Tigers were managed by Charles "Suitcase" Mason, a home run champ with the Bacharach Giants of a decade earlier. Mason was up in years, Davis says, but could still field, in spite of the oversized feet that accounted for his nickname.

They traveled by bus and played in fairgrounds around the upper midwest, across North Dakota, into Montana. "Wasn't too bad, wasn't too bad," he remembers. "Some places we couldn't find no place to stay. We slept in jails or go to the fairgrounds and sleep before the game." In some towns, they slept in a rooming house for Negro Pullman porters.

Playing for Westfield, Alabama, in 1937, Piper broke his leg sliding into second and had to turn down an offer to play with the Birmingham Black Barons of the Negro American league. (The Birmingham white Barons played in the Southern league.)

Piper went to work for TCI, the Tennessee Cast Iron pipe company. "I was with the construction crew building a tin mill," he says. The crew got laid off just after Christmas, and by March, they still hadn't been hired back. So Davis went on the road again. He joined a touring team in Yakima, Washington, managed by the great left-hander, Big Bill Foster, perhaps the best black lefty of all time. They played the bearded House of David club from South Dakota to Seattle, then back into Idaho and Kansas, on their way to St. Louis before heading back to Yakima.

But the team ran into bad luck. In Montana, they got "rained out and cold out" for a week. They tried to sleep in a ballpark, but the wind gusts sent bark "flying around the infield."

The players ate on credit at a black hotel, but when they couldn't pay their room rent either, the hotel confiscated their bags. As they attempted to slip their suitcases out the window into the bus, the lady who ran the rooming house caught them and rode along with them to the next town, where they finally got a game in and made enough to pay her.

Usually, the traveling secretary sent the receipts back to Yakima, to the team owner, who mailed back money to pay the players. But with no money coming in, there was none to mail back. Davis and the others couldn't even collect their 75 cents a day eating money. Foster left the team to go home to Mississippi. He saw the situation, so he didn't stay long.

"What we did, to get some money, we took all the secretary's papers, told him we were going to hold the gate receipts and split them between us, we weren't going to send the owner anything."

When they drove into Missouri, the sheriff met them with a lien from the owner against the bus. They explained their plight to the official, who winked that "the lien didn't get here in time to deliver" and let them go on their way. At the next town, they were met by another sheriff with another lien, and they told him the same tale. "When we got to St. Louis, I said I wasn't going any further, so I caught the bus and came home to Birmingham."

Piper impressed the coach of the ACIPCO (American Cast Iron Pipe Com-

Ed Steele (left), Artie Wilson, a member of the New York Giants, 1951, and Piper Davis (right), at the East-West Game in Comiskey Park. (Photo: from the author)

pany) team and got a job working and playing for them for three dollars a day. He played second, opposite second baseman Artie Wilson, who later played with the New York Giants. In the winter, Davis also played basketball with the Savoy Five, who wore the jerseys of Bob's Savoy Cafe.

In 1941, Candy Jim Taylor, manager of the Black Barons, offered Piper $150 a month. "I said, 'No, I tried that once. One hundred fifty to go back on the road? I don't think I'll go.'"

But the following year, Piper was playing Sundays with the Black Barons for $7.50 a game. They raised him to $10, and finally, in '43, gave him $250 a month, plus a $500 bonus.

By that time, Wingfield Welch was managing the Barons. Tom Hayes, who inherited a funeral parlor and insurance company, owned the team; and Abe Saperstein, owner of the famous Globe Trotters, was general manager and promoter. When Saperstein found out Davis could shoot baskets too, he gave him an extra $50 a month, plus a job with the Trotters in the off-season. So, at the age of almost 26, Piper Davis became a rookie in the Negro National league.

In addition to his $300 salary, Davis drew meal money, which was one or two dollars a day. "And they gave you a dollar if you rode at night. Sometimes you had some long rides, pardner, from Kansas City to Washington, and played the next night."

Piper started out at first base, but the shortstop was booting away so many games that Welch moved Davis to short. "Man, I haven't played shortstop in five years," he protested. But Welch gave him a fielder's glove and slapped some grounders to him between games of a doubleheader. Piper started the second game at short, made the All-Star team at that position, batted .386*, and led the league in doubles.

It was in 1943 that Piper impressed Giles of the Reds. The Cincinnati short-stop was Eddie Miller, a fine fielder but a .234 hitter. Beginning in '43, the Reds finished second, third, seventh, and sixth. One wonders how they would have done with Davis at short.

Piper helped lead Birmingham to the pennant. They took the famous Home-stead Grays, whose roster included Josh Gibson and Buck Leonard, to seven games before losing the World Series.

As soon as the Series was over, Davis was on the road again, this time with the Globe Trotters. "I was a pretty good basketball player with the Globe Trotters about four years," Piper remembers. He played guard and center, along with Babe Presley, Duke Cumberland, Bernie and Al Price, and Sam Sharp.

They played in the Chicago area, getting into shape, then played small towns in Illinois and Wisconsin before striking west on the same circuit the Omaha Tigers had followed: Omaha, Bismarck, Coeur d'Alene, Pocatello, Salt Lake City, Ogden, Spokane, and Walla Walla. "Some places were pretty cold," Davis recalls. Then they played down the coast: Seattle, Tacoma, Portland, Eugene, Sacramento, Oakland, San Francisco, Los Angeles—and across the south: El Paso, Houston, Dallas, Baton Rouge, New Orleans, Birmingham, and Atlanta. Some years they did the eastern swing: Detroit, Cleveland, Erie, Montreal, Connecticut, New York, New Jersey, Philadelphia, Baltimore, and Charleston. "I've been in every big city in the United States except Galveston, Texas," Davis says.

They spun the ball on their fingertips, played "football" (kicking the ball through the hoop), and "baseball" (running imaginary bases). They hid the ball under their shirts, or dribbled between the defender's legs (known as a "leg job"). "My specialty was bouncing the ball on the floor and catching it with my legs. The fellow that's guarding you wouldn't know where the ball was." Some-times Piper would put the ball on the floor, run away, then run back, pick it up, and sink a basket.

The clowning was prearranged, usually for the beginning of the third quarter, for instance. Since they played a different team every night, the opponents didn't know what to expect. "Sometimes we run up against a team we couldn't afford to clown, so we put it on after the game."

The team usually went on the road in early November. By the time they got home, it was March or April and time to start the baseball campaign.

Welch managed the Trotters as well as the Black Barons. Sitting at a hotel one night, he remarked that if he had another outfielder and a little more pitching, he could win the pennant again in '44.

"Who's gonna play short?" Davis asked.

"You," Welch replied.

---

*Based on a review of original box scores.

"I know a shortstop can beat me playing shortstop—Artie Wilson. We played four years together out at ACIPCO, me at second, him at shortstop."

"You think you can get him to leave home?" Welch asked.

"Sure I can get him."

The first thing Artie asked was, "Do you get all your money?"

"Yeah, I got it and more," Piper replied.

"Okay," said Wilson, "I'll go."

So in 1944, Wilson played short, hitting .346. A left-handed batter, he sliced every pitch to left field, somewhat like Pete Runnels or Wade Boggs in later years. In 1949, Art led the Negro league with a .401 average. But when he joined the Giants in '51, manager Leo Durocher insisted that Wilson pull the ball, which he couldn't do. He hit .182 and was released to make room for Willie Mays.

Meanwhile, Davis returned to first base, though he went into a slump at bat and hit only .150. But the Barons did win the pennant.

They were on their way back home to start the Negro World Series with the Homestead Grays when their bus plowed off the highway. Catcher Lloyd "Pepper" Bassett, the famous rocking chair catcher, and outfielder Leander "Gal" Young ("he had a big ol' butt like a gal") were hurt slightly. Third baseman Johnny Britton "had a hole in his head," and Tommy Sampson broke both his legs.

Davis was rushed into second base, and though the Barons lost the Series in five games, one of baseball's great infield combinations was born. No rival in white baseball of that era comes to mind; and in black baseball, only Dick Seay and Willie Wells of the Newark Eagles compare, though Wells was getting old and Seay was a banjo hitter.

Piper and Artie were Mutt and Jeff, one tall, the other short. But size didn't make any difference, Wilson insisted. He liked playing next to Davis. "He was a smart ballplayer. He knew what he was going to do with the ball before he caught it."

In '45, Davis bounced back at bat with .345 to Wilson's .346. They were probably the best double-play combination in America.

Piper recalls arriving late for a game in Chattanooga. "That old ballpark was high up, you go in over the stands, then go down to the dugout. We walked in the stadium, hollered, and told them we were there." They changed and dashed onto the field. From their years together at ACIPCO, "we knew each other like a book." With a man on first, the batter slapped a ball up the middle. Instead of going for the ball, Davis knew Wilson could handle it, so he broke for the base instead. Sure enough, Artie under-handed the ball to him for another of their patented DPs. "Now," said the announcer, "wasn't that worth waiting for?"

The Barons finished second to the Cleveland Buckeyes, who starred Sam Jethroe, later two-time National League base-stealing champ.

That winter the news was out: Jackie Robinson of the Monarchs had signed with the Brooklyn Dodgers.

In 1947, Piper turned down an offer from the St. Louis Browns, who had just signed Hank Thompson and Willard Brown of the Kansas City Monarchs. "They were going to give me $500 a month to go to Toledo" [their American

Association farm]. "But I was making 700–800 a month in Birmingham. And I wasn't going to get any part of the sales price." He turned them down. But he and Birmingham owner Tom Hayes agreed that henceforth Davis would get a percentage of any sales price.

Davis stayed with the Barons, hitting .360, according to the published statistics.

That winter he joined other U.S. black stars, such as Thompson, Jethroe, and Monte Irvin, for the Cuban season, hitting .303. A kid named Julio Becquer, who later played for the Washington Senators, remembered him as "one of the classy guys. I always liked clothes, and one of the things impressed me was how this guy looked—dressed to kill."

In the spring, Piper returned to Birmingham.

Surprisingly, quite a few whites came to see the Black Barons—they got the choicest segregated seats, of course—and the white Birmingham *News-Herald* gave the games good press coverage. "We had an average of no less than 500 whites, but when we played the Kansas City Monarchs with Hank Thompson, Willard Brown, and Jackie Robinson, or when we played the New York Cubans, Indianapolis Clowns, or Homestead Grays, we'd have anywhere from 800 to 1200 whites."

Years later, when Davis was working as a security guard for South Central Bell, an elderly white lady stopped and asked, "You're Piper Davis, aren't you?" He admitted that he was. "My goodness," she exclaimed, "I've seen you play ball many Sundays. I'm an avid fan, didn't miss a game."

Blacks also could attend the white Barons' games in the same park, Rickwood Field, though they had to sit in the bleachers. In 1948, after integrated major league teams played exhibitions in Birmingham, police chief Bull Connor—later infamous for playing fire hoses, and siccing dogs, on civil rights marchers—ordered whites to sit in the bleachers for Black Baron games. "We didn't have a hundred whites after that."

Too bad. They missed the chance to see an historic event, the professional baseball debut of Willie Mays.

"They told me there was a pretty good kid in Fairfield named Willie Mays," recalled Davis, who had become manager of the Black Barons. Davis had played with Willie's father, "Cat" Mays. "They said he was a hell of an athlete," Davis says of Willie—"football, basketball, and baseball. He had scholarships already. Colleges were looking at him for basketball and football. I said, 'What grade is he in?' "

"The eleventh grade," he was told.

"I can't do nothing with him," Piper concluded regretfully.

But that June, toward the end of the school semester, Mays and his weekend semipro team were playing in Chattanooga with only one black hotel available, the same one the Barons were staying at. Piper and Willie found each other like two magnets. "You still want to play, you have your daddy call me," Davis told him.

When the elder Mays phoned, "I told him to have Willie at the Birmingham ballpark at 12:30 that Sunday."

Mays was a shortstop, but Davis had a solid infield already, with himself at

Piper Davis. (Photo: from the author)

second and Artie Wilson at short.* "What I needed was an outfielder that could throw." So he told the kid to work in the outfield.

The Barons took Mays down to Montgomery with them for a Sunday game, then hustled him home in time for school the following day.

When school was out, Davis decided that Willie would be his regular center fielder, replacing Jim Zapp, and quietly taped the lineup on the dugout wall

---

*Wilson would go up to the New York Giants in 1951. Ironically, he was cut from the squad to make room for a new rookie sensation by the name of Willie Mays.

before batting practice. The news stunned Zapp and his buddy, right fielder Ed Steele, who put their heads together, whispering angrily.

"There's the lineup, fellows," Davis said. "If anyone doesn't like it, there's the clubhouse. You can leave and cash your pay checks. I know you've got enough salary to pay for your uniforms." That stopped the whispering right away.

"Don't sign a contract," Piper advised the kid, knowing that, without one, he could probably collect a nice bonus from a white big league club. So Willie played for $250 a month on a handshake.

Davis gave Willie only one pointer on his fielding, and that was to charge ground balls and get the ball away fast. If he fumbled, Davis told him, don't throw home but catch the runner going into second to avoid drawing an error.

As for his hitting: "I didn't try to change him at all, with one exception." Mays tended to step into the ball, leading with his shoulder. "Pitchers in the Negro league were meaner than in organized ball." They threw spitballs, emery balls, and beanballs. When they saw Willie offering his shoulder as a target, "you know where they were throwing it."

Later, at an old-timers' reunion, Mays would recall going down in a heap from one beaning. He looked up to see Davis striding out of the dugout toward him. "Can you see first base?" the manager asked, bending down.

Willie nodded weakly.

"Then get up and get on it," Davis told him and walked back to the bench.

"You taught me to survive," Mays told his old skipper simply.

Davis also taught him how to escape future beanings: Stride more toward third base, he advised. "If a guy throw you a fastball inside, get that hip out of there fast." Willie could do it and still hit the pitch, Piper said, "because he had good wrists."

Mays hit .262 that year, with one home run. Davis hit .353 with seven homers, his lifetime high in huge Rickwood Park, and led the Black Barons to the pennant, beating the Monarchs in a seven-game play-off but losing again to the Grays and Luke Easter in the World Series.

That winter, Davis was on the west coast with Satchel Paige's All-Stars, playing Bob Feller's and Ewell Blackwell's Stars. Usually, Feller and Paige would pitch three innings to draw a crowd; but for the final game, they agreed to go nine innings all the way. "Men, get your rest," Satchel ordered. "You know we don't get too many runs off Feller. I might beat him with one run, but two will do." They won it 8–0, as Davis got two hits, one of them a homer "after Feller had tired a little bit."

Joe Black was a hard-throwing hurler for the Baltimore Elites before the Dodgers signed him. "He struck me out a couple times in Baltimore one Sunday and put his glove to his mouth and winked his eye at me."

The next night, the teams met again in Philadelphia. The Barons got a rally going, and Black hurried from the bullpen to face Davis again. "I punched the computer," Davis says; that is, he did some mental calculating. "He struck out on that little old dinky curveball he's got," Piper told himself, "so that's what you should hit this time. Wait on that pitch." Sure enough, the first pitch was a fastball and the second was "that dinky curve," and Piper hit it on the roof of Shibe Park. "When I got around to shortstop, I winked my eye at him."

Thirty-five years later, the two slapped hands at an old-timers' reunion. "I always thought I was a pretty good hitter," Piper told Joe, "but after you got in the big league, winning 18–19 ball games, I *know* I was a good hitter!"

Another Dodger pitcher, Dan Bankhead, "I also hit pretty good." The night that Brooklyn signed him, the Barons were playing him in Memphis. All their players came over to ask, "Let him look good."

"Heh," Artie Wilson told them, "I want to look good too. Somebody may want *me*."

Actually, the Yankees and Indians both signed Wilson. Cleveland eventually prevailed and later traded him to the Giants.

In 1949, the scouts were out watching Junior Gilliam of Baltimore when the Barons came to town for a doubleheader. "I got four-for-four, all the balls were hit pretty well. The first time up in the second game, I hit a line drive to left field." While they were changing clothes after the second game, the club secretary told Piper, "Somebody wants to see you."

"Me?"

"Yeah."

"I'll be out in a few minutes."

"I think he's from the Boston Red Sox."

"Then let him in!"

Larry Woodall, former coach and scout, entered and chatted for a while.

The next night, in East Haven, Connecticut, Woodall returned. "We came to take you to Boston," he announced.

"Man, I ain't got nothing but my shaving kit," Piper said.

"Well, that's enough," Woodall replied. They caught a train to Boston and checked Piper into the team hotel.

The next morning, Sox general manager Joe Cronin called to talk contract. First of all, Piper said, the Red Sox would have to buy his contract from Hayes, and Davis had been promised a percentage of the sale price. Second, he says, Cronin agreed to an "under the table deal"—the Red Sox would pay him the major league minimum if he was still on the organization's payroll the following May 15. Piper promised to confer with Hayes and let Cronin know his decision.

"I'm 33," Davis reminded his owner, "and I've got a chance to play in the major leagues." The Red Sox thought he was 31—back in '47, the Browns had taken two years off his age, and Piper discreetly never corrected it.

Tom advised him to hold out for $7,500 on signing and another $7,500 if he was with the organization on May 1—no black player had ever fetched over $10,000 before. "I'll give you $1,500 of the first $7,500, and we'll split the next $7,500 fifty-fifty," Hayes promised. They phoned Cronin, who agreed to the deal. The understanding on the pay raise was not in the contract, but remained "under the table."

So in March, Davis reported for spring training with the Red Sox' Scranton farm club in Cocoa, Florida. "I can't stay in the hotel with the club," he says. "I stayed out of the city with one of the waiters. They paid him to let me stay at his home and bring me down to the hotel. I ate breakfast in the waiters' quarters, then I'd go out the waiters' door and go around the front and get in the bus and go to the ballpark. How do you like that?"

When the team broke camp to play its way north, through Georgia, the Carolinas, and Virginia, Piper went home to Birmingham, then flew to Scranton to join his teammates as the new first baseman. He started strong, hitting .333 after 15 games; he was leading the team in home runs and RBIs and was tied in stolen bases. He was moved to third base to replace the injured Frank Malzone; while at shortstop, Piper's old position, Milt Bolling was kicking games away with his glove. Meanwhile, Walt Dropo, the big first baseman on the Louisville farm team, was having a great spring and was promoted to the Red Sox. Most people assumed Davis would move up to Louisville to replace him. Piper looked confidently toward the 15th of May.

That morning, he found his regular $500 check in his locker, but no raise. The Scranton general manager said he didn't know anything about Cronin's secret deal. After the morning workout, Davis went to a movie, then returned to the hotel. "Did you ever get in touch with the ball club?" his landlady asked. "They want to see you in the ballpark." Piper hopped in a cab.

Back at the park, the general manager told Davis he had to let him go.

"Why?" Piper asked.

"He said, 'Economical conditions,'" Piper reports. But the real reason, Davis suspects, was the pay raise and the extra $7,500 sales price, both due on May 15. He assumes that when Scranton asked Boston what to do, the Red Sox front office replied, "Release him; we got Dropo and don't need him." Dick Gernert would be promoted to Scranton to play first.

"That was a shocker," Piper says today. "I'm assuming that he had called Cronin, because the general manager is the one got to do the releasin.'"

Several Scranton fans threatened to boycott the team in protest, and Piper was interviewed on Scranton radio. Was he a victim of race prejudice? "That's what the reporters were trying to get me to say. They wanted me to 'cut' the Red Sox." But Piper didn't know what was really behind the decision. He refused to criticize the team.

Years later, Davis read that age was the reason. "I would have felt better if they had told me that instead of 'economical conditions.'"

Was he angry? the reporter asked. No, he answered, "more hurt than angry."

It would be nine more years before the Red Sox would integrate, the last team in the majors to do so.

The Scranton club didn't even give him transportation money to get home, and Davis bought his own train ticket. At Washington, as he got off the train to change to the Jim Crow car, he bumped into Cronin, who was on his way to Louisville. "Heh, Slugger, you're supposed to go first class," Joe said.

"I'm going where my money can afford," Piper answered. When he got home, a check for the train fare and meals was waiting.

Meanwhile, his replacement, Gernert, hit .265, and Scranton finished last, 36½ games behind. Dropo enjoyed one good rookie season at Boston before the pitchers learned to curve him, his average fell to .239, and the Red Sox let him go. It would be 19 years before they would win a pennant.

Meanwhile, Davis went to Mexico to play, then finished the season with Birmingham, hitting .383.

His protege, Mays, had matured into a .330 hitter, and the New York Giants grabbed him for a bonus, just as Davis had predicted. A grateful Willie always maintained that Piper was "like a father to me."

Oakland, a Giant farm club in the Pacific Coast league, offered Davis a job in

'51, and he stayed with them for four years. Manager was Mel Ott, the old home run hitter from Louisiana. Center field was Sam Chapman, who had become famous as the race-baiter who had ridden Jackie Robinson so mercilessly in 1947. Davis' average dropped to .265. He ended the year at Ottawa in the International league in a trade for his old buddy, Wilson. For the year, Piper hit .265, Wilson .255 after being released by New York.

In '53, he led the Oaks' team at bat with .296 with 13 homers, his personal high. By comparison, Chapman hit .263, future Hall-of-Famer Ray Dandridge .268, and rookie Jim Marshall, .273.

Like Willie Mays, the 21-year-old Marshall, the baby of the team, calls Davis "almost like a father to me."

"He certainly helped me get to the big leagues," Marshall says today. "He drew people to him without doing anything but being himself. Triple-A was a big challenge to me, and I spent a lot of time in his room. He used to sit in his room and smoke that pipe. He helped me mainly in helping me relax and do the best I could—and try to do better than I could. We shared a lot of good times together; we used to talk a lot about basketball. And he was a good friend to all of my children.

"I reminisce about him a lot," the future Cub manager says. "He was a very special person in my life. I don't know whether he realizes that or not."

The next year, Marshall raised his average to .285 (to Davis' .288). The other players called Piper "Lipper." "Any high fastball around his lips, he could really hit it," Marshall says. "And he was very good at stealing pitchers' signs; he knew what was coming a lot of times."

Piper played every position, even catcher. Oakland wanted to reward him with a "day," but feared dissension if they did so. Instead, they advertised him to play all nine positions, and the newspapers hailed it as his day.

Davis studied the opposition, including Los Angeles second baseman Gene Mauch, later manager of the Phils, Angels, and other teams. "I was catching for Oakland, and Mauch came to bat," he recalls. "A man on first, they were leading by one run. I saw his stance, waiting on a curveball to shoot it to right field—a short right field fence in Los Angeles. Our hardest throwing pitcher was throwing that day, so I called for a fastball up and in. Strike one."

The second pitch was also a fastball, high and tight. Strike two. Piper crouched and put down one finger for another high fastball. The pitcher stepped off the mound. The "book" called for a waste pitch, but Piper insistently put one finger down again. The hurler shrugged and threw. "Bam!" Davis smiles. "Strike three." Cursing, Mauch threw his bat away.

In '55, Piper was traded to Los Angeles, and the first man to greet him was Mauch. "Glad to have you with us, I know you're going to help us out," he said. "But one thing I want to know: How in the hell can you throw three straight fastballs when you're behind in a double play situation?"

"The element of surprise, my dear brother," Piper grinned, "the element of surprise."

Davis got a kick out of imitating his teammates. When he went in to substitute for Mauch, he copied Gene's every mannerism, even to brushing his hair back behind his ears. The fans loved it.

Piper hit .316, Mauch, .348, and Los Angeles wrapped up the Pacific Coast league pennant by 16 games. (Two other infielders in the league on their way to the majors were Bill Mazeroski, .306, and Frank Malzone, .296.)

When I called Mauch some three decades later to ask about his old teammate, Gene was stunned. I thought the phone connection had gone dead. At last Mauch managed to say, "Is he a charming person or what? What a beautiful guy.

"When I think of Piper Davis, I think of the consummate gentleman—that's the first thing that comes to mind.

"The second thing is his versatility and his complete understanding of the game. He understood baseball as well as, or better than, anyone in the Pacific Coast league, including me. He could play first base, third base, center field, any place. And he had a way with other players on his team of making them feel like they were the best.

"Usually, I don't like people to call me and ask about baseball, but I've really had a kick out of talking about Piper Davis."

Davis ended his career with Fort Worth in the Texas league in 1958 as player-coach to help manager Lou Klein out with the young players. Piper hit over .300, and again helped lead his club to the flag.

After finally retiring, Piper scouted for the Detroit Tigers, managed a bowling alley, worked for the major league scouting bureau as its token black, and finally signed on with the Cardinals as scout.

In May 1958, his old Los Angeles teammate, pitcher Jim Brosnan, met Davis again. Jim had just been traded to the Cards from the Cubs, with whom he had spent his entire career. "I was very upset," he recalls. Piper and Buster Clarkson, another old Negro leaguer, met the pitcher in a Pittsburgh hotel. The two old battle-scarred veterans of many a bus ride "took me in hand" and took turns telling of the bad old days, contrasting them with the future Jim had in front of him. "When they walked me out to catch a cab, I was feeling great!" Jim, who had been 3–4 with the Cubs that spring, was 8–3 with the Cards the rest of the year.

"I always thought Piper would wind up as a coach," Brosnan says. But nobody wanted him.

Mauch recalled that he was using Piper's glove in 1956, when Gene was sold to the Red Sox. He tried to give it back, but Davis insisted, "No, you keep it, man, that's the only way that glove's going to get to the big leagues."

Davis, Lorenzo "Piper"   BR   TR   6'3"   187 lbs.
B. July 3, 1917, Piper, Ala.

Year	Team	G	AB	H	2B	3B	HR	SB	BA	Psn
1942	Bl Barons	2	4	0	0	0	0	0	.000	if
1943	Bl Barons		57	22	9*	1	1	1	.386	if
1944	Bl Barons	64	253	38	3	3	2	7	.150	if
1945	Bl Barons	58	211	66	10	7	3	7	.313	if
1946	Bl Barons	4	11	3	0	1	0	0	. —	2b
1947	Bl Barons	56	228	62	1	0	2	0	.360	if
1948	Bl Barons	76	295	104	19	8	7	6	.353	if
1949	Bl Barons	82	299	113	—	—	—	—	.378	if
1950	Scranton	15	63	21	4	0	3	0	.333	1b,3b
	Bl Barons	42	149	57	10	2	3	4	.383	2b,ss
1951	Oak–Ottawa	157	567	150	26	4	7	12	.26	
1952	Oakland									
1953	Oakland	174	670	198	39	8	13	1	.296	
1954	Oakland	120	365	105	19	2	9	3	.288	
1955	Oak–LA	125	309	90	19	1	6	1	.244	
1956	LA	64	152	48	9	0	6	1	.316	
1957	Ft Worth									

Ersatz Octobers: Baseball Barnstorming

ROBERT COLE

"Did you have to work in the winter?"
Kevin Bass of the San Francisco Giants asked Willie Mays.
"My first few years," Mays said,
"I made more barnstorming than I did with the Giants."
"What's barnstorming?" Bass asked.
NEW YORK TIMES, APRIL 7, 1991

On October 16, 1962, Bobby Richardson of the Yankees caught a line drive smashed by Willie McCovey of the Giants in Candlestick Park, San Francisco; the World Series ended after 12 days of rain and excitement; and Willie Mays ran to catch a plane.

Willie landed in Wichita, Kansas, where, on October 17, he joined the last postseason barnstorming tour of major league baseball players in America, and was the star of the exhibition game with three base hits.[1] The tour was organized by Mack Massingale, a former player for the Kansas City Monarchs of the old Negro National League, who was trying to revive a custom that went back to the beginning of professional baseball.

Barnstorming games were those arranged after the season by players themselves or by independent promoters, between touring teams, or between a touring team and a local team—as opposed to the officially scheduled league games. Barnstorming games had to be squeezed into the few weeks after the World Series ended, and before cold weather made it impossible to play the summer game. In many parts of the country, it was strictly an October undertaking. The exhibitions often were played much less seriously than official games—out of a concern for avoiding injury to the players—and often the advertised players made only token appearances. But baseball is a game that can be played fairly impressively without great intensity by the players. Many games were quite serious, and barnstorming generally was popular, as Jules Tygiel described in *Baseball's Great Experiment* (1983):

> During the first half of the twentieth century, barnstorming constituted an integral feature of America's cultural landscape. . . . Each fall squads of major

leaguers brought baseball to American communities, entertaining the faithful, while supplementing their own incomes. Though billed as all-star teams, they often included only one or two name stars and a variety of lesser lights and minor leaguers. No one complained. When a major league barnstorming team appeared, towns took on a festive air. Businesses closed, schools might be given a half-holiday, and parades welcomed the Olympian visitors.[2]

But by 1962, unfortunately for Mack Massingale's tour, this custom was passing away. *The Sporting News,* a St. Louis weekly newspaper known as the "Bible of Baseball," put it this way in an article on October 20: "Barnstorming trips after the World Series once were a regular part of the fall sports schedule, but diminishing crowds in recent years dimmed the lure of the road. No troupes went out on exhibition tours last fall."[3]

Although it would be difficult to prove that no major leaguer attempted to arrange an informal postseason game in this country after Massingale's failure, none were reported in *The Sporting News,* which was the only place the exhibitions ever had been reported nationally. (And even *Sporting News* coverage was not very complete until after World War II.) One of the few surviving experts on the subject, William Heward, now on the faculty of Ohio State University, and from 1971 through 1975 manager of the famous barnstorming team, the Indianapolis Clowns, told me in a telephone conversation that "with great confidence I can say that no one [from the major leagues] was doing it then."[4]

The "diminishing crowds" *The Sporting News* referred to were turning to pro football and to television, which began to be available across the country in the 1950s, carrying the image of baseball into areas where it had been seen only fleetingly in theater newsreels, destroying the game's existence as a tantalizing newspaper novelty, demythologizing the game and its heroes. As early as 1951, Birdie Tebbetts, a successful barnstormer for three years, drew poor crowds with his annual New England tour and observed, "In other years, fans would have packed the ballparks to get a close-up view of these players, but not this year. The fans already had seen them in their living rooms. . . . [For] any place that has good reception of TV, these postseason tours are a thing of the past."[5]

But in a larger sense, the passing of barnstorming was part of the passing of a time when the major leagues extended only from Boston to St. Louis, the west coast was the other side of the moon, and large parts of the United States still existed in rural isolation from the big-city sports markets. These areas subsequently were opened up not only by exposure to television, but also by shifts in industry and population, and by the networking of the interstate highways, all of which made the big leagues more accessible to millions of people. Something colorful and picaresque was lost in the transformation—the barnstorming that was baseball's equivalent of the carnival or the gypsy camp on the edge of town, vaudeville, the lonesome whistle of the passing freight train, and the traveling salesman.

The romance of barnstorming was rooted in two fantasies, one of which was realized regularly, the other only occasionally: The first was the visit to the distant city or the hick town of the big-league stars who previously had existed only in newsprint or in occasional radio broadcasts—the folks down home finally got to *see* their heroes.[6] The second was the eternal hope that some wonderful baseball player (a natural) might be blooming almost unseen in a remote burg, and the local hero would be discovered ruefully by the big-league tourists in the exhibition game against the town team. This American myth is best depicted in Bernard Malamud's novel, *The Natural,* in which heroic Roy Hobbs is found by a bird dog scout in the west, who brings him to the city (by train, naturally), rough and untutored. Roy shows his stuff by striking out big-league slugger Whammer Wambold when the two face each other by chance at a carnival in a jerkwater town where the train has been stopped. The novel was adapted into a popular movie of the same name in 1984 (starring Robert Redford as Roy), and the myth of the country hero was one of the few elements faithfully preserved.[7]

There were some real-life Roy Hobbses. Pitcher Rube Bressler, famous in the twenties, said he got his shot with the pros when, as a 17-year-old railroad worker, he beat Earle Mack's Philadelphia All-Stars in Renovo, Pennsylvania.[8] Earle Mack was a lifetime barnstormer, leading expeditions from the 1910s through the 1940s.[9] Mack was the son of Philadelphia Athletics Manager Connie Mack, and two years later Bressler was with the Athletics.

Wes Ferrell of the Boston Red Sox made a delightful confession of the discovery, at his own expense, of another country Roy. This one came to bat against Ferrell in a game at Reidsville, North Carolina, wearing bib overalls and smoking a cigarette. When Ferrell got two strikes on him, the farmer flipped away the cigarette and drove Ferrell's next pitch over the center field fence— went long tater on him.[10] A loudmouthed farmer came out of the stands at a Philadelphia Phillies exhibition in Fort Wayne, Indiana, in 1920, claiming he could outhit the pros, and astonished the crowd by whaling out several long balls. He turned out to be Casey Stengel in disguise.[11] And although it never got him to the big time, Apples Jaworski was considered some punkins around Wilkes-Barre, Pennsylvania, in 1931 for being able to beat major league barnstormers even though he was just a batting practice pitcher, not a regular, for the town's minor league team.[12]

This myth of the unknown star added poignancy to the histories of black ballplayers like Satchel Paige, Josh Gibson, and Cool Papa Bell, who rode up and down this country in rattlers, pursuing the sun that was always shining somewhere, yet doomed by racial segregation to play their game in the obscurity of the black major leagues.[13] They reportedly preferred barnstorming against white major league players to the competition in their own leagues.[14] The interracial rivalries were fierce, especially before blacks were allowed to play in the major leagues in 1947. Bob Feller, the largest-scale player–promoter in barnstorming, said the games between blacks and whites were "real grudge fights."[15] Mickey Vernon, another long-time barnstormer, said, "The games with colored teams were very competitive. Somebody would get knocked down. But in the small towns, they'd be more casual, because there were no colored fans in the stands."[16] Cool Papa Bell said the black teams would win the short series, where reserves were no factor, and recalled Dizzy Dean's once asking a black team to go easy on him.[17] Winning was the blacks' only reward, except for the somewhat empty one of gaining heightened reputations today in a less racially biased time. A special committee has elected some of the black players to baseball's Hall of Fame, and major leaguers often have testified to their ability. Regarding Paige, for example, Dizzy Dean said he was the best pitcher Dean ever saw,[18] and Joe DiMaggio said, after his last season with the San Francisco Seals, that he thought he was ready to play for the Yankees because he got a hit off Paige.[19] Paige's view of big leaguers was not as generous: He said Charley Gehringer was the only one who ever gave him trouble, and he wished he could have pitched to Babe Ruth.[20]

*   *   *

The examples so far have been of the most common kind of barnstorming in the United States—the domestic, postseason tours run mainly by the players, which are the focus of this essay. However, since the term "barnstorming" referred to an informal business, it often was used loosely, and, indeed, there were other kinds of barnstorming. From the earliest history of the game, teams had to tour to find opponents, if only because there were fewer opponents available at the beginning. As baseball has evolved, the different kinds of barnstorming have been defined mainly by who was promoting the tours, players or club owners. The postseason domestic tours were the domain of the players, who were trying to capitalize on their national or hometown fame, and who, typically, were financed and managed by promoters and agents who were independent of the ownership of the players' Organized Baseball teams.

Official major league club owners also entered the barnstorming market, but mainly to arrange spring training tours between their teams and other major league teams—or occasionally to arrange international tours for the official teams, mainly to Japan. The spring training tours usually matched two major league teams from different leagues, playing each other in a series of small towns as the teams worked their way from spring training camps in the south and southwest back to their home cities in the north and midwest. The Cleveland Indian–New York Giant series was the oldest (begun in 1934) and among the best of these, most of which ended almost the same year as autumn barnstorming, in 1960 when scheduling exhibitions was complicated by the fact that the two leagues opened a week apart.[21] That was one of the many changes in baseball in the 1960s that forever altered the profile of the professional game and prevented the return of barnstorming.

International tours went back to 1874, when Harry Wright, founder of the first professional baseball team, the Cincinnati Reds, wanted to take America's new game back to his home country of England. Wright hoped the new game would replace cricket, and hired A. G. Spalding to be his advance man to arrange a series of matches at cricket clubs in Great Britain. The tour impressed the British, but lost money; and in 1888, Spalding, now a baseball club owner and sporting goods salesman, arranged an around-the-world tour to further both his interests, and had it end in England after stops in Australia, Ceylon, Egypt, Italy, and France. He also saw his players as missionaries for the American way of sport. His tour, like Wright's, was a propaganda success and a financial failure.[22]

Later the New York Giants and Chicago White Sox played each other around the world in 1913,[23] and again in 1924, when they were observed in London by George Bernard Shaw, who called the American game "mad."[24] But by far the most popular tour stop was Japan, where baseball became established as the national sport after visits from American ballplayers in 1913, 1921, 1928, 1931, 1934, 1949, 1951, 1953, 1955, 1956, 1958, 1962, and 1966, according to an historical review by *The Sporting News* in 1966.[25] The 1913 team was from the Pacific Coast League. Ty Cobb, Babe Ruth, and Joe DiMaggio each went at the end of his career, in 1928, 1934, and 1951, respectively; and DiMaggio hit his last home run in Japan. Starting in 1953, the tours were by official teams, not the earlier all-star squads, typified by the Los Angeles Dodgers, who, in 1966, took an official party of 80, including owner Walter O'Malley. Star pitcher Sandy Koufax did not go, however; and while the team was in Japan he announced his retirement at age 30 because of an arthritic elbow.[26] There have been several tours since, up to the one in 1990 built around Cecil Fielder, the Detroit Tiger home run king who had played in Japan.[27] A 1968 tour by the St. Louis Cardinals had considerable impact on baseball because Steve Carlton said it was on that tour that he taught himself to throw the slider with which he won 329 games. He developed the pitch as a defense against Sadaharu Oh, the Japanese home run champion.[28]

The club owners not only did not promote the postseason domestic tours, they attempted to control the players' tours because the owners were, in fact, opposed to them. Their opposition stemmed from fear of injury to players in games on rough country diamonds; the often ethically questionable, if not fraudulent, business practices of some postseason promoters, which could reflect badly on baseball; and the fact that the players often made "too much" money barnstorming. It was "too much" money if the amounts approached or exceeded World Series shares, as they did in the early years of the century and right after World War II. The owners saw the players' big barnstorming profits as creating at least the appearance of evil in a sport that could not tolerate any suspicion of its integrity after the gambling scandals of the early years. The fear was that the public might reason: well, if these ballplayers can make more money barnstorming than they can playing in the World Series, why would they hustle to make it to the Series? So, starting in 1947, the players' shares of the World Series receipts were increased, and barnstorming was not allowed to begin until 10 days after the regular season ended. That way, players would not even have to consider whether they'd rather be in the Series or be out barnstorming.[29]

The rules were spelled out in the *Baseball Blue Book*. The length of the barnstorming season was prescribed, and games were not allowed with semipro teams whose lineups included players ineligible for professional baseball (usually because of gambling convictions and other moral problems). Also, no more than three players from an official team could play on the same barnstorming team.[30]

Cheating practices of some barnstormers included false advertising, phony identities, no-shows, short games, and announcements of phony attendance figures, either to make the tour seem more successful than it was, or to disguise the take. The largest crowd for a barnstorming game in the United States was supposed to have been 27,462 to see Bob Feller and Satchel Paige pitch on October 6, 1946, at Yankee Stadium.[31] But even though some of the tours reported what appeared to be specific attendance figures and averages, there was no convenient way to check these numbers, and sportswriters often challenged them.[32]

These problems were at their worst in the informal early years of baseball. Various rules were passed early in the century in attempts to curtail barnstorming, especially after independent promoters began to organize touring pick-up teams each fall to exploit the World Series that began in 1903. The promoters would give their teams the same names as the ones that had played in the Series, even though often only a couple of players from the real teams were barnstorming, and then would tour the country, in effect continuing the World Series.[33] Owners first tried to control players' barnstorming with 12-month contracts in 1910, then ruled in 1911 that no player who had played in the World Series could barnstorm that year, then tried in 1914 to write player contracts that banned barnstorming.[34] The 1911 rule was the most effective, and was seen by the players to be unfair, because they were keenly aware that theirs was a brief, chancy business in which they had best gather their dollars while they could.

As late as 1951, barnstorming was marred by misleading advertising similar to that of the earlier years. The largest baseball crowd in the history of Denver, and one of the largest in American barnstorming (over 20,000 at Bears Stadium on October 14, 1951) was disappointed by the lineups for a game between Fido Murphy's American League and National League All-Stars: Many of the Americans were absent and the Nationals won 10–1. "A. L. All-Stars, Ugh!" chided *The Sporting News* headline.[35] Despite the high fees he supposedly received, Satchel Paige was a notorious no-show,[36] and Bobby Avila of the Cleveland Indians, the 1954 American League batting champion, had something of that reputation—even in his native Mexico, where he was a national hero.[37] This was not a new thing. Fans in his hometown of West Frankfort, Illinois, planned a day in honor of successful rookie pitcher Paul Derringer of the Cardinals on October 11, 1931, but he didn't show.[38]

This consumer fraud could be caused by many of the vagaries of life on the road—carousing, oversleeping, running late. The chance to spend a golden autumn day stalking a deer or a dear tempted many an adventuresome young man away from a pseudo-game at Podunk Park against the local hotshots.[39] And on many of the tours, there was such a tone of playfulness and such a low margin of profit that prankish and unprofessional behavior was almost inevitable. Quality control was difficult, and exploitation was the name of the game: Promoters tried to sign up novelties such as a clown like Al Schacht, Max Patkin, Jackie Price, or Shorty Potato, or a hometown hero or an Indian outfielder or an infield made up of the four (or five) Schoendienst brothers, or the four Ferrell brothers, or the first outfield comprised of the three DiMaggio brothers, or Virgil Trucks and his father to pitch a doubleheader.[40] Satchel Paige would entertain the crowds with demonstrations of his uncanny control by knocking a cigar out of a batter's mouth from the mound, or show the power of his pitches by driving a nail into a plank with one.[41] When Commissioner

Kenesaw Mountain Landis let Alabama Pitts into organized baseball after Pitts got out of Sing Sing in 1935, it was with the stipulation that Pitts play no exhibition games—so that his prison record could not be exploited.[42]

Baseball "outlaws" tried to exploit their notoriety, but had a tough time with the establishment. The Chicago Black Sox, banned from baseball because they allegedly threw the 1919 World Series, barnstormed in various combinations, and several of the players ended up as a town team in Hibbing, Minnesota. Commissioner Landis was so unforgiving of them that he banned even an amateur who played second base for them,[43] and suspended the most famous of honest Sox, Dickie Kerr, for once playing in an exhibition against them.[44] In 1948, when Max Lanier, former ace lefthander of the St. Louis Cardinals, still was considered an outlaw for having jumped to the Mexican League in 1945, he formed an all-star team that included two other famous jumpers, Sal Maglie and Danny Gardella of the New York Giants. They played colleges and semipros up the Mississippi Valley, won 55 in a row, and suddenly found they couldn't get games. Lanier blamed Commissioner A. B. (Happy) Chandler, who threatened to ban from professional baseball anyone who played against Lanier. In 1949, the jumpers all were reinstated to baseball.[45]

Owners also raised the objection that barnstorming sometimes competed with the World Series, and generally was seen to be demeaning to professional baseball—all those famous players racing around the country, sometimes playing twice daily in different towns, grubbing for quick bucks in ersatz competition, even clowning and letting women play (like the time Jean Marlowe of the All-American Girls Baseball League pitched an inning for Danny Litwhiler's Pennsylvania All-Stars at Wilkes-Barre, Pennsylvania, in 1951)[46]—and all this with no managers, coaches, or front office people from the big clubs around to apply any restraint. *The Sporting News* often spoke for the owners, and did so in a 1947 editorial, "Too Many Pitfalls in Barnstorming," when it said: "After the last man is called out in the World Series, it would be better for all concerned if the players retired to their homes."[47]

Not very serious or professional, but apparently appealing, was the skylarking that big leaguers might improvise while free-lancing out in the sticks away from the constraints of serious team play in a fierce pennant race. A standard bit of showboating was to have all the fielders, except the pitcher and catcher, sit down, and allow those two worthies to dispose of the local yokels. This was a Satchel Paige shtick,[48] but is on record as having been staged as far back as 1921 by the infamous Chicago Black Sox.[49] Likewise, the two-man defense has been done as recently as 1948 by Birdie Tebbetts' All-Stars at a frolic at Glens Falls, New York. The batter in Tebbetts' game was retired when he hit a line drive to left field that huge Walt Dropo caught while relaxing on his back.[50]

However it was played, barnstorming retained the physical risks of any sport, to the great distaste of the club owners to whom the players represented assets. To avoid injury to their star, in 1946, the Boston Red Sox paid Ted Williams $10,000 *not* to barnstorm, more than he was offered to tour. The Detroit Tigers did the same for pitcher Hal Newhouser, who had won at least 25 games in each of the three previous years.[51] Barnstormers got hurt, occasionally seriously. Probably the most publicized injuries were those to Jimmy Foxx of the Philadelphia Athletics in 1933 and 1934, when he was in the midst of a Hall of Fame career as a home run hitter. In 1933, he suffered a broken toe from a horseplay accident in a hotel room; and in 1934, he was admitted to a hospital in Winnipeg, Canada, after being beaned.[52] But he recovered each time and led the league in home runs in 1935, the first of six more prime power-hitting seasons he had. But Glenn Chapman, the Dodgers' rookie shortstop, broke his right leg sliding in a barnstorming game at Richmond, Indiana, in 1934 and never played in the majors again.[53] Taft Wright broke his throwing arm in Hartsville, South Carolina, in 1947 (and continued in the game),[54] and Phil Rizzuto was chastised by *New York Daily News* columnist Jimmy Powers for injuries he sustained against the Brooklyn Bushwicks—an exceptional semipro team and frequent opponent of major league all-star teams—in 1949.[55] Luke Easter collided with a teammate in Houston in 1950 and needed stitches to close a wound in his head.[56] Suitcase Simpson had his wrist broken by a pitch in Texas in 1953; and Willie Mays hurt his shoulder sliding in Austin, Texas, in 1956.[57] There were other risks, too: Dominic DiMaggio of the Red Sox was sued for $11,600 in damages by a fan after Dom's bat hit the fan in the stands at Wrigley Field, Los Angeles, during an exhibition game October 4, 1941.[58]

But whatever the risks, there were more heroics: Doc Creamer remembers Babe Ruth made good his boast and became the first man to hit a ball out of the boundless field in Billings, Montana.[59] Charlie Maxwell hit a home run over the five-story cell block for Virgil Trucks' all-star team in its annual game against the convicts at the Michigan State Reformatory in 1956.[60] And big Luke Easter hit 20 homers in 36 games while touring the south in 1953—the equivalent of a whopping 86 homers in the regular 154-game season.[61] Surely those were legitimate, not hit off grooved courtesy pitches. And if you never had seen a big-league ballplayer, how exciting it must have been to watch.

Also, it was a lot of fun for the players, the kind of traveling and playing that made the game magical all the way back to its beginnings. There were town teams before there were leagues, and the teams tried to find opponents by going from town to town. Wahoo Sam Crawford, who would go on to the Detroit Tigers and baseball's Hall of Fame, recalls how it was in Nebraska in the innocent 1880s before he turned pro:

> . . . I remember when I made my first baseball trip. A bunch of us from around Wahoo, all between 16 and 18 years old, made a trip overland in a wagon drawn by a team of horses. . . . It had room to seat all of us—I think there were 11 or 12 of us—and we just started out and went from town to town, playing their teams.
>
> One of our boys was a cornet player, and when we'd come to a town he'd whip out that cornet and sound off. People would come out to see what was going on, and we'd announce that we were the Wahoo team and were ready for a ball game. . . . We didn't have any uniforms or anything. . . .
>
> We were gone three or four weeks. Lived on bread and beefsteak the whole time. We'd take up a collection at the games . . . and that paid our expenses. . . . We'd get 12 pounds [of round steak] for a dollar and have a feast. We'd drive along the country roads, and if we came to a stream, we'd go swimming; if we came to an apple orchard, we'd fill up on apples. We'd sleep anywhere. . . .[62]

That kind of male bonding and sense of freedom helps explain the appeal of barnstorming to many players, except that major leaguers usually stayed in the best accommodations they could find. They were older than the players from Wahoo, but they still were baseball boys, now seeking happy trails away from Maxine and the kids. As late as 1957, in the waning years of the roadrunning, Nellie Fox, who also would be elected to the Hall of Fame, when asked why his irregulars were playing for little profit before small crowds in Altoona and other central Pennsylvania outposts, replied, "more or less for fun."[63]

They endured a lot to have fun. Birdie Tebbetts' team had to use a flamethrower to dry a field in Presque Isle, Maine, to play a game in 1948. Hal White's team played a game "in the middle of nowhere," on a country field 28 miles west of Williamsport, Pennsylvania, in 1953. Ted Lyons and crew had games canceled at Statesville and Joliet, Illinois, prisons because of a prison break at Statesville on October 9, 1942. Clint Courtney's team, running out of players when some guys quit, played a night game in Wichita Falls, Texas, then drove till 3:30 A.M. to play the next afternoon in Tucumcari in 1956—in the rain.[64]

*   *   *

A representative team from the final days of barnstorming was Danny Litwhiler's Pennsylvania Major League All-Stars, who were on the mountain roads of the Quaker State from 1948 until 1952. In any of those years, there were 15 to 20 teams of major leaguers barnstorming in this country, and most of them had much in common. In 1950 for instance, Birdie Tebbetts and Mickey Harris had teams in New England; Allie Reynolds in Oklahoma; Dick Sisler in the midwest; Al Evans in the Carolinas; Satchel Paige and Bob Lemon in California, and— touring more widely—Jackie Robinson, Roy Campanella, Luke Easter, George Digby (a scout) and Harry (The Hat) Walker in the south.[65] Sometimes they played each other, but they usually tried to stake out their own ground and play local teams, or, in the case of the black players' teams, play other touring teams from the Negro Leagues. Litwhiler had been a National League outfielder and a barnstormer since before World War II.[66] While working as a substitute physical education teacher at Scott Township High School near Bloomsburg, Pennsylvania, he got the idea to form his own team for the fall of 1948. He was encouraged by his principal, Earl Davis, who volunteered to handle the business arrangements—typical of the deals players struck to have their tours managed. They needed help with finances, because most of them weren't used to handling large sums of money. In those days of lower salaries, part of the motive for barnstorming was the need most players had for winter income. People were reluctant to hire ballplayers just for the winter. For example, although he was a two-time batting champion, Mickey Vernon played for the poor-paying Washington Senators and had to work winters at everything from an oil refinery to a haberdashery shop.

Litwhiler recruited 14 players for his regular roster. He tried to limit it to Pennsylvania residents, and would schedule games in the players' hometowns or in towns where they had had successful minor league seasons—Bloomsburg for Litwhiler, York for Ken Raffensberger, Newport for Billy Cox, etc. (Litwhiler would, however, sign up outlanders if they were hunting buddies of his and Carl Furillo's, as was Vern Bickford of Richmond, Virginia.) The owners of their big league teams cooperated by letting the players use their regular uniforms. Litwhiler also would arrange games in small towns in his area where major leaguers lived who were not on his touring team, and then contract to have such a player join the All-Stars for a single game in his hometown. For example, he would schedule a game at Brownsville, Pennsylvania, because Pat Mullin lived there, or pick up Harry Perkowski for a game in Charleston, West Virginia.

Litwhiler said his standard financial arrangement was a 70–30 split with the local promoter, the 70 per cent coming off the top to the touring team. If it rained, Litwhiler collected $1,000 a game. Litwhiler supplied the baseballs, stamped "Pa. Major League All-Stars," which Earl Davis sold to the local club. Tickets were $3.00 and $1.00, and "we had our guy right there on the gate," so no shorting would be done, Litwhiler said. The team's headquarters was the Magee Hotel in Bloomsburg, and from there they raced all over Pennsylvania and four other states—almost always on two-lane roads except when they could use the Pennsylvania Turnpike.

In 1950, after four games in two days against Jackie Robinson's team in Virginia, Litwhiler's gypsies returned to their home state. Between October 11 and October 29, with only October 13 and 27 off, they played 17 games in 19 days. They played at Bloomsburg, then drove 95 miles south to York for their next game, 60 miles west to Greencastle, 135 miles north to Williamsport, 200 miles east to Paterson, New Jersey, 100 miles west to Wilkes-Barre, 300 miles farther west to New Castle, 135 miles east to Roaring Spring, 100 miles west to Brownsville, 300 miles farther west to Portsmouth, Ohio, 100 miles southeast to Charleston, West Virginia, 225 miles northwest to Dayton, Ohio, and 225 miles back to Charleston, 200 miles farther south to Bristol, Virginia, 100 miles north to Bluefield, West Virginia, 125 miles northeast to Buena Vista, Virginia, and 150 miles south to Winston-Salem, North Carolina. This was barnstorming, if not masochism. Well, Litwhiler said, "remember, big leaguers drove good cars, and anyway, most of us had knocked around a lot, and had been in service," and were used to cramped quarters and inconvenience. They traveled two or three to a car, sometimes driving fast, sometimes driving with abandon. Litwhiler recalls leading the motorcade down the turnpike one day in his Buick, when Ron Northey in his Mercury came alongside and called out, "Wanna race?" Litwhiler hit 100 miles per hour before Northey passed him.

Litwhiler said players felt like heroes everywhere they went, and "you kind of owned the hotel." When they played local teams, he said, the locals were "scared to death" they would be humiliated like the four batters Bobby Shantz struck out on 12 pitches in Bloomsburg. Litwhiler also remembered one day when Dick Sisler, joining the Pennsylvanians, got scared. Sisler, who stuttered, had just pulled into a service station when the attendant, a big man, asked, "W-w-w-what can I d-d-d-do for you?" Sisler said, "F-f-f-fill it up," and the man looked daggers at him. Later, when the players were back on the road, Sisler commented, "J-J-J-Jesus, I wanted oil, too, b-b-b-but I wasn't g-g-g-going to ask h-h-h-him for it."

Litwhiler used the tour to learn a new position, first base, which he had been told he would play the following spring. Outfielder Don Mueller also played out of position, catching, even though he had broken fingers. "Hell, I can catch," he said. "Mueller would play, regardless," Mickey Vernon said. "He had that makeup. He was unusual." "He was *tough*," Litwhiler said.

*   *   *

While Danny Litwhiler's barnstormers were representative in the modest income and considerable enjoyment they got from their tours, there were a small number of star players who did very well financially. To them, money was the name of the game. Whereas the accounts of championship baseball games in *The Sporting News* are almost exclusively devoted to explanations of the runs, hits, and errors, the accounts of the barnstorming activity almost always led with the size of the crowds at the games, and commentary as to whether those crowds represented profit or loss for the barnstormers. As late as 1958, a player could say of the Willie Mays–Roy Sievers tour of Mexico, "We made mucho dinero."[67]

In fact, the history of major league barnstorming could be delineated in terms of the dominant barnstormers of successive eras, starting with Babe Ruth in the 1920s. Babe was mostly done with barnstorming by 1929, except for playing three games in Los Angeles in 1931 that benefitted a children's clinic operated in the name of movie actress Marion Davies[68] and for a fantastic tour of Japan in 1934,[69] the year before the Babe's last season in the majors.

Following Ruth would come Leroy (Satchel) Paige, the legendary fastballer, who, according to his Hall of Fame plaque, pitched in the Negro Leagues from 1926 to 1947, and in the major leagues off and on from 1947 through 1965. He barnstormed most of those years, against major leaguers until he was allowed in himself, and was a coach on the Mack Massingale–Willie Mays tour in 1962.[70] The last record of his barnstorming was with the Indianapolis Clowns in 1967, at age 61, according to his birthday in the *Baseball Encyclopedia*. In her biography of Paige, Kathleen Long Humphrey said he occasionally would pitch an inning even after 1967, but not on the road.[71]

A frequent pitching opponent of Paige, Dizzy Dean (with his brother Paul) was the big draw from 1932 through 1936, when Dizzy was enjoying a brief period of extraordinary success and popularity as a pitcher for the St. Louis Cardinals.[72]

Then came Bob Feller of the Cleveland Indians, whose attraction as a barnstormer began in the last couple of years before World War II. He reached unparalleled heights of barnstorming success right after the war, from 1945 through 1949. Feller capitalized on the postwar baseball boom, and on his spectacular 1946 season, when he won 26 games and set a major league record for strikeouts, by chartering two DC-3 airliners and flying two teams on a coast-to-coast tour that earned him $80,000, more even than his enormous 1946 salary of $45,000.[73]

Satchel Paige, barnstorming in Winston-Salem, North Carolina, in September 1959. (Photo: from the author)

Finally came the last days of major league barnstorming in the United States, the 1950s, when black players, only recently allowed into the majors, drew the biggest barnstorming crowds. They were led first by Jackie Robinson from 1948 through 1953, then Roy Campanella from 1951 through 1954, and finally, by Willie Mays and Don Newcombe from 1955 through 1958.

In the twilight of barnstorming, it was necessary to leave the United States to make a profit, to go to a Latin American country or Japan where the people hadn't been saturated with baseball by television. But until the late fifties, most of the U.S. was a barnstormer's market. In 1946, players could make more money barnstorming than playing in the World Series,[74] and famous players in particular profited from the desire of backwater fans to see their heroes in person. Babe Ruth is said to have made double his regular salary barnstorming in 1919 and 1920, his last season with the Boston Red Sox and first with the New York Yankees, when he first became known as a home-run hitter.[75]

The player who gained most fame as a barnstormer was Satchel Paige, who spent most of his career in the powerful but obscure Negro leagues that were the stunted fruit of racial segregation in the U.S. until the 1950s. Barnstorming was an economic necessity for the poorly-financed black teams, who might have to supplement their ticket sales by playing a hundred exhibition games around a

130-game "regular season."[76] They even barnstormed their World Series, playing it in various cities instead of only in the home cities of the competing teams.[77]

The black baseball barnstorming tradition went back to the 1880s.[78] In that desperate context, Paige became famous for beating major league barnstormers before blacks were allowed into organized baseball in 1946. (Paige himself made it in 1948, at a rare advanced age for a player, and did well.) But the most money Paige claims to have made barnstorming was $2,800 for a game during World War II against Dizzy Dean.[79] Paige said in his 1948 autobiography that he usually got $500 for pitching three innings of an exhibition game for the Kansas City Monarchs.[80] With Bismarck, North Dakota, he got a .22 rifle for winning one game, a car clock he coveted for winning another.[81]

No one made as much as Babe Ruth, who probably was the best-known person in the United States in his day. Even so, Babe knew as well as anyone how chancy his chosen career was, and wanted to make money while he was still young and able. He felt that way after his team, the New York Yankees, lost the Series in 1921, and directly defied Commissioner Landis by going on a barnstorming tour of New York and Pennsylvania—one that lost money because inclement weather canceled several games. Landis cost Ruth even more money by withholding his Series share and then suspending him for the beginning of the 1922 season.[82] Ironically, the rule against barnstorming by Series players was dropped that year.[83]

After playing in several exhibitions for $1,500 each in 1920 (a year the Yankees *didn't* win the pennant), Ruth reportedly made $40,000 barnstorming in Cuba, but lost it all betting on horses, and had to borrow money from his wife to get home.[84]

One of the Babe's barnstorming strategies was to try to profit from both his own name and that of his less colorful teammate, Lou Gehrig, another prodigious homer hitter. They went out as opposing teams called the Larrupin' Lous and the Bustin' Babes, and Babe would play first base to save his legs.[85] Novelty names and identities like those were common, such as the Bloomer Girls of the 1910s, most of whom were men in dresses, and one of whom was young Rogers Hornsby, beginning his pro career,[86] or the House of David teams of the 1930s and later, supposedly representing their religious order in their trademark beards, but riddled with ringers like Grover Cleveland Alexander, who ended his alcohol-diluted career with the team.[87]

The Babe's last performance as a barnstormer was in 1934, his next-to-last year as an active player, when, at age 39, he was the main attraction of a tour to Japan arranged by Connie Mack. Ruth was incredibly popular in a country where baseball was the national sport, and the Mack/Ruth tour drew huge crowds, including an 80,000 sellout in Osaka. Babe played every inning of the 22 games and hit 13 home runs.[88] Within a decade, Japanese soldiers would be fighting U.S. soldiers and taunting them by yelling "to hell with Babe Ruth!"[89]

But the Babe was passing, and that same year of the visit to Japan a new generation of barnstormers was hitting the road, led by the fireballing, big-talking St. Louis Cardinal pitcher, Jay Hanna (Dizzy) Dean, who had just had his best year, winning 30 games. But he couldn't beat Satchel Paige, who had been doing this kind of thing for a disputed number of years. Dean and Paige dueled often for the next decade, but never more memorably than in 13 innings at Hollywood Park, before Satch won, 1–0.[90]

This was during the Depression, but somehow fans found money to buy tickets for barnstorming exhibitions. Leo Durocher, one of Dean's St. Louis teammates, told in his autobiography, *Nice Guys Finish Last,* how Dean and Pepper Martin (another Cardinal) would hustle up a crowd in a small town by arriving early in the day, stationing themselves on opposite corners of the main street, and hollering back and forth to each other compelling reasons to go to that afternoon's game.[91]

Dizzy Dean was a barnstormer from his first year as a professional, 1931, when, as a 20-year-old whiz with Houston, he set a Texas League strikeout record of 303 in his only year in the minors. One of his exhibition games, at Charleston, Missouri, made the front page of *The Sporting News* because Elam Vangilder, who was 35 and a former St. Louis Browns star, struck out 22 in beating Diz. Another game, at Joplin, Missouri, was canceled because the promoter wouldn't pay Diz a $150 guarantee.[92] But the most unusual tour was to Atkins, Arkansas, where Diz found a long-lost brother, and said he planned to make a catcher of him.[93]

In 1933, after winning 20 with the Cards, Dizzy was invited to pitch in Los Angeles. He also pitched against his older brother, Elmer, at Houston, where Elmer, a failed professional player, was a peanut vendor at the ballpark. He hit a triple off Diz. And Diz beat his younger brother, Paul, who had pitched that year for Triple-A Columbus, Ohio.[94]

The next year, Diz and Paul had the most sensational year any two ballplaying brothers ever had, Diz having his best season at 30–7 and Paul going 19–11 as they pitched the Cards to the pennant and then starred in the World Series. They then went barnstorming under the management of the well-known promoter Ray Doan, and, according to a page one story in the November 1 *Sporting News,* earned more than their Series shares. Each was said to have made over $15,000 in the off-season, including $5,716 barnstorming, $5,309 for the World Series, $1,625 from vaudeville at the Roxy Theatre in New York City, and $2,759 from other income.[95] But it was not all profit. As the headline in *The Sporting News* said, "The Deans Discover All Isn't Gold That Glitters." Paul was said to have developed a sore arm (to the extent that owner Sam Breadon called and told him to throw easy in the exhibitions).[96] And what came to be called "the Dizzy Dean scandal" grew out of an incident in Milwaukee in which the brothers did not pitch as many innings as the promoter expected them to, and angry fans stormed the box office wanting their money back.[97] That led *The Sporting News* to call for "Curbing the Barnstormers" and prompted American League president William Harridge to urge the end of barnstorming, as *The Sporting News* reported:

> [Harridge] has gone on record as favoring an *absolute ban on all barnstorming* by major league players and expects some action to be taken on a proposal he will make at the annual winter meeting of the National and American Leagues ending exhibitions at the close of the season. Harridge cited the injury to Jimmy Foxx, the unpleasantness at Milwaukee when the fans stormed the box office . . . and other

instances to show the undesirability of these postseason games. Players are now permitted to barnstorm until October 31, except in special cases, as in the trip to the Orient. . . . The National League, however, is not likely to make any move toward further restrictions on barnstorming . . .[98]

But Commissioner Landis cleared the brothers of any wrongdoing in Milwaukee, saying their contract called only for personal appearances there;[99] Paul recovered and won 19 again in 1935; and barnstorming flourished, with the Deans touring against Satchel Paige. But their flush years soon passed. Paul was 5–5 in 1936 and over the hill. Diz was almost done after he had his toe broken by a line drive in the 1937 All-Star game at the height of his powers, and although he continued to manage barnstorming teams for years—even a badminton tour in 1938—he didn't pitch many more exhibitions. Ray Doan had turned to managing the new star of barnstorming—the adolescent Bob Feller.

Nor did the travel restrictions of World War II stop barnstorming, especially on the west coast where there were a lot of fans flush with defense factory wages. The big promoter out there was Joe Pirrone of Los Angeles. Buck Leonard, a Negro League player, said that Commissioner Landis once stopped a barnstorming series between a black team and a white team in California, possibly because he was touchy about the white major leaguers losing to the blacks (as major league officials long had been), or possibly because some of the white players were failing to show up for scheduled games.[100]

One practice that did not survive World War II was the barnstorming of minor league teams. It was common in the 1930s for league champions to tour in their regions and sometimes to play series against each other. Such an example was the Charlotte Hornets of the Class B Piedmont League winning a series 3–2 from the Charleston Senators of the Class C Mid-Atlantic League, with the decisive game at Beckley, West Virginia, October 4, 1931. Minor league even made international tours. A Class D New York–Pennsylvania League all-star team (chosen by the player running the tour) sailed October 8, 1931, on the SS *Caribobo* for a tour of Puerto Rico and South America to end January 18.[101] The Memphis Chicks of the Southern Association played nine games against teams in Mexico in 1931, and although other minor league teams were scheduled to tour there, this was a rare thing. The report on the Chicks tour said: "The Chicago White Sox took a trip to Mexico back in 1907, but no other representative of organized baseball appeared [t]here until 1921, when Dallas and San Antonio came for a series." An American League all-star team went in 1933.[102] The end of World War II and the intense interest in the restoration of baseball to its prewar excellence (after the highly compromised wartime seasons, when most good players were in service) created one last stretch of go-go years for barnstorming, 1945 to 1951.

Rapid Robert Feller, a returning Navy hero, was responsible for most of the success the players had then. He was 27, and, like only the best players, had been barnstorming since he turned pro at 17 in 1936. He had received $4,000, a generous rate, from Ray Doan, a promoter with whom Feller worked well into the 1940s.[103] His first big year of touring was 1937, when, at age 18, he pitched up and down the West Coast, and struck out 12 in his Van Meter, Iowa, "homecoming" game. The homecoming game was a tradition that went way back in baseball, and in the case of Preacher Roe of the Dodgers, was continued even after he retired to his home town in Arkansas. Feller said in a November 20, 1990, telephone conversation with me that he regularly flew to Seattle to pitch against Fred Hutchinson of the Tigers in his homecoming game. In 1938, Feller and Hutchinson, both 19, drew 8,000 for the game.[104]

Ambitious and self-disciplined, Feller had got rich off his fastball and fast curve. As he was always willing to say, he knew his strong right arm was a perishable asset and he wanted to cash in on it while he could. As soon as he returned to baseball in 1945, he asked the new commissioner, Happy Chandler, to change the rule that allowed players to schedule only 10 days of exhibition games after the season ended. Feller appealed for 30 days, and finally prevailed by arguing that returning war veterans should be given the chance to recoup financial losses the war had cost them. Feller himself had enlisted right after Pearl Harbor, served in combat, and lost almost four full seasons in the prime of his baseball life.[105] Given a chance to prosper in the extended exhibition season, Feller kept barnstorming on the front page of *The Sporting News* as it never had been before and would not be again. The only other player to make the cover story for barnstorming was Birdie Tebbetts, for his successful tour of New England in 1948. Tebbetts was the subject of the cover cartoon (by Gene Mack) characteristic of the newspaper in that era; it showed Birdie flying over New England under the heading, "Opening Up a New Northeast Passage."[106]

Feller was not discharged from the Navy until August 1945, so he didn't have time to promote a full-scale barnstorming tour that October. In fact, his tour got less attention in *The Sporting News* than the one run for Pete Gray, the one-armed outfielder who had played his only major league season that year with the St. Louis Browns.[107] Gray, 28, chartered a plane for a series of games on the west coast. He took along as mascot a one-armed boy who had become attached to him, and played against a team with a one-armed black outfielder, Jess Alexander.[108] Gray drew big crowds, but the stress of the major league season and the barnstorming—especially the flying, which Gray was not used to, because most teams still traveled by train then—was too much for him. He returned to his home in Nanticoke, Pennsylvania, exhausted.[109]

But neither Pete Gray nor Babe Ruth, nor anyone, ever equaled Bob Feller's barnstorming success of 1946. Feller took months to plan it, incorporated himself as Ro-Fel, Inc., invested thousands of his own money—and personally grossed as much as $80,000 from the 32 games he scheduled for his touring team that fall.[110] Bob had worked for other promoters on his previous tours—except for the annual "homecoming" game in Van Meter, Iowa—but when he toured his own way it was unprecedented, and all Feller.

Competing with other barnstorm promoters, Feller started recruiting players at the All-Star game that July, getting both batting champions, Stan Musial and Mickey Vernon, and other stars such as Spud Chandler, Charlie Keller, Johnny Sain, Ken Keltner, Jim Hegan, and Bob Lemon. Feller wanted Ted Williams and Hal Newhouser, but their employers paid them each $10,000 bonuses not to risk their expensive bodies barnstorming. Feller's team started playing in New York the day after the regular season ended, and played all the way to the west coast, flying in a chartered airliner. Many of their games were against Satchel Paige's

Negro All-Stars, flying in another plane chartered by Feller. (The next year, Feller took pains to route the flights so as to avoid as many mountain ranges as possible.[111]) He attended to an unusual number of details himself, even though he hired a traveling secretary, a trainer, a lawyer, and a publicist for the trip. He was, therefore, a playing manager in the fullest sense of the word, for in addition to handling arrangements, he pitched two to five innings in most games. He missed only one game, when he had to fly back east for a personal appearance at Atlantic City.[112]

Critics (mostly *The Sporting News,* major league executives, and the sportswriters they controlled) questioned whether Feller wasn't wearing himself out with this frantic activity (an extraordinary amount of travel for those days), and especially wondered about the strain on his arm.[113] Feller, always outspoken, scoffed in reply: "Sure I'm tired. . . . My arm is in great shape, though. . . . After all, you know, a fellow is only young once, and I'm going to make as much money as I can, while I can."[114]

The trip was so successful that the players made $3,500 each, almost as much as the Cardinals got for beating the Boston Red Sox in the World Series that year. But there were problems. First, in a bit of rhetorical irony, Feller, famous for throwing strikes on the ball diamond, was plagued by labor strikes throughout his tour: A power strike prevented a night game in Pittsburgh. A strike of streetcar workers interfered with the game in Columbus, Ohio. An airline pilots' strike forced him to start the Sacramento game early, with fans still arriving. And a shipping strike complicated the game in Hawaii.[115] Then Ray Doan sued Feller over management of the 1945 tour,[116] and Satchel Paige, who called him "Bob Rapid,"[117] sued Feller over money in Los Angeles.[118] Feller finished the tour by playing Jackie Robinson's touring team, then was criticized for saying that no Negro players he had seen "combine the qualities of a big league player . . . not even Jackie Robinson."[119]

The tour also established a lasting gain for all major leaguers, leading to an increase in their World Series shares, so that no one, skeptically, could ever wonder if the players would rather barnstorm than play in the Series.

Feller tried to adjust to the 1947 rules by flying his troupe to the barely exploited territory of Mexico, another big baseball country. His team was treated lavishly by the Pasquel brothers, who ran Mexican baseball and who had been raiding major league rosters; but for the whole tour, Feller still drew smaller crowds than in 1946. Average attendance for all games dropped from 7,760 to 5,482, and the headline in *The Sporting News* gave Bob's accurate opinion of the new arrangement: "Late Start Dooms Tours—Feller."[120] As for recurrent fears that he'd get a sore arm, Feller said, "That's the least of my worries. I worry more about the weather, the size of the crowd, and the number of baseballs we lose in batting practice." He said he saw no harm in pitching 30 barnstorming games, predicted he would pitch seven more years (he pitched nine),[121] and took pride in the fact that his total innings pitched for the regular season and barnstorming games equaled the totals of some of the workhorse pitchers from the 1910s with whom he and other modern pitchers were disparagingly compared.[122]

Also, Feller almost made the owners' worst nightmare come true when his chartered plane had trouble taking off from Mexico City for the trip home. Some scared players got off in San Diego.[123]

Ironically, Feller did not barnstorm in 1948 because his regular team, the Indians, reached the World Series for the first time since 1920—and won it, four games to two, over the Boston Braves. But poor Bob lost both games, including a rout before the largest crowd in baseball history. He decided to forego touring that fall, except for the annual homecoming game in Iowa, when his fears about lost baseballs came true: They used up 50 new ones and had to quit after eight innings. Only 1,500 people showed up on a bitter cold day, the smallest crowd ever, and the next year Feller moved to Texas.[124] He gave team barnstorming one last shot in 1949,[125] and then tailed off until he retired as an active player in 1956. In the "late sixties, early seventies," as he recalls todays, he began his one-man, one-night visits to minor league parks, which included giving instructional clinics and even pitching to local folks.[126]

After Feller, the black major leaguers, especially the Brooklyn Dodgers, were the most successful barnstormers. Most of the best-attended games matched teams of black major leaguers against teams from the Negro major leagues, which were in their last stages of decline. These games were played in the south and southwest, and fewer on the west coast. According to *The Sporting News,* most of the crowds were black people—a striking disproportion, even though many games were played in areas where the populations of cities included far higher percentages of blacks than the national 12 per cent. *The Sporting News* said of a hugely successful tour by Jackie Robinson in 1951: "The attendance in some cities was estimated as running as much as 90 per cent Negro."[127] Many of the cities, of course, had had teams in the Negro major leagues, so that barnstorming, in its last days, was returning to one of its roots.[128]

These attendance patterns also reflected the significance of the first entry of black players into the majors. The Brooklyn Dodger organization had pioneered this movement, starting in 1946, and it was clear in the 1950s that the only barnstorming teams that could draw large crowds in this country were those led by Dodgers—with the exception of those featuring Willie Mays. When barnstorming attendance was off by 50 per cent in 1956, Curtis A. Leake, traveling secretary for Willie's all-stars, said, "The reason for the poor attendance is a matter of much conjecture. However, we've been badly hurt by the lack of any Dodgers on the team."[129] Alex Pompez, the famous New York Giant scout who was one of the backers of Mays's team, had said the same thing earlier.[130] In addition to their appeal to black fans, the Dodgers were generally attractive and highly publicized at this time, winning the National League pennant five times in the eight seasons from 1949 through 1956.

A preview of this barnstorming trend occurred in 1946, after Jackie Robinson's first season in organized baseball, at Montreal. Robinson, 27, the first black man in the modern game, attracted large crowds in his first touring, but otherwise the trip was troublesome. In *The Jackie Robinson Story,* by Arthur Mann (1950), Robinson claimed that some black businessmen from Pittsburgh who promoted his tour cheated him of thousands of dollars, including the $3,500 bonus he received for signing with the Dodgers (158–159). The trip ended on the west coast, where he had a run-in with Bob Feller over a guarantee for a game in Los Angeles, threatening to withhold his players from the game until his financial terms were met. The game was played, but Robinson got into more controversy by complaining about ball-and-strike calls.[131]

All this unpleasantness was resurrected in 1969 when Feller and Robinson appeared at a ceremony in Washington honoring the hundreth anniversary of baseball. They rehashed their old differences at a press conference, Feller saying Robinson "has always been bush." Two witnesses, a promoter, and a sportswriter who umpired the 1946 game, supported Feller's view, and Robinson called it all "a damned lie."[132]

One of the players on Robinson's 1946 barnstorming team was Al Campanis, a teammate at Montreal, who filled in because Robinson couldn't get enough good black players. In 1987, Campanis lost his job as vice president of the Dodgers by saying on national television that black players "may not have the necessities" to be field managers or general managers.[133]

Robinson went on a brief barnstorming tour after his rookie year, 1947, when the Dodgers lost a seven-game World Series to the Yankees; he spent more time making personal appearances in theatres (Mann, 199). The next year Robinson barnstormed longer, and his team drew good crowds in the south, including 13,100 at New Orleans on October 17.[134] A crowd of 2,000 or more would have been considered decent by most barnstorming teams, but in 1949, Robinson's stars averaged 5,942 for 25 games in the south. *The Sporting News* called it "one of the most successful barnstorming tours in history."[135] The Robinsons opened in Newport News, Virginia, on October 12, three days after the Dodgers had lost the five-game World Series to the Yankees again. Unlike some big leaguers, Jackie did not shortchange the fans who came out to see him after his batting champion/Most Valuable Player season, and played all but 10 innings of the 25 games.[136] In a game at Columbus, Georgia, he offered refunds to anyone who thought it was too cold to attend that day, but he got no takers.[137] In 1950, at age 31, he said he would not barnstorm again, despite drawing crowds that averaged 3,703, because the touring kept his stomach upset.[138] He had taken Campanella, Newcombe, Larry Doby, and others along for a series against the Indianapolis Clowns, a black barnstorming team.

But Robinson went at it aggressively in 1951, winning a bidding war for the best black players against Campanella, who was National League MVP that year and was heading his first team. Robinson got most of the big names—Doby and Luke Easter of the Indians, Sam Jethroe of the Boston Braves—except for the rookie Willie Mays, Newcombe, and Monte Irvin of the Giants, who went with Campanella.[139] Mays couldn't play many games, however, because he had to leave the team October 14 at Newport News to report for his preinduction physical examination for the Army October 23 at Birmingham, Alabama.[140] Years later, Mays's agent, Carl Kiesler of New York, said Willie probably went with Campanella because he was close friends with Campanella and Newcombe.[141] The 1951 tour was another success: "All Dixie turns out again to greet Jackie's troupe," read *The Sporting News* headline.[142] The tour started in the south and ended in Los Angeles, where there was a Jackie Robinson Welcome

Day Nov. 4, since he had lived in Pasadena as a boy and played sports at UCLA.[143] Whereas these homecoming days were common for white players, few for blacks were reported in *The Sporting News*.

Jackie's last tour was 1953, when he was 34, and after the Dodgers had lost the World Series to the Yankees for the second straight year. His team played against the Negro American League all-stars, and included three white players, Gil Hodges of the Dodgers, Ralph Branca of the Detroit Tigers (a former Dodger), and Bobby Young of the minor league Baltimore Orioles. These white players were not allowed to play in a game in Birmingham October 18, but homeboy Willie Mays, 22, got a furlough from the Army and played—and was the star, getting two hits and a delayed steal of home that thrilled a crowd of 6,200, the biggest of the tour.[144]

One of Robinson's last gestures as a barnstormer was to play a game at Natchez, Mississippi, October 24 to benefit a local Negro Catholic school, to fulfill a promise he had made the year before to the pastor, Father Amos Gaudette.[145] Another highlight of Robinson's final tour was the ferocious slugging of Luke Easter of the Indians, who had 20 home runs in the 36 games[146]—which would be 86 homers in 154 games—after having missed most of the regular season because of a broken foot. It was Big Luke's last hurrah after three years of power hitting for the Indians. He played only six games in 1954, and was gone from the majors, although he did play more in Triple-A.

Robinson's departure from barnstorming was just another sign that the practice was passing away. His last year, 1953, also marked the last time that a team led by a white player had a successful tour—and that team had to go to Japan to find crowds. New York Yankee pitcher Ed Lopat was the leader of a team that toured Japan playing a series against the New York Giants that drew more fans in a month than five major league teams had drawn for that entire season—tens of thousands in most major Japanese cities.[147] The star of the tour was Hank Sauer of the Chicago Cubs, who hit 12 home runs in 12 games, and reminded people of Babe Ruth in 1934.[148] In turn, Japanese teams were touring the Philippines profitably. The Giants played in Manila November 15 and 16, after a game against an inter-service team on Okinawa November 12.[149]

For the entire Far East tour, Lopat's players were said to have made $5,500 each, compared with the World Series record share at that time, $6,772 to Cleveland players in 1948. Lopat said the money had been deposited for the players in American banks before they left for Japan.[150] The tour was underwritten by the Mainichi newspaper chain, as were many of the big league tours to Japan. One anonymous Giant player, complaining that the sponsors gave away too many tickets, said the Giants got only $660 each, but that he liked the goodwill aspects of the tour.[151] But the baseball owners thought it unseemly for their players to be profiteering in Japan, so the new commissioner, Ford Frick, "advised against" a return trip in 1954.[152] Lopat was limited to a tour of Hawaii and the west coast, which did poorly—and which inspired his agent to say that baseball barnstorming could never again be profitable in the U.S.[153]

These signs of the times had been posted since 1950, when an elaborate baseball all-star tour directed by the tennis pro, Bobby Riggs, and promoted to an extraordinary extent with full-page advertisements in *The Sporting News*,[154] had been ruined by cold weather and closed early. "Jachym–Riggs All-Stars Quit $64,000 in Red," was *The Sporting News* banner headline,[155] the Jachym referring to promoter John Jachym of Jamestown, New York. The Jachym–Riggs team had played 13 games of its 32-game schedule, and had only one black player listed on its roster, Sam Jethroe, which may have helped explain the poor attendance.

In 1952, every tour except Roy Campanella's hit bad weather in early October and canceled remaining games.[156] In 1954, Campy's crowds were down by 50 per cent, even though he was touring with stars like Newcombe and Jim Gilliam of the Dodgers, Larry Doby of the Indians, Minnie Minoso of the Chicago White Sox, and Brooks Lawrence of the Cardinals.[157] Only 56 people came to see a game rookie Al Kaline promoted in his hometown of Baltimore in 1955.[158] In 1956, the Dodgers' black stars didn't tour, and no one made any money.[159] *Sporting News* headlines told the story: Aspirin Required by Barnstormers— Gates Off 50 Pct.; Low Crowds Doom Future Shea Treks; Few Barnstorm Tours This Fall—Pickings Lean.[160]

By 1959, even Mexico City did not pay off. A team featuring Don Newcombe and Harmon Killebrew quit there after drawing poor crowds.[161] Hank Aaron had left that team after one game, and when he jumped a team in 1960 and was fined, *The Sporting News* said, "annual barnstorming of negro all-star teams may be a thing of the past after this year."[162]

Despite all that, by 1955, Willie Mays had become the last great barnstormer. The year before, the Giants had won the pennant and swept the Indians in the World Series, and Mays had had his first great season, capped by the famous catch he made off Vic Wertz in Game 1 of the series. But that year Willie had elected to play winter ball in Puerto Rico instead of to barnstorm. Teammate Monte Irvin criticized Willie for this, saying he should rest in the off-season and not risk injury.[163]

Willie, 24, had been touring since he was 17 and playing for the Birmingham Black Barons, but 1955 was the first year that a team went out under his name. He had hit 51 home runs that season and people wanted to see him—25,000 the first week. He was not a businessman like Bob Feller and some of the others, but he was a player who went at it with the same verve on skin infields that he showed at the Polo Grounds. His barnstorming teams won 49 games in a row in 1955 and 1956, and lost the 50th one when Willie didn't play in Victoria, Texas, October 30, 1956, because he had hurt his shoulder sliding in Austin, Texas, the day before.[164]

There are only three successful domestic postseason barnstorming tours mentioned in *The Sporting News* after 1954—one each in 1955, 1957, and 1958, all in the name of Willie Mays. The first record of his barnstorming glory was in 1950, the year Mays played at Trenton, New Jersey, in the Class B Interstate League, after signing with the Giants. Only 19 that fall, he went touring the south with Luke Easter's Negro All-Stars, and *The Sporting News* said "Willie Mayes" hit three triples at Houston October 22.[165] In 1955, Willie hit several home runs while touring, including one in Atlanta that went 460 feet,[166] one off Charlie Pride (later a popular singer, then a pitcher for the touring opponent),[167] and another with two on and two out in the ninth that won a game in Los

Angeles. Willie hit a single, a triple, and a home run as his team drew an overflow crowd of 4,174 at Longview, Texas, with a block-long line of fans waiting for tickets.[168]

In 1956 at Little Rock, he twice allowed himself to be caught in rundowns between third and home, and, as *The Sporting News* put it, "befuddled his pursuers to emerge from the traps on both occasions."[169]

But the crowds were diminishing; and when Willie, 25, got back to New York after the 1956 tour, a reporter quoted him as saying, in one of the few stories about barnstorming to lead *The Sporting News,* under the banner, "Willie's Not Chilled by Freeze in Sticks": "We hit some towns in Texas where they had television down there for the first time this year. The people all watched the World Series on TV and I guess they just got a little too much baseball and didn't want to come out and see us play. Imagine that. People getting tired of baseball. I just can't understand it." Willie said he still had faith in barnstorming, and would have liked to play in the Puerto Rican winter league, but was ineligible after two years in the majors.[170]

Willie went to Mexico in 1957, and came back to play in an exhibition in San Francisco because the Giants were moving there for the 1958 season. He hit a 450-foot home run in Seals Stadium on the first pitch after he had been knocked down by a fastball thrown by Marino Pieretti, a tough little right-hander whose career had been interrupted in 1951 when he was slashed with a knife in a barroom fight.[171] The home run sailed over a clock in center field that bore an advertisement by a local funeral director with only his name and the word, "Eventually." But, good as he ever was, Willie didn't draw crowds in his west coast barnstorming. Observers said people now preferred pro football. Willie did cause something of a stir, however, with his criticism of the condition of center field at Seals Stadium. Matty Schwab, the Giants' groundskeeper, said he would have to raise the infield and harden the outfield for Willie.[172]

In 1958, the last year anyone made much money barnstorming, Willie was half the draw for a Willie Mays–Mickey Mantle all-star game before an unusually large exhibition crowd of 21,129 at Yankee Stadium.[173] The game became known for being the subject of a very good baseball book by George Plimpton, *Out of My League* (1961), the first of a series that made Plimpton famous as the author who played in professional sports events and then wrote about his experiences. One of his passages describes pitching to Mays: Willie popped to short (92–93).

After the New York game, Willie and slugger Roy Sievers led another successful tour of Mexico in the fall of 1958. The first game, October 17, attracted a sellout crowd of 23,537 to Social Security Stadium in Mexico City. Mays's team beat Sievers's, 10–3, but fans apparently were unhappy with the game because the Sievers' stars made six errors, three by Roy at first base.[174] The fans unnerved the players by constantly whistling in derision,[175] and for the next two games in Mexico City, attendance was only 13,762 and 14,635—great for a barnstorming game in the U.S., but below expectations for Mexico City, a place fanatic in its love for baseball. On October 26 in Tampico, Willie excited the crowd by making two great catches in center field, once reaching over the fence to steal a home run.[176] This was what the fans in the hinterlands came to see—

the big star gracing the small-town field, giving a hint of how the game is played at the top, somewhat like a circuit rider journeying to minister to the faithful far back in the hills. For 21 games in Mexico, the teams drew an average of 6,122 per game. "We made mucho dinero," one of the players said.[177] But those lush days were nearly over.

The next year, 1959, Willie played in a sellout exhibition at Syracuse, New York, again with Mantle, but then decided not to go on the trip to Mexico. The tour folded after two games.[178] In 1960, apparently there was an unusual amount of disenchantment with barnstorming, as six advertised players failed to show up for an exhibition in Birmingham, Alabama, between the American and National League Negro All-Stars.[179] Commissioner Frick fined three of the no-shows—Bad Henry Aaron of the Milwaukee Braves $1,000 for his second offense, and Charley Neal and Maury Wills of the Dodgers $500 each for their first.[180]

No one went out in 1961 except for Roger Maris, Harmon Killebrew, and Jim

In the fall of 1961 Roger Maris of the Yankees, right, tried to capitalize on the fame he achieved for hitting 61 home runs that season. He barnstormed through North Carolina with these other two sluggers, putting on hitting exhibitions. At left is Harmon Killebrew of the Minnesota Twins, and in the middle, Jim Gentile of the Orioles. Killebrew was the most active barnstormer of the three, having led trips to Mexico in the late 1950s. (Photo: from the author)

Gentile, trying to cash in on Maris's 61 homers by putting on a series of hitting exhibitions in North Carolina.[181]

Unfortunately for Mack Massingale's attempt to revive barnstorming in 1962, his tour folded after four games, for the usual reasons: poor weather, poor publicity, and, consequently, poor crowds. The players, one team of black big leaguers and another of black and white players, got only $50 each per game, instead of the $100 they had been promised. *The Sporting News* did not say exactly what Willie Mays, the star of the tour, received, other than that it was a guarantee and a percentage of the gate.[182] But years later, Mays's agent, Carl Kiesler, said Mays told him that "Willie got $10,000 to $15,000 up front plus percentage [of the gate], paid every night. In 1962 that was a lot of money, even though he was 31. He would get paid every day, it wouldn't be as if he was owed it at the end of the tour."[183]

Mays had said just before the World Series that he wished he had not signed to go on the tour, but probably remembering the fine Aaron had received two years before for failing to fulfill a barnstorming contract, Willie went. It was the first time since he began his professional career in 1948 at age 17 that Willie had not been eager to play all winter. He was now 31 and a national hero, and if his love for the road had died, maybe it was time for barnstorming to die, because no modern player typified fly-by-night baseball like the perennially young Say-Hey Willie Mays. In late October and early November 1957, for instance, he played in five games in Mexico, four in the Dominican Republic, flew to Miami for one, came back to Panama for three, then on to San Francisco, Sacramento, and Los Angeles for five games in a week—and had two canceled in Tijuana because he forgot to get work permits.[184] But by the time Mack Massingale tried to make a buck with Willie in 1962, it's hard to see how barnstorming could have been revived on any significant scale. The major leagues now had teams in Kansas City, Los Angeles, San Francisco, and Houston, and soon would have teams in Atlanta and Seattle, so there were few areas left without representation. Games were being televised nationally every weekend, the season was extended from 154 to 162 games in 1961, and extended more by the play-offs in 1968. Soon salary scales would rise incredibly, and players wouldn't need the money. Winter leagues in the Caribbean grew and attracted minor leaguers, Latin major leaguers, and other players with less than two years' experience in the majors, greatly depleting the pool of possible barnstormers. Fewer small towns were so remote from TV and travel that the sight of a major league player was a novelty. There was no longer room anywhere for barnstorming. It had vanished like those white patches that once were used to indicate "unexplored territory" on the old maps.

NOTES

1. *The Sporting News,* October 27, 1962, p. 35. Because of the generalized nature of headlines on most *Sporting News* accounts of barnstorming news, and because most accounts are unsigned, these articles will be referred to only by date and page number of publication.

2. Jules Tygiel, *Baseball's Great Experiment: Jackie Robinson and His Legacy* (New York, 1983), p. 26. Tygiel also writes a lot about preseason (spring training) barnstorming, especially in Chapter 14, "The Unwritten Law of the South."

3. *The Sporting News,* October 20, 1962, p. 29.

4. Telephone conversation, August 29, 1990. Professor Heward wrote a modern history of the Clowns with Dimitri V. Gat, *Some Are Called Clowns* (New York, 1974).

5. This was a view generally held among barnstormers, such as Tebbetts, Bob Feller, and Willie Mays, and expressed frequently in *The Sporting News.* Typical remarks appeared October 24, 1951, p. 20 (by Tebbetts); November 9, 1949, p. 4 (Feller); November 21, 1956, p. 1 (Mays).

6. As Danny Litwhiler, a veteran barnstormer, said in interviews with the author on November 15–16, 1981, "There were a lot of people around Bloomsburg who had never seen a major league ballplayer. . . . We felt like heroes."

7. Bernard Malamud, *The Natural* (New York, 1952), pp. 19–25.

8. Lawrence S. Ritter, *The Glory of Their Times* (New York, 1966), p. 190.

9. *See The Sporting News,* October 10, 1940, p. 4, and October 16, 1946, p. 23, for typical tours by Mack.

10. Donald Honig, *Baseball When the Grass Was Real* (New York, 1975), pp. 17–18.

11. Robert Creamer, *Stengel: His Life and Times* (New York, 1984), p. 131.

12. *The Sporting News,* October 8, 1931, p. 5.

13. This subject is treated extensively in Robert W. Peterson's history of black baseball, *Only the Ball Was White* (Englewood Cliffs, N.J., 1970), especially in Part 2, "Way Down in Egypt Land."

14. Peterson, *Only the Ball Was White,* p. 99.

15. *The Sporting News,* October 17, 1951, p. 4.

16. Interview with the author, November 15, 1981.

17. *Baseball When the Grass Was Real,* pp. 157, 159.

18. *Only the Ball Was White,* p. 129.

19. (No author), "Green Pastures at Last," *Dell 1949 Major League Baseball,* pp. 37–38.

20. Leroy (Satchel) Paige (as told to Hal Lebovitz), *Pitchin' Man* (Cleveland, 1948), p.46.

21. Bob Addie, "Barnstorm Fun on Way North Just a Memory," *The Sporting News,* April 13, 1960, p. 12.

22. The Wright and Spalding tours are described in Peter Levine, *A. G. Spalding and the Rise of Baseball: The Promise of American Sport* (New York and Oxford, 1985), especially Chapter 6, "Touching Bases around the World: The Social Promise of Sport." *See also* David Q. Voigt, *American Baseball, Vol. I* (Norman, Okla., 1966), pp. 47–49.

23. *The Glory of Their Times,* p. 187.

24. George Bernard Shaw, "Baseball Is a Mad Game," *London Evening Standard,* October 1924, reprinted in *Yesterday in Sport* (New York, 1968), pp. 72–73.

25. *See* Hal Drake's history of U.S. teams in Japan, *The Sporting News,* October 29, 1966, p. 26.

26. *The Sporting News,* December 3, 1966, p. 41.

27. Claire Smith, "The Return of Cecil: An Event in Japan," *New York Times,* November 4, 1990, p. 8:4.

28. Interview with Steve Carlton on videotape history of Philadelphia Phillies, "Centennial! Over 100 Years of Philadelphia Phillies Baseball" (Philadelphia, 1987).

29. *See* Burton Hawkins, "Bob Feller's $150,000 Pitch," *The Saturday Evening Post,* April 19, 1947, p. 170. Hawkins, a Washington sportswriter who was traveling secretary for Bob Feller's incomparably successful 1946 barnstorming, is explaining the anxiety that club owners felt over the large profit Feller's tour would make.

30. The *Blue Book* was published annually, but barnstorming rules hardly changed for years. Typical wording for the postwar period under discussion here would have been on pp. 532–533 of the 1950 edition (Fort Wayne, Indiana: Heilbroner, 1950).

31. *The Sporting News,* October 16, 1946, p. 23, and October 22, 1958, p. 25.

32. *See* the skepticism of Harold Rosenthal of the *New York Herald Tribune* toward the announced attendance at the Mays–Mantle exhibition in New York in 1958 (*The Sporting News,* October 22, 1958, p. 25), and J. G. Taylor Spink's questioning of a crowd of 14,000 Bob Feller claimed for an October 24, 1947, game in Mexico City (*The Sporting News,* November 5, 1947, p. 2).

33. Robert Creamer, *Babe: The Legend Comes to Life* (New York, 1974), pp. 242–243.

34. These rules are summarized in *Baseball,* pp. 190–191.

35. *The Sporting News,* October 24,1951, p. 15.

36. *See,* for example, *The Sporting News,* October 16, 1941, p. 6, and October 8, 1942, p. 9.

37. Avila was one of the missing American League All-Stars in Fido Murphy's big game in 1951.

38. *The Sporting News,* October 15, 1931, p. 1.

39. Mickey Vernon, a tactful man, said in an interview with the author on November 15, 1981, that he did not remember groupies being around during his barnstorming days in the 1940s and 1950s, and observed that, "We were in and out [of town] too fast for women. We'd have a beer and go." As for groupies, he thought "there's probably more of it today—because there are *more* players." He chuckled at this. As for deer, hunting was a main attraction for the barnstormers who went into New England with Birdie Tebbetts and Frank Shea, as *Sporting News* accounts show. A deer even ran into Shea's car one moonlit night in Maine as the seven-car entourage was rolling on to Calais for the next game (November 3, 1948, p. 18). Several of the players built a hunting lodge at Milo, Maine, in 1950 which they called the "Milo Bullpen" (November 1, 1950, p. 18). In 1951, Shea killed a 350-pound bear in Maine (October 31, 1951, p. 21).

40. Red Schoendienst and his less famous brothers cavorted together on diamonds in the midwest in 1948 and later. All were pro players (*The Sporting News,* October 27, 1948, p. 16). The four Ferrell boys were similarly active in North Carolina (October 26, 1933, p. 6); the three DiMaggios in California (November 17, 1938, p. 17); and O. T. Trucks and his son Virgil in Mobile, Alabama, where they lost both ends of the doubleheader (October 12, 1939, p. 13).

41. *Pitchin' Man,* p. 68, and Bill Veeck, with Ed Linn, *Veeck as in Wreck* (New York, 1962), p. 182.

42. J.G. Taylor Spink, *Judge Landis and 25 Years of Baseball* (New York, 1947), p. 224.

43. Pete Dexter, "Black Sox Blues," *Esquire,* October 1984, pp. 265–267.

44. Harold Seymour, *Baseball, Vol. II, The Golden Age* (New York, 1971) p. 334.

45. *Baseball When the Grass Was Real,* p. 203, and Richard J. Durrell, "The Night the Stars Nearly Fell in Minnesota," *Sports Illustrated,* October 17, 1988, unpaged.

46. *The Sporting News,* October 24, 1951, p. 20.

47. *The Sporting News,* November 11, 1947, p. 14.

48. *Pitchin' Man,* p. 54.

49. *Esquire,* pp. 265–267.

50. *The Sporting News,* November 3, 1948, p. 18.

51. *See* Ted Williams, as told to John Underwood, *My Turn at Bat: The Story of My Life* (New York, 1969), pp. 105–106.

52. *The Sporting News,* November 2, 1933, p. 5.

53. *The Sporting News,* October 11, 1934, p. 4.

54. *The Sporting News,* November 5, 1947, p. 14.

55. Ed Fitzgerald, "The Scooter That Carried the Yanks," *Sport,* January 1950, p. 27.

56. *The Sporting News,* November 1, 1950, p. 22.

57. *See The Sporting News,* November 4, 1953, p. 17, and November 7, 1956, p. 19.

58. *The Sporting News,* October 16, 1941, p. 6.

59. *Baseball When the Grass Was Real,* p. 188.

60. *The Sporting News,* October 31, 1956, p. 20.

61. *The Sporting News,* December 2, 1953, p. 18.

62. *The Glory of Their Times,* pp. 66–67.

63. *The Sporting News,* October 23, 1957, p. 27.

64. *See The Sporting News,* November 3, 1948, p. 18; October 28, 1953, p. 18; October 22, 1942, p. 10; October 31, 1956, p. 20.

65. *The Sporting News,* October 11, 1950, p. 33.

66. The following description of Danny Litwhiler's barnstorming is based on the author's interviews with him November 15 and 16, 1981.

67. *The Sporting News,* November 19, 1958, p. 17.

68. *The Sporting News,* October 15, 1931, p. 5.

69. *The Sporting News,* November 8, 1934, p. 1.

70. Paige's barnstorming is detailed in Kathryn Long Humphrey's biography, *Satchel Paige* (New York, 1988), and in *Pitchin' Man,* and elsewhere. His presence on the Mays–Massingale tour is noted in *The Sporting News,* November 3, 1962, p. 24.

71. Humphrey, *Satchel Paige,* pp. 86, 92. Paige's 1967 tour with the Clowns was the subject of a short feature in *The Sporting News* which showed that the old pitcher had become an anachronism (July 15, 1967, p. 27).

72. This inference is drawn from (1) two articles in the 1934 *Sporting News:* "The Deans Discover All Isn't Gold That Glitters" (October 25, p. 7) and "Dizzy Dean to Demand $25,000, / Paul $15,000 for Next Season" (November 1, p. 1), both of which dealt with the brothers' barnstorming; and (2) a reading of the spotty coverage of barnstorming given by *The Sporting News* in these years. Unlike the fairly thorough coverage after World War II, the prewar coverage missed most games, and often was so carelessly collected and edited that it might, for instance, include three separate references to one barnstorming tour under one heading of the "Caught on the Fly" column, instead of combining them into one unified report—and the references might not even be in chronological order reading from the beginning of the column. *See* for example *The Sporting News,* October 26, 1933.

73. The fullest account of Feller's success in 1946 is Burton Hawkins' article, "Bob Feller's $150,000 Pitch," in the April 19, 1947, *Saturday Evening Post,* pp. 25, 148, 170.

74. "Feller's Bonanza Tops Ruth's Riches and Take," *The Sporting News,* November 6, 1946, p. 1.

75. Creamer, *Babe: The Legend Comes to Life,* p. 243.

76. *Baseball When the Grass Was Real,* p. 157.

77. *Only the Ball Was White,* pp. 99–100.

78. Ibid., p. 146.

79. *Pitchin' Man,* p. 43.

80. Ibid., p. 43.

81. Ibid., pp. 52–53.

82. *Babe,* pp. 244–245.

83. Ibid., p. 249.

84. Ibid., p. 234.

85. "Baseball in the Big-Bang Era," *The National Pastime* (Garrett Park, Md., 1989), pp. 38–39. In his autobiography, *Now Pitching, Bob Feller* (with Bill Gilbert, New York, 1990), Feller says that in 1928, as a boy of nine, he saw the Ruth–Gehrig tour in Des Moines. He says he saved money for his ticket by catching gophers around his home of Van Meter for the 10-cent bounty the county paid, and then bought a Ruth–Gehrig autographed ball with some of the rest—"my first gopher ball," Feller said (pp. 20–21).

86. *The Glory of Their Times,* p. 149.

87. Jack Sher, "The Ups and Downs of Old Pete," *Sport,* April 1950, pp. 56–57.

88. *Babe,* pp. 380–381.

89. Ibid., p. 13.

90. *Veeck as in Wreck,* p. 182.

91. Leo Durocher, with Ed Linn, *Nice Guys Finish Last* (New York, 1975), p. 83.

92. *The Sporting News,* October 15, 1931, p. 1; October 29, p. 8.

93. *The Sporting News,* November 12, 1931, p. 8.

94. *The Sporting News,* October 26, 1933, p. 22.

95. *The Sporting News,* November 1, 1934, p. 1.

96. *The Sporting News,* October 25, 1934, pp. 4, 7.

97. *The Sporting News,* October 25, 1934, p. 4.

98. *The Sporting News,* October 18, 1934, p. 4.

99. *The Sporting News,* November 1, 1934, p. 8.

100. Joe Pirrone's name appears repeatedly in the Caught on the Fly columns in the 1930s' *Sporting News,* typically like this: "A number of major league players who winter on the Pacific coast will be in the lineup of the Pirrone All-Stars, who have been organized to play in the Winter

League in California" (November 18, 1934, p. 8). Buck Leonard refers to him as "Joe Perroni." *Only the Ball Was White*, pp. 152–153.

101. *The Sporting News*, October 15, 1931, p. 5.

102. *The Sporting News*, November 12, p. 1, 1931, and October 26, 1933, p. 8.

103. Bob Feller, *Strikeout Story* (New York, 1947), pp. 109–111, and *The Sporting News*, November 15, 1945, p. 13.

104. Roe's homecoming is in *The Sporting News*, October 24, 1956, p. 24, and Fred Hutchinson's October 13, 1938, p. 1.

105. *Strikeout Story*, p. 236, and "Major Leagues to Play Around World to '46," *The Sporting News*, September 27, 1945, p. 1.

106. *See* Tebbets on the front page of the October 27, 1948 issue, and Feller on the following covers: *The Sporting News* front pages for October 23, 1946; November 6, 1946; November 13, 1946; August 20, 1947; November 5, 1947; December 12, 1947.

107. *The Sporting News*, September 27, 1945, p. 1; October 11, 1945, p. 13; October 18, 1945, p. 17.

108. Richard Goldstein, *Spartan Seasons* (New York, 1980), p. 210.

109. *The Sporting News*, October 18, 1945, p. 17.

110. Hawkins, "Bob Feller's $150,000 Pitch," p. 25.

111. *The Sporting News*, December 12, 1947, p. 2.

112. Besides being covered in Hawkins' article, these details are also in *The Sporting News*, November 6, 1946, pp. 1–2, and November 9, 1949, p. 4.

113. *See,* for example, an item on p. 10 of *The Sporting News* for October 30, 1946, quoting an anonymous source about the risk to Feller's arm, and a *Sporting News* editorial, November 5, 1947, p. 14, and Hawkins in the *Saturday Evening Post*.

114. *The Sporting News*, November 6, 1946, p. 2.

115. Regarding the strikes, see *The Sporting News*, October 30, 1946, p. 9 (TWA pilots' strike); November 6, p. 2 (power strike and street car strike); November 13, p. 1 (shipping strike).

116. *The Sporting News*, October 16, 1946, p. 23.

117. *See Pitchin' Man,* Chapter 19, "Stick With Feller," pp. 73ff.

118. *The Sporting News*, November 5, 1946, p. 2.

119. *The Sporting News*, October 30, 1946, p. 9.

120. *The Sporting News*, December 12, 1947, p. 1.

121. *The Sporting News*, October 29, 1947, p. 25.

122. *Strikeout Story*, p. 236.

123. *The Sporting News*, December 12, 1947, p. 2.

124. *The Sporting News*, October 27, 1948, p. 9.

125. *The Sporting News*, November 9, 1949, p. 4.

126. Telephone conversation with me, November 20, 1990.

127. *The Sporting News*, November 7, 1951, p. 19.

128. Barnstorming by Negro League teams is described best by Robert W. Peterson in Part II of *Only the Ball Was White* (Englewood Cliffs, NJ, 1970), pp. 52–181.

129. *The Sporting News*, November 7, 1956, p. 19.

130. *The Sporting News*, October 31, 1956, p. 20.

131. *The Sporting News*, November 6, 1946, p. 2.

132. *The Sporting News*, August 9, 1969, p. 9.

133. Joseph Thomas Moore, *Pride Against Prejudice* (New York, 1988) p. 128. This is a biography of Larry Doby of the Cleveland Indians, the first black man to play in the American League.

134. *The Sporting News*, October 27, 1948, p. 16.

135. *The Sporting News*, November 9, 1949, p. 13.

136. *The Sporting News*, November 9, 1949, p. 20.

137. *The Sporting News*, November 9, 1949, p. 13.

138. *The Sporting News*, November 1, 1950, p. 7.

139. *The Sporting News*, October 17, 1951, p. 28.

140. *The Sporting News*, October 24, 1951, p. 15.

141. Author's telephone conversation with Kiesler, January 1, 1991. Mays declined to be interviewed for this chapter, but spoke through Kiesler.

142. *The Sporting News*, October 24, 1951, p. 15.

143. *The Sporting News*, November 7, 1951, p. 19.

144. *The Sporting News*, October 28, 1953, p. 18.

145. *The Sporting News*, November 4, 1953, p. 18.

146. *The Sporting News*, December 1, 1953, p. 18.

147. *The Sporting News*, November 11, 1953, p. 15.

148. *The Sporting News*, November 25, 1953, p. 16.

149. *The Sporting News*, November 25, 1953, p. 18.

150. *The Sporting News*, November 25, 1953, p. 16.

151. *The Sporting News*, November 25, 1953, p. 16.

152. *The Sporting News*, November 10, 1954, p. 1.

153. *The Sporting News*, November 3, 1954, p. 21.

154. *The Sporting News*, October 11, 1950, p. 36.

155. *The Sporting News*, November 1, 1950, p. 7.

156. *The Sporting News*, October 29, 1952, p. 13.

157. *The Sporting News*, November 10, 1954, p. 19.

158. *The Sporting News*, November 2, 1955, p. 23.

159. *The Sporting News*, November 7, 1956, p. 19.

160. *The Sporting News*, October 24, 1956, p. 24; October 31, 1956, p. 20; October 8, 1958, p. 31.

161. *The Sporting News*, November 11, 1959, p. 20.

162. *The Sporting News*, November 9, 1960, p. 23.

163. *The Sporting News*, November 3, 1954, p. 21.

164. *The Sporting News*, November 7, 1956, p. 19.

165. *The Sporting News*, November 1, 1950, p. 22.

166. *The Sporting News*, October 26, 1955, p. 23.

167. Author's telephone conversation with Carl Kiesler, Mays's agent, January 2, 1991. Kiesler said this was one of the few specific memories Mays said he had of barnstorming games.

168. *The Sporting News*, November 16, 1955, p. 14, and November 9, 1955, p. 18.

169. *The Sporting News*, October 31, 1956, p. 20.

170. *The Sporting News*, November 21, 1956, pp. 1–2.

171. *The Sporting News*, October 24, 1951, p. 21.

172. *The Sporting News*, November 13, 1957, p. 7.

173. *The Sporting News*, October 22, 1958, p. 25.

174. *The Sporting News*, October 29, 1958, p. 25.

175. *The Sporting News*, November 19, 1958, p. 17.

176. *The Sporting News*, November 12, 1958, p. 26.

177. *The Sporting News*, November 19, 1958, p. 17.

178. *The Sporting News*, November 11, 1959, p. 20.

179. *The Sporting News*, November 2, 1960, p. 22.

180. *The Sporting News*, November 9, 1960, p. 23.

181. *The Sporting News*, October 25, 1961, p. 26.

182. *The Sporting News*, November 3, 1962, p. 24.

183. Author's telephone conversation with Kiesler, January 2, 1991.

184. *The Sporting News*, November 13, 1957, p. 7.

Too Good to Be True

W. P. KINSELLA

For me, the baseball season ended abruptly on a Tuesday night last August, at the exact moment that Manny Embarquadero killed the general manager's dog.

Manny came late to our ball club. In a season scheduled to end August 31, he arrived July 15, supposedly as the organization's hottest prospect, a recent import from some tropical island where the gross national product was revolution, and the per capita income seventy-seven dollars a year. A place where, it is rumored, because of heredity and environment, or a diet heavy in papaya juice, young men move with the agility of panthers, and have arms capable of throwing a baseball from Denver to Santa Fe on only one hop.

According to what I had read in *USA Today,* there were only two political factions in Courteguay, Manny's tropical paradise: the Government and the insurgents, factions that changed identity with depressing regularity, depending on which one was currently in power. One of the current insurgents was a scout for our organization, reportedly receiving payment in hand grenades and flamethrowers, when he spotted Manny Embarquadero in an isolated mountain village (on Manny's island, a mountain was anything more than fifteen feet above sea level) playing shortstop barefooted, fielding a psuedo-baseball supposedly made from a bull's testicle stuffed with papaya seeds.

An even semicompetent player would have been an improvement over the shortstop we had, a slow-footed fellow from Stockton, California, who was batting .211, and was always late covering second base on double play balls.

"The organization's sending us a phenom," our manager, Dave "The Deer" Dearly, told us a few days before Manny's arrival. Dearly was a competent manager, who, with his players, was a pleasant, laid-back guy. A former all-star second baseman with the Orioles, he knew a lot about baseball and was able to impart that knowledge to his players. But on the field during a game, he was something else.

"Been swallowing Ty Cobb meanness pills," was how Mo Chadwick, our center fielder, described him. Dearly was developing a reputation as an umpire-baiting bastard, a manager who flew off the handle at the call of a third strike, screamed like a rock singer, kicked dirt on umpires, punted his cap, and heaved water coolers onto the field with little or no provocation.

"Got to have a gimmick," he said to us out of the side of his mouth, one night on the road, as he strutted back to the dugout after arguing a play where a dim-witted pinch runner had been out by thirty feet trying to steal third with two out. Dearly had screamed like a banshee, backed the umpire halfway to the left field foul pole, and closed out the protest by punting his cap into the third row behind our dugout. The opposing fans loved to boo him.

Before Manny Embarquadero arrived on the scene, my guess was that of all the people on the squad, Dave Dearly would be the only one to make the Bigs.

I planned all along on quitting organized baseball at the end of the season. My fastball was too slow and didn't have enough action; my curve was good when it found the strike zone, which wasn't often enough. I was being relegated to middle relief way down here in A ball—not a positive situation. I felt I could probably make it as far as Triple A and be a career minor leaguer, but I wasn't that in love with minor league baseball. I had one semester to a degree in social work. A few weeks earlier, I'd enrolled in classes for the fall.

I agreed with Dearly that you needed a gimmick. Unless you were Roger Clemens or Ken Griffey Jr., you needed a gimmick. As it turned out, Manny Embarquadero had a gimmick. If the ball club hadn't been so cheap that we had to bunk two-to-a-room on the road, I never would have found out what it was.

Manny Embarquadero looked like all the rest of those tropical paradise ballplayers, black as a polished bowling ball, head covered in a mass of wet, black curls, thin as if he'd eaten only one meal a day all of his life, thoroughbred legs, long fingers, buttermilk eyes.

On the day Manny arrived, the general manager, Chuck Manion, made a rare appearance in the clubhouse to personally introduce the hot new prospect.

"Want you boys to take good care of Manny here. Make him feel welcome."

Manny was standing head bowed; he was definitely dressed in ghetto-Good-will-store style: black dress shoes, cheap black slacks and a purple pimp-shirt with most of the glitter worn off.

"Manny not only doesn't speak English," Chuck Manion went on, "he doesn't speak. He's mute. But he's not a deaf mute. Unfortunately, no one is sure what language, if any, he understands. He knows no English or Spanish, but he's able to follow general instructions in basic sign language.

"The amazing thing is he's hardly played any baseball at all; he wandered out of the mountains, was able to communicate to our scout that he was seventeen years old, and had never played competitive baseball. He truly is a natural. I've seen video tapes. If he can play the way he does on one month's experience, he'll be in the Bigs after spring training next spring."

While Dave Dearly was a nice guy, Chuck Manion, the general manager, was a jerk. He was about forty, a blond, red-faced guy who looked as if he had just stepped out of a barber's chair, even at eleven o'clock at night. Anytime he came to the clubhouse, he wore a $400 monogrammed jogging suit and smelled of fifty-dollar-an-ounce aftershave. His family owned a brewery—and our team. Chuck Manion played at being general manager of "the Club," as he referred to us, just for fun.

"I bet he thought he'd get laid a lot, was why he wanted a baseball team as a toy," said my friend Mo Chadwick, on a night when Manion, playing the benevolent, slumming employer, accompanied a dozen of us players to a bar after a game.

He seemed extremely disappointed that there weren't dozens of women in various stages of undress and sexual frustration crawling all over us players.

"Dumb sucker thought he'd buy one round of drinks and catch the overflow," said Mo Chadwick.

I think he was right. Manion only hung around long enough for one drink and a few pointed questions about Baseball Sadies. As soon as he discovered that minor league ballplayers didn't spend all their time beating off sex-crazed groupies, he vanished into the night.

"Going down to the airport strip and cruise for hookers in his big BMW," said Mo Chadwick, and again I had to agree.

After we all shook hands with Manny Embarquadero and patted him on the shoulder and welcomed him to the club, Chuck Manion made an announcement.

"We're gonna make Crease here"—and he placed a hand on my shoulder— "Manny's roommate, both at home and on the road. Crease reads all the time so he won't mind that Manny isn't much of a conversationalist." Manion laughed at his own joke.

I did read some. In fact, the year before I'd been involved in a real brouhaha with my coaches because I sat in the bull pen reading a book, passing the time until my dubious expertise was needed on the mound. The coaches insisted that reading would ruin my control. I read anyway. I was threatened with unconditional release. I learned to hide my book more carefully.

Management rented basement housekeeping rooms within walking distance of the ballpark; I'd been alone since my last roommate had gone on a home-run-hitting binge and been promoted to Triple A Calgary, a place where, they say, if it isn't snowing, the air is so dry it makes your nose bleed.

My nickname, Crease, came about because ever since Little League I'd creased the bill of my cap right down the middle, until it's ridged like a roof above my face. I always imagined the sharp crease in the middle of my visor allowed me to draw a straight line from the V in the bill of my cap to the catcher's mitt.

"This guy is too good to be true," Mo Chadwick said to me after we'd watched Manny Embarquadero work out. "Something's not right. If he's only played baseball for one month, how come he knows when to back up third base, and how come he knows which way to cheat when the pitcher's going to throw off-speed?"

"Ours not to reason why," I said. "He's certainly a rough diamond. If he's played as little as they say, he will be in the big leagues come next spring."

If Manny Embarquadero hadn't talked in his sleep, I never would have found out what a rough diamond he really was.

The day Manny arrived we left town on a road trip. On our first night together, I woke up in humid blackness on a sagging bed, to the sound of loud whispering.

The team had reserved the whole second floor of a very old hotel, so at first I assumed the sounds I was hearing were players or management in the hallway. But the whispering continued, and as I became wider awake, I realized it was coming from the next bed.

Apparently no one was certain what language Manny Embarquadero understood, if he understood any language.

"Our scout says he may understand one of the pidgin dialects from the mountain country of Courteguay," Chuck Manion said the day he introduced Manny. The mountains Manny wandered out of bordered on Haiti, so there was some speculation that Manny might understand French. Needless to say, we didn't have any French-speaking players on the team.

I moved out of bed quietly and raised the tattered blind a few inches to let a little street light into my room, just enough to determine that Manny was alone in bed. What I was hearing was indeed coming from his mouth, but it wasn't Spanish, or French, or some mysterious Courteguayan dialect. It was ghetto language, inner-city street talk pure and simple. I didn't learn a lot except that Manny Embarquadero wasn't mute, at least when he was sleeping.

He mumbled a lot, but also spoke several understandable phrases, as well as the words "Mothah," and "Dude," and "Dee-troit." At one point, he said clearly, "Go ahead girl, it ain't gonna bite you."

At breakfast in the hotel coffee shop, Manny, using basic hand signals and facial expressions, let me know he wanted the same breakfast I was having: eggs, toast, hashbrowns, large orange juice, large milk, large coffee.

When we got home, The Deer, showing more imagination than most managers were capable of, had three cards made for Manny, one with the sun rising, one with it at high noon, another with the sun setting, while on the back of each was printed an order for a reasonable breakfast, lunch, and dinner.

"I think we should have a talk," I said to Manny as soon as we got back to our room after breakfast.

Manny stared at me, his face calm, his eyes defiant.

"You talk in your sleep," I said. "Don't worry, I'm not going to tell anyone, at least not yet. But I think you'd better clue me in on what's going down."

Manny stared at me for a long time, his eyes appeared to be all whites, with black-bullet pupils boring into me. It looked as though he was considering doing me some irreparable physical damage.

"If I was back home, mon, that stare would have shriveled your brain to the size of a pea," Manny said in a sing-songy Caribbean dialect.

"Don't play games with me," I said. "Your home, as far as I can tell, is in Detroit, and from what you've said, somewhere with a close-up view of the Renaissance Center. So don't give me this island peasant shit. When I look at you closely I can tell you're no more seventeen than I am. You're older than me, and I just turned twenty-three. I don't know why you're running this scam, and I don't particularly care. But if we're gonna room together you're gonna have to play it straight with me."

"Fuck! Why couldn't they assign me a roomie who's a heavy sleeper? I really thought I'd trained myself to stop talking in my sleep."

The accent this time was pure inner-city Detroit.

"So what's the scam? Why are you pretending to be a mute, hot-shot, child prodigy of a shortstop from the hills of Courteguay?"

"I just want to play baseball, man."

"That's no explanation."

"Yes, it is. I played high school ball. I didn't get any invites to play for a college. I went to every tryout camp in the country for three years. Never got a tumble. 'You're too slow, you don't hit for power. Your arm is strong but you don't have enough range,' was what I heard again and again.

"So I started looking around for an angle. If you ain't the most talented, then you got to play the angles. You got to have a gimmick, I decided. I looked around some more and I seen that all the shortstops were coming from Courteguay, and they're black, and I'm black, so I figured if I went over there and kept my mouth shut and pretended to be an inexperienced kid from the outback, I'd get me a chance to play."

"Shows a hell of a lot of desire," I said.

"I even tried the Mexican Leagues, but I couldn't catch on."

"I bet nobody's ever pulled a scam like this before. But in a month or so, when you don't improve fast enough, this team is going to send you packing. Only, aren't they liable to send you back to Courteguay?"

"I'm gettin' better every day, man. I'm gonna make it. People perform according to expectations. Everyone figures I'll play my way into the Bigs next spring, and I'm not going to disappoint them."

"There's a little matter of talent."

"I have more than you can imagine."

"Lots of luck."

The next night, when Manny played his first game, the play-by-play people mentioned that Manny was mute but not deaf. By the eighth inning, there were a dozen people behind our dugout shouting to Manny in every language from Portuguese to Indonesian. Manny only shrugged his shoulders and smiled in a friendly manner, displaying a faceful of large, white teeth.

I kept Manny's secret, though I took to watching him carefully from my spot in the left field bullpen. He was a one hundred percent improvement on our previous shortstop. I could see what the scouts, believing him to be seventeen and inexperienced at baseball, had seen in him.

He had an arm that wouldn't quit. He could go deep in the hole to spear a ball on the edge of the outfield grass, straighten effortlessly, brace his back foot on the grass, and fire to first in time to get the runner. He displayed uncanny anticipation; he covered only as much ground as was necessary, never seeming to extend himself, but the thing was that he covered whatever ground was necessary in order to reach the ball.

Of course, his name wasn't Manny Embarquadero.

"I am one anonymous dude. Jimmy, with two m's, if you must know, Williams with two l's. Hell, there must be two thousand guys in Dee-troit, Michigan, with the same name as mine. And all us young black guys look alike, right?

"I had a gramma, probably a greatgramma, but she died. I think I was her granddaughter's kid. But that girl went off to North Carolina when I was just a baby and nobody ever heard from her again. Once, Gramma and I lived for three years in an abandoned building. We collected cardboard boxes and we made the walls about two feet thick. It gets fucking cold in the winter in Dee-troit, Michigan. Gramma always saw to it that I went to school, even if we didn't have a real roof over our heads."

Two nights later, there was a buzz among the players that there was a scout from the Big Show in the stands. Everyone who got in the game pressed a little, some pressed a lot, and everybody except Manny managed to look bad at one time or another. Manny was unbelievable. There was one play where the ball was hit sharply to his right and deep in the hole, a single if there ever was one. The left fielder had already run in about five steps expecting to field the base hit, when he saw that Manny had not only fielded the ball, but was directly behind it when he scooped it up and threw the runner out by a step. What he did was humanly impossible.

"How did you do that?" I asked as he flopped on the bench beside me after the inning had ended. Manny just smiled and pounded his right fist into his left palm.

Later, back at the hotel, I said, "There was something fishy about that play you made in the sixth inning."

"What fishy?"

"You moved about three long strides to your right and managed to get directly behind a ball that was hit like lightning. There's no major league shortstop could have gotten to that ball. I think you did something illegal, or magical. You're not a magician, are you?"

"I'm not anything but a shortstop, man." But he looked at me for a long time, and there was a shrewdness in his stare.

What I could not understand was that no one else had noticed what Manny had done. No one else noticed that one second he was starting a move to his right, making a valiant effort to snag a sure base hit, and an instant later he was behind the ball, playing it like a routine grounder. No one commented. When I carefully broached the subject, no one showed any interest. He had not been overwhelmed by congratulations when he came in from the field. Was I the only one who saw what Manny had done?

The trouble between Chuck Manion and Manny Embarquadero began on a hot Saturday afternoon. We were at home and scheduled for a twi-night doubleheader. Chuck Manion, wearing a gray, monogrammed sweat suit, worth more than I was getting paid every month, showed up to work out with the team. He was accompanied by his hateful little dog, a nasty spotted terrier of some kind, with mean, watery eyes and a red ass. Manion sometimes left the dog in the clubhouse while he was attending a game, where it invariably relieved itself on the floor.

"After losing an extra-inning game, it's a real fucking joy to come back to a clubhouse that smells of dog shit," The Deer said one evening.

"Tell him where to stuff his ugly, fucking dog," one of the players suggested. We all applauded.

"Wouldn't I love to," said Dearly. "Unfortunately, Manion may not always be right, but he is always the owner and general manager. His family actually puts money into this club. In the eyes of the executives of our big league club, an owner like that can do no wrong."

On that humid Saturday afternoon, Manion brought the dog out onto the playing field. Dearly spat contemptuously from where he was hitting out fungoes, but said nothing.

Spotting Manny and I tossing the ball on the sidelines, Manion stopped in front of me and, pointing to Manny, said, "Tell Chico to take Conan here for a couple of turns around the outfield."

"His name is Manny," I said. "And he can understand simple sign language. Tell him yourself."

"You're the one who's retiring at the end of the season, aren't you?" Manion said to me in a snarky voice.

"Right."

"And a goddamned good thing."

He walked over to Manny, put the leash in his hand and pointed to the outfield, gesturing to indicate two circles around the outfield.

I wondered what Manny Embarquadero would do. I knew what Jimmy Williams would do. But which one was Manion dealing with, the timid ballplayer from the hills of Courteguay, or the street kid from Dee-troit?

It didn't take long to find out.

Manny Embarquadero let the leash drop to the grass, and with the same hand that dropped the leash, he gave Manion the finger, staring unflinchingly at him with as much contempt as I had ever seen pass from one person to another.

Manion snarled curses at Manny and turned away to hunt down Dave Dearly. At the same moment, the dog, Conan, nipped at Manny's ankle. Manny's reaction was so immediate I didn't even see the kick. But I heard the yelp, and saw the dog fly about fifteen feet into left field, his leash trailing after him.

Manion found Dave Dearly, and the curses piled up and multiplied trying to get out of his mouth. He demanded that Manny be fired, traded, deported, or arrested.

When Dearly tried to soothe the irate general manager, he too was threatened with every penalty imaginable.

"Goddammit, Chuck," Dearly was saying, "I got enough trouble babysitting and handholding twenty-five players, most of them rookies, without having you and your goddamned mutt riling things up."

The mutt, Conan, apparently undamaged, was busy relieving himself on the left field grass, baring his pearly fangs at any ballplayer who got too close to him.

Manion continued to froth at the mouth, demanding Manny's immediate dismissal and deportation, threatening Dearly with dismissal if he didn't comply.

At that moment, Dearly must have remembered he was building himself a reputation as an umpire-baiter, for he suddenly went from the defensive to the offensive. His face turned stop-sign red as he breathed his fury onto Chuck Manion, backing him step-by-step from the area of third base toward the outfield, scuffing dirt on Manion's custom jogging outfit. Manion had only anger on his side. He was not experienced in on-field confrontation.

"Take your ugly fucking dog and get the fuck off my baseball field," roared The Deer, turning away from Manion as suddenly as he had confronted him. Dearly punted his cap six rows deep in the empty stands, where it landed right side up, sitting like a white gull on a green-painted grandstand seat.

Manion retrieved the dog's leash and headed for the dugout, still raging and finger-pointing.

"From now on walk your own fucking dog on your own fucking lawn," were Dearly's parting words, as Manion's back retreated down the tunnel to the dressing room.

The players applauded as Manion disappeared from view.

"Way to go, Skip," several of us said.

"You better watch out," I said to Manny, over a late supper at a Jack-in-the-Box. "Manion's gonna get your ass one way or another."

"Fuck Manion, and his ball club" said Manny Embarquadero. "And fuck his dog, too."

Manion didn't show his face on the field all the next week, but if we looked up, he could be seen in the owner's box, a glass wall separating him from the press table, pacing, smoking, often taking or making telephone calls.

Manny continued his extraordinary play.

"Did you see what I did there in the second inning?" Manny asked when we were safely in our apartment after the game.

"I did."

"I can't figure out how I did it. If anybody but you sees, and if they figure that I'm getting help . . . what would they do, bar me from the game? Do you have any idea?"

In the second inning, Manny Embarquardero had gone up the ladder for a line drive. The ball was far over his head, but what I saw was a long, licorice-colored arm extend maybe four feet farther than it should have to catch the ball. No one else, it seemed, saw the supernatural extension of the arm. Dearly and the other players patted Manny on the back when he came off the field; they apparently saw only a very good play, not an extraordinary or impossible one.

"Want to tell me how you do what you do?" I said.

Manny had made at least one impossible play in each of the last dozen games. What he did at the plate was less obvious, but probably magically inspired as well, for he was, without any fanfare, batting over .400 since he had joined the club.

"I guess I can tell you," Manny said. "Must be because you know who I really am that you can see what I do. Besides, no one else would believe you if you spilled your guts. I'm just a poor, mute, black, immigrant ballplayer."

"I've no intention of spreading your secrets around. I'm going to be through with baseball for good in a few weeks."

"If you want a professional career, I might be able to arrange it. It would involve a trip to Courteguay. And I don't know about you being white and all."

111

"Not interested."

"There's a factory down there in Courteguay. They sing and chant over your body, wrap it in palm fronds, feed you hibiscus petals, and lots of other things. After a week or so, you emerge from the factory with an iron arm and the speed of a bullet, and the ability to be in more than one place at a time.

"It's just like a magic trick, only instead of the hand being quicker than the eye, the whole ballplayer is quicker than the eye. They send a couple of guys up to the Bigs each year. I just lucked out. I didn't even suspect anything unusual was going on in Courteguay. I really thought I'd stand a chance of getting a professional contract if I came from a backwater like Courteguay.

"The reason I got into the factory, got the treatment, was I got caught stealing food that supposedly belonged to this guerrilla leader, Dr. Noir, a man who looked like Idi Amin, only not so friendly. . . ."

"What was the price?" I asked. "What do you have to do in return?"

"You don't want to know," said Manny.

"I reckon I don't. You're actually kidding me, aren't you? There's no factory in Courteguay that turns out iron-armed infielders."

"Think what you want, man. This Dr. Noir was from Haiti originally: voodoo, dancing naked around a fire all night, cutting out people's spleens and eating them raw. At the moment Dr. Noir leads the insurgents in Courteguay, but someday soon he'll be president of the Republic."

"You're right," I said. "I don't want to know."

A week later, the night we got home after a short road trip, came the news that Dave Dearly had been fired. We were in first place by a game, thanks mainly to Manny Embarquadero's fielding and hitting.

The grapevine reported that Chuck Manion had been unable to convince the executives of the parent club to get rid of Manny. The big league club's prime interest was in quality baseball players, so no matter what Manion threatened, they wouldn't part with a phenom-prospect just because Manion didn't like him.

Dave Dearly was another matter. Since Manion and his family put large amounts of their own money into the stadium and the team, the top dogs decided that it was good business to keep a wealthy owner as happy as possible, and if keeping him happy, no matter how unreasonable he was, meant jettisoning a minor league manager, so be it.

The third base coach, a young guy named Wylie Keene, managed the club the next night. Between innings, Manny would hiss questions into my ear. He wanted me to quiz Keene about Dave Dearly's departure; the who, what, why, and when of the firing.

"It was primarily because The Deer went to bat for your Courteguayan friend over there," Keene told me. "Chuck Manion wanted Manny given the bum's rush out of baseball. But the Deer stood up to him.

"He told the parent club that Manion acts as if the players are his personal slaves, and he said he wouldn't have his players treated that way, and life was too short to work for an asshole like Manion, no matter how much money he puts into this club.

"But, we all know money is the bottom line, so The Deer is gone. He thinks there'll be other jobs, that the organization will find another place for him."

"What do you think?"

"I don't know. He's a good man. He'll catch on somewhere, but not likely in this organization."

When we got home I passed all that information to Manny.

"Manion is a son of a bitch," Manny said. "I'd love to get him to Courteguay for a few minutes. I'd like to leave him alone in a room with Dr. Noir, who, you're not gonna believe this, has a degree in a chiropractics from a college in Davenport, Iowa.

"Dr. Lucius Noir. I saw his diploma. According to rumors, he deals personally with political prisoners. Just dislocates joints until they confess to whatever he wants them to confess to. Wouldn't I love to hear Manion scream."

"There's not much you can do," I said. "Look, you're gonna be out of this town in a few weeks. You'll never have to see or hear of Manion again."

"Maybe there is something I can do," Manny said. "Come on," he said, heading for the door.

"It's after midnight."

"Right."

We walked the darkened streets of the city for over half an hour. Manion lived in the richest suburb, his house overlooking the eighteenth tee of a private golf course. The house loomed up like a mountain in the darkness.

"Listen," I said. "I'm not going to let you do something you'll be sorry for, or get arrested for. . . ."

"Don't worry, I'm not going to hurt Manion physically. In fact, I'm not gonna touch him. The only way you can hurt rich people is by taking things away from them, taking away things they value. Manion's such an asshole, he probably loves that stinking little dog. . . ."

Manny said that as we were crawling through a hedge and creeping across Manion's patio. I'm sure I would have left if Manny had decided to break into the house. Basically, I have a law-abiding heart. But he didn't. Just as we were crossing the moon-silvered patio, Conan came sniffing around the corner of the house, stopped abruptly, and stood stiff-legged, his fangs bared, a growl deep in his throat.

"Pretty doggie," said Manny Embarquadero, holding a hand toward the hairless, red-assed mutt. They stood like that for some time, until the dog decided to relax. It moved forward one step as Manny continued crooning softly to it.

Manny struck like a cobra. The dog was dead before it could utter a sound.

We turned to leave.

"I should have killed Manion. But I've got places to go."

"Somebody's gonna find you out."

"How? Are you gonna tell?"

"You're the most likely suspect."

"In Courteguay they'd barbecue that little fucker and smack their lips over him. In Courteguay dogs are a delicacy."

"You're not from Courteguay."

Manny was going to get caught. There was no doubt in my mind. He was going to ruin a promising baseball career, which may or may not have been aided by the supernatural. Personally, I had a lot of doubts about Manny's stories.

"Manny Embarquadero is pure magic. They'll never lay a hand on me," said Jimmy Williams, late of Dee-troit city.

"You forget," I said "there really isn't anyone named Manny Embarquadero."

"Oh, yes there is," he said, his eyes piercing me like awls. "Oh, yes there is."

As we crawled through the hedge, I let a branch take the creased cap off my head. When it fell I made no effort to retrieve it. There was a bus that passed through town at four A.M., and I'd be on it.

Rituals: The Oiling of the Glove

BILL MEISSNER

My father said a good ballplayer keeps his glove oiled, and never lets it get in the dust, and I've always remembered his advice. After dinner, my son and I sit on the cement front porch steps of our house, oiling our gloves with neat's-foot oil and soft cloths. There's a tenderness about it, this oiling: We oil the joints and hinges of the gloves, the darkened pockets, the intricate web and lacings, the scraped places on the back where we scooped against the earth again and again to pull up the sinking line drives. The air fills with the scent of oil, a baseball player's perfume. I think about the great fielders, about Willie Mays and Ty Cobb and Dimaggio. When we're finished oiling our gloves, the skin of our fingers is moist and pliable, and will smell of the fragment scent of oil and leather all evening.

"Why do you always have to oil a glove?" my son asks.

"If you oil it enough, you'll play better," I respond automatically.

"But won't you play better if you *practice*?"

"Yeah," I agree with a chuckle. "That too. But if you don't oil a glove, it'll dry out and crack."

I think about Willie Mays, and his famous over-the-shoulder catch in the 1954 World Series. I think about Willie, lovingly oiling his glove before that World Series. Then I recall going to Milwaukee County Stadium with my father in 1958 for my first major league ball game, catching a foul ball, bare-handed, from Willie Mays on the third pitch of the game.

"Oil your glove and you'll always be ready," I add. "That's what Grandpa always used to say."

"Ready for what?"

"Ready for anything. Ground ball or line drive. Ready for whatever comes your way."

"Was Grandpa a good ballplayer?" my son asks.

"Good," I say. "Really good. Best fielder in his league."

In the old days, baseball gloves were no more than thin pieces of leather fitted over the palm and fingers. Over the years, they've grown wider, thicker, and longer, and the good ballplayer seems obsessed with softening the glove, getting it broken in so it's sure and flexible, making it feel small on the hand again. The dream glove is a glove that becomes one with the hand.

Some people believe you can tell your future just by staring at your hand. They believe you can read your past, and predict the events to come. Palm readers stare at the hand, and the hand tells all.

Sometimes I wonder, as all fathers wonder: What will my son be when he grows up? Will he follow his crooked dreams and aspire to be a pro baseball player? Or will he be like his grandfather, forced to take a series of odd sales jobs, driving the highways to peddle Nutrena dog food and washing machine parts. My son's only nine, but I know what he thinks about doing.

"Think I could ever be a major leaguer?" he asked earlier this summer.

"Only one out of a million kids make it," I say flatly.

"What if I'm that one?"

I give him a half-smile but don't answer. I think of four-time Gold Glove winner Kirby Puckett saying, in an interview, that he never doubted he'd be that one in a million. But my son's no Puckett—he has the style of a young ballplayer, but not the deft, instinctive fielding skills. And his hitting ability is above average, at best.

It's just a dream, I want to tell him, the chances remote and distant. It's just a dream of boys across America, a dream so many of us share when we grow up, until the real world, with all its practicality, hits us in the face like a line drive and we wake one morning at 17 or 18 knowing it will never happen.

Sometimes, as we drive toward the little league field, I talk to my son about the great major leaguers. I tell him about Mickey Mantle, Hank Aaron, Willie Mays, Ted Williams.

"What team do they play on now?" he asks.

"They don't play," I explain. "They're retired. When you reach 35 or so, your career is about finished."

"Why?" my son asks.

"You're getting old, that's why." I sigh. "Your reflexes slow down a little, you lose your speed. Your knees and elbows start to go."

"So what do they do?"

"Retire."

"And then what?"

"I don't know. They go into business. Or sales. Johnny Bench does ads for house paint. Joe Dimaggio sold coffeemakers on T.V."

"Who's Joe Dimaggio?" he asks, blinking.

"Should we go in?" my son asks again as he gets up from the porch step.

"No," I reply. "Let's stay out a while longer."

I stand up, pick up my glove and stroll to the middle of the yard. My son follows automatically and we play catch, throwing back and forth in silence, the only sound the snapping of the ball in the damp leather pockets.

We play until dusk, until I can barely see the ball. I see my son's arm swing down but see no ball until it appears a few feet in front of my face, a dark shape emerging from the darkness.

"Give me a high long one," he says. "I'll make a Willie Mays catch."

When I tell him it's time to quit, he insists on throwing a few more. I squint at the ball, flickering through the shadows as it spins toward me, and a couple of throws skim off my glove and bounce behind me on the grass.

I sit back down on the porch step, and he walks over and lays his glove beside me. He'll grow out of this glove, I think, as I stare at it. He'll grow out of it soon.

"Did Grandpa ever want to be a major leaguer?" he asks.

"I don't know," I confess, putting the cap back on the neat's-foot oil. "But he was on a championship amateur team." I recall the black and white photo of the 1934 team in Iowa, and my father's smooth face squinting into the sun.

"Then why didn't he keep playing?" he asks. "Why didn't he try out for the majors?"

I shrug.

I lean back against the hard cement step. I want to tell him that, as we get older, we all go through this: these cycles of expectation and loss, these dreams that ripen, then dry up and become brittle. Instead I remain silent. The chosen few make it: the Wagners, the Cobbs, the Ruths, the Gehrigs, but then they, too, are eclipsed by time, and they turn into fading gray pictures in old record books. Yet somehow—and this is the timeless beauty of baseball—these men and their

Bill and Nathan Meissner and gloves. (Photo: from the author)

legendary feats stay alive in the collective memories of baseball fans. Somehow, like fathers and hopes and dreams, they can never die.

My son and I stare out at the evening sky, the patterns of light and darkness, the bright red rim coating the horizon. We live our lives as best we can. We keep our gloves oiled just in case. We keep our gloves oiled and hope they'll catch the ball better than we ever could. We sit on the front porch, gently sliding our gloves on and off our hands.

Bibliography of Baseball Books: January 1990–April 1991

COMPILED BY RICHARD W. ARPI

This bibliography is in two sections: books published in 1990 and those published in the first quarter of 1991. Each part has individually numbered entries that are grouped into nine categories: Anthologies, Book Reviews, and Literary Analysis; Biographies and Personal Accounts; Fiction and Poetry; Histories and General Works; Hobby; Humor and Trivia; Instruction, Fitness, and Rules; Juvenile; and Reference, Statistics, and Annual Works.

I have tried to provide the following information for each entry: author; complete title; writers of introductions and forewords; city of publication; publisher; existence of photographs, illustrations, indices, notes, and bibliography; price (for both hardcover and paperback); and ISBN numbers for both. Also, I note if a book is a reprint and the date and publisher of the first edition. I list the addresses of authors of self-published books, when known. Although it is possible for some books to fall under more than one category, they are listed only once, under the most likely category.

Information is as complete and as accurate as I have been able to verify by early May of 1991. Readers should note that while I acknowledge the existence of media guides (1990, item 316) and yearbooks (1990, item 349), I do not list them all. Other than that, I have tried to be as comprehensive as possible, but I make no claims to have listed every baseball book published in the time period stated above. However, I believe I have listed practically all of the new releases.

I gratefully acknowledge the assistance of members of the Society of American Baseball Research's Bibliography Committee, especially Bernie Esser, Andy McCue, and Bobby Plapinger.

SECTION I: ANTHOLOGIES, BOOK REVIEWS, AND LITERARY ANALYSIS

1. Admoties, Paul, editor. *The SABR Review of Books: A Forum of Baseball Literary Opinion, Volume V.* SABR: P. O. Box 93183 Cleveland, Ohio 44101 (147 pp., $7.00 p) 0-91037-42-0, annually since 1986

2. Allen, Lee. *Cooperstown Corner: Columns from the Sporting News by Lee Allen, 1962–1969.* Introduction by Steven P. Gietschier. Foreword by Paul Adomites. SABR. (181 pp., index, $10.00 p) 0-910137-41-2

3. Bjarkman, Peter, editor. *Baseball and the Game of Life: Stories for the Thinking Fan.* Introduction by Peter Bjarkman. Birch Brook Press Box 293 Otisville, New York 10963 (230 pp., $40.00 h plus $2.00 p/h) 15 stories by Coover, Kinsella, Neugeboren, Roth, & others. 0-913559-15-6

4. Boswell, Thomas. *Game Day: Sports Writings, 1970–1990.* New York: Doubleday. (394 pp., $19.95 h) 0-385-41617-2, football, boxing, basketball, golf, Olympics, tennis, baseball

5. Bowering, George, editor. *Taking the Field: The Best of Baseball Fiction.* Red Deer, Alberta: Red Deer College Press, (296 pp., $14.95 p)

6. Dagavarian, Debra, editor. *A Century of Children's Baseball Stories.* Westport, CT: Stadium Books (192 pp., $7.95 p)

7. Falk, David, editor. *The Cubs Reader: The Best Writing Done on Baseball's Most Loveable Team.* Ventura Arts: P.O. Box 6093 Thousand Oaks, California 91360 (195 pp., $9.95 p) 0-941913-03-1 similar books on Yanks, Dodgers, Bosox

8. *Great Baseball Stories.* NY: Mallard Press (301 pp., $15.98 h) 20 stories both fiction and nonfiction

9. Grossinger, Richard and Kevin Kerrane, editors. *Into the Temple of Baseball.* Celestial Arts: P. O. Box 7327 Berkeley, Calif. 94707 (230 pp., photos, $18.95 p) 0-89087-598-7

10. *The Ol' Ball Game: A Collection of Baseball Characters and Moments Worth Remembering.* Order from Stackpole Books, Cameron & Kelker Streets, P. O. Box 1831, Harrisburg, Pa 17105 (178 pp., $14.95 h) 0-8117-1081-1; 29 original essays by Broeg, Hall, Holway, Kaplan, Macht, and others

11. Schulman, L. M., selector. *The Random House Book of Sports Stories.* Illustrated by Thomas B. Allen. New York: Random House. (246 pp., $15.95 h) 0-394-82874-7; contains Thurber's "You Could Look it Up," Ring Lardner's "Harry Kane," and Jay Neugeboren's "Ebbets Field."

12. Sloan, David, editor. *Best Sports Stories 1989. (46th Annual Sports Journalism Awards)* St. Louis: The Sporting News. (285 pp., $10.95 p) 0-89204-353-9; includes many other sports besides baseball

SECTION II: BIOGRAPHIES AND PERSONAL ACCOUNTS

13. Allen, Maury. *Baseball: The Lives Behind the Seams.* New York: Macmillan. (308 pp., photos, index, $18.95 h) 0-02-501341-6

14. Anderson, Sparky with Dan Ewald. *Sparky!* New York: Prentice-Hall. (264 pp., photos, index, $18.95 h) 0-13-109463-7

15. Aylesworth, Thomas and Benton Minks. *The Encyclopedia of Baseball Managers: 1901 to the Present Day.* New York: Crescent Books. (224 pp., photos, index, $15.99 h) 517-67909-4

16. Baylor, Don with Claire Smith. *Don Baylor: Nothing But the Truth: A Baseball Life.* New York: St. Martin's Press. (338 pp., photos, $4.95 p) 0-312-92106-3; reprint, St. Martin's, 1989

17. Berra, Yogi with Tom Horton. *Yogi: It Ain't Over.* New York: Harper & Row. (305 pp., photos, $4.95 p) 0-06-100012-4; reprint, McGraw-Hill, 1989

18. Bouton, Jim. *Ball Four, 20th Anniversary Edition.* Edited by Leonard Shecter. New York: Colliers. (472 pp., photos, index, $12.95 p) 0-02-030665-2; reprint, World Publishing Co., 1970 & 1981; new epilogue by Bouton.

19. Bryan, Mike. *Baseball Lives: Men and Women of the Game Talk about their Jobs, their Lives, and the National Pastime.* New York: Fawcett Columbine. (345 pp., $9.95 p) 0-449-90510-1; reprint, Pantheon, 1989

20. Caray, Harry with Bob Verdi. *Holy Cow!* New York: Berkeley Books. (230 pp., $4.50 p) 0-425-12238-7; reprint, Villard, 1989

21. Craft, David and Tom Owens, *Redbirds Revisited: Great Memories and Stories from the St. Louis Cardinals.* Foreword by Warner Fusselle. Chicago: Bonus Books. (246 pp., photos, $19.95 h) 0-929387-12-0

22. Creamer, Robert W. *Stengel: His Life and Times.* New York: Fireside Books (349 pp., photos, index, $9.95 p) 0-671-70131-2; reprint, Simon & Schuster, 1984

23. Dravecky, Dave with Tim Stafford. *Comeback.* San Francisco: Harper & Row and Grand Rapids, Michigan: Zondervan Pub. (252 pp., photos, $17.95 h) 0-310-52880-1

24. Drysdale, Don with Bob Verdi. *Once a Bum, Always a Dodger: My Life in Baseball from Brooklyn to Los Angeles.* New York: St. Martin's Press. (278 pp., photos, index, $18.95 h) 0-312-03902-6

25. Etkin, Jack, Bob Nightengale, Kevin Scarbinsky, & Rick Weinberg. *Bo Stories. (Bo Jackson): A Fun and Exciting Look at the Feats of One of the Most Electrifying Young Talents of Our Time.* Illustrations by Bill Wilson. St. Louis: The Sporting News. (176 pp., photos, $6.95 p) 0-89204-350-4

26. Feller, Bob with Bill Gilbert. *Now Pitching, Bob Feller: A Baseball Memoir.* Birch Lane Press (Carol Publishing Group, 600 Madison Ave, NY 10022): (231 pp., photos, index, $18.95 h) 1-55972-005-0

27. Garvey, Cynthia and Andy Meisler. *The Secret Life of Cyndy Garvey* New York: St. Martin's Press. (362 pp., photos, $4.95 p) 0-312-92203-5; reprint, Doubleday, 1989

28. Gildner, Gary. *The Warsaw Sparks.* Introduction by Albert E. Stone. Singular Lives, Iowa Series in North American Autobiography. Iowa City,

Iowa: University of Iowa Press, 52242 (239 pp., $12.50 p) 0-87745-276-8; university professor coaches baseball team in Poland

29. Gorman, Bob. *Double X (Jimmie Foxx)*. from author, 2430 Guenther Court, Baldwin, New York 11510 (213 pp., photos, bibliography, stats, $10.00 SABR members, $12.00 others)

30. Gregg, Eric and Marty Appel. *Working the Plate: The Eric Gregg Story*. New York: William Morrow. (220 pp., photos, index, $16.95 h) 0-688-09089-3

31. Harwell, Ernie. *Tuned to Baseball*. New York: Ballantine Books. (239 pp., photos, index, $3.95 p) 0-345-36125-3; reprint, Diamond Communications, 1985

32. Heiman, Lee and Dave Weiner and Bill Gutman. *When the Cheering Stops: Former Major Leaguers Talk About Their Game and Their Lives*. New York: Macmillan. (308 pp., photos, index, appendix, $18.95 h) 0-02-550765-6

33. Hershiser, Orel with Jerry B. Jenkins. *Orel Hershiser: Out of the Blue*. New York: Charter Books. (246 pp., photos, $4.50 p) 1-55773-341-4; reprint, Wolgemuth & Hyatt, 1989; includes one updated chapter

34. Holmes, Tot. *Brooklyn's Babe: The Life and Legend of Babe Herman*. Holmes Pub. P.O. Box 11, Gothenburg, Nebraska 69138 (242 pp., $19.95 h) 0-943716-12-8

35. Jackson, Bo and Dick Schapp. *Bo Knows Bo*. New York: Doubleday. (218 pp., photos, career stats, $18.95 h) 0-385-41620-2

36. Johnstone, Jay and Rich Talley. *Some of My Best Friends are Crazy: Baseball's Favorite Lunatic Goes in Search of His Peers*. New York: Macmillan (241 pp., photos, $18.95 h) 0-02-559560-1

37. Jordan, David M. *A Tiger in His Time: Hal Newhouser and the Burden of Wartime Ball*. South Bend: Diamond Communications (271 pp., photos, $18.95 h) 0-912083-49-2

38. Joyce, Gary. *The Only Ticket Off the Island*. Toronto: Lester & Orpen Dennys (229 pp., $24.95 h Can.) 0-88619-324-9, account of one Dominican Winter League Season; also paper 0-88619-326-5

39. Kerr, John. *Calvin: Baseball's Last Dinosaur. (Calvin Griffith)* Forewords by Pat Reusse and Shirley Povich. Dubuque: William C. Brown Pubs. (206 pp., photos, $12.95 p) 0-697-11237-3

40. Madden, Bill and Moss Klein. *Damned Yankees: A No-Holds Barred Acount of Life with "Boss" Steinbrenner*. Cartoons by Ed Murawinski. New York: Warner Books. (292 pp., photos, index, appendix, $19.95 h) 0-446-51544-2

41. Niekro, Phil and Joe with Ken Picking. *The Niekro Files: The Uncensored*

Letters of Baseball's Most Notorious Brothers. Chicago: Contemporary Books. (227 pp., $7.95 p) 0-8092-4132-3; reprint, Contemporary, 1988

42. Odenkirk, James E. *Plain Dealing: The Biography of Gordon Cobbledick of the Cleveland Plain Dealer.* (may not be exact title). $16.95 plus $2.00 p/h from Spider-Naps Publications, c/o James E. Odenkirk P. O. Box 50925 Phoenix, Arizona 85076-0925; features newspaper articles of Cobbledick's on Cleveland sports

43. Pallone, Dave with Alan Steinberg. *Behind the Mask: My Double Life in Baseball.* New York: Viking Press (331 pp., photos, $18.95 h) 0-670-83312-6; the life and times of a gay umpire

44. Peary, Danny, editor. *Cult Baseball Players, The Greats, The Flakes, The Weird, and The Wonderful: Famous Writers and Celebrities Profile their All-Time Favorite Baseball Stars.* New York: Fireside Books. (383 pp., photos, index, $10.95 p) 0-671-67172-3

45. Robinson, Ray. *Iron Horse: Lou Gehrig in His Time.* New York: W. W. Norton. (300 pp., photos, index, appendices including lifetime stats and list of Lou Gehrig Award winners 1955–1989, $22.50 h) 0-3930-2857-7

46. Ryan, Nolan and Harvey Frommer. *Throwing Heat: The Autobiography of Nolan Ryan.* New York: Avon Books. (249 pp., photos, $4.95 p) 0-380-70826-4; reprint, Doubleday, 1988

47. Sokolove, Michael Y. *Hustle: The Myth, Life and Lies of Pete Rose.* New York: Simon and Schuster. (304 pp., photos, index, $19.95 h) 0-671-69503-7

48. Strawberry, Darryl with Don Gold. *Hard Learnin'.* New York: Pocket Books. (275 pp., $4.50 p) 0-425-12651-X

49. Thrift, Syd and Barry Shapiro. *The Game According to Syd: The Theories and Teachings of Baseball's Leading Innovator.* New York: Simon & Schuster. (304 pp., index, $18.95 h) 0-671-68410-8

50. Wagenheim, Kal. *Babe Ruth: His Life and Legend.* Waterfront Press, 52 Maple Ave., Maplewood, NJ 07040 (274 pp., photos, stats, $12.95 p) 0-943862-41-8; reprint, Praeger, 1974

51. Walton, Jerome and Jim Langford. *Rookie: The Story of a Season.* South Bend: Diamond Communications. (157 pp., $8.95 p) 0-912083-44-1; also $18.95 h 0-912083-45-X

52. Williams, Dick and Bill Plaschke. *No More Mr. Nice Guy: A Life of Hardball.* San Diego: Harcourt, Brace, Jovanovich. (344 pp. index, photos, $19.95 h) 0-15-166728-4

53. Winegardner, Mark. *Prophet of the Sandlots: Journeys with a Major League Scout.* New York: Atlantic Monthly Press. (279 pp., appendix $18.95 h) 0-87113-336-9; story of Tony Lucadello

54. Yastrzemski, Carl and Gerald Eskenazi. *Yaz: Baseball, The Wall, and Me.* New York: Doubleday. (300 pp., photos, stats, $19.95 h) 0-385-26769-X

55. Zimmerman, Tom. *A Day in the Season of the Los Angeles Dodgers.* New York. Shapolsky Publishers. (175 pp., photos, bibliography, $16.95 h) 0-944007-89-9

SECTION III: FICTION AND POETRY

56. Brock, Darryl. *If I Never Get Back: A Novel.* New York: Crown Publishers. (424 pp., $18.95 h) 0-517-57345-8

57. Cronin, Justin. *A Short History of the Long Ball.* Council Oak Books 1428 S. St. Louis, Tulsa, Ok. 74120 (90 pp., $12.95 h) 0-933031-23-8

58. Everson, David. *Comeback.* New York: Key Books (Ballantine)

59. Gardner, Steve. *O Baseball, O Columbus.* (poems). Matchbooks Publications. 5683 N. Shuffle Creek Road, Unionville, In. 47468 ($2.50 plus $.65 p/h)

60. Irvine, Robert. *Gone to Glory.* New York: St. Martin's Press. (231 pp., $16.95 h) 0-312-04321-X, adult mystery

61. Kiraly, Sherwood. *California Rush.* New York: Macmillan. (242 pp., $17.95 h) 0-02-563570-0

62. Leavy, Jane. *Squeeze Play.* Garden City, NY: Doubleday. (373 pp., $18.95 h) 0-385-26300-7

63. Lelchuk, Alan. *Brooklyn Boy.* New York: McGraw-Hill. (298 pp., $19.95 h) 0-07-037163-6

64. Lyle, Sparky and David Fisher. *The Year I Owned the Yankees: A Baseball Fantasy.* New York: Bantam Books. (313 pp., $17.95 h) 0-553-05750-2

65. Manfred, Frederick. *No Fun on Sunday: A Novel.* Norman: University of Oklahoma Press. 73019 (287 pp., $19.95 h) 0-8061-2273-0

66. Slattery, Marty. *Diamonds Are Trumps: A Pitcher's First Novel.* St. Luke's Press, 4210 B. F. Goodrich Blvd. Memphis, Tenn. 38118 (264 pp., $16.95 h) 0-918518-78-4

67. Zubro, Mark Richard. *Why Isn't Becky Twitchell Dead?* New York: St. Martin's Press (189 pp.) adult mystery

SECTION IV: HISTORIES AND GENERAL WORKS

68. Adomites, Paul. *October's Game.* World of Baseball Series. Alexandria, Va.: Redefinition, Inc. (185 pp., photos, $17.72) 0-924588-06-3

69. Alvarez, Mark. *The Old Ball Game.* World of Baseball Series. Alexandria, Va.: Redefinition, Inc. (187 pp., photos, $17.72) 0-924588-09-8

70. Angell, Roger. *The Summer Game.* New York: Penguin Books. (303. pp., $7.95 p) 0-14-013121-3; reprint, Viking, 1972

71. Aylesworth, Thomas G. *Baseball's Great Dynasties: The Cubs.* New York: Gallery Books (W. H. Smith Pubs.) (79 pp., photos, index, stats, $7.98 h) 0-8317-0657-0

72. Bjarkman, Peter C. *Baseball's Great Dynasties: The Dodgers.* New York: Gallery Books (80 pp., photos, index, team records, $7.98 h) 0-8317-0655-4

73. Bjarkman, Peter C. *Baseball's Great Dynasties: The Toronto Blue Jays.* New York: Gallery Books. (79 pp., photos, index, stats, $7.98 h) 0-8317-0659-7

74. Bock, Hal. *The Associated Press Pictorial History of Baseball.* New York: Mallard Press (imprint of BDD Promotional Book Co., 666 Fifth Ave. 10103 (208 pp., photos, $29.98 h) 0-792-45371-9

75. Bosco, Joseph. *The Boys Who Would Be Cubs: A Year in the Heart of Baseball's Minor Leagues.* New York: William Morrow. (351 pp., photos, index, stats, $21.95 h) 0-688-08261-0; the 1988 season of the Peoria Chiefs of the Midwest League

76. Boswell, Thomas. *The Heart of the Order.* New York: Penguin Books. (363 pp., $8.95 p) 0-14-012987-1; reprint, Doubleday, 1989

77. Bowman, John and Joel Zoss, editors. *The Pictorial History of Baseball. Fourth Edition.* New York: Gallery Books. (247 pp., $22.98 h) 0-8317-6914-9

78. Cohen, Stanley. *Dodgers! The First 100 Years.* New York: Birch Lane Press (Carol Pub. Group, 600 Madison Ave. 10022) (240 pp., photos, index, bibliography, $19.95 h) 1-55972-030-1

79. Cole, Milton. *Baseball's Greatest Dynasties: The Red Sox.* New York: Gallery Books (79 pp., photos, index, stats, $7.98 h) 0-8317-0658-9

80. Coleman, Ken and Dan Valenti. *The Impossible Dream Remembered: The 1967 Red Sox.* Lexington, Mass.: Stephen Greene Press. (260 pp., photos, index, $10.95 p) 0-8289-0769-2; reprint, Stephen Greene, 1987

81. Curran, William. *Big Sticks: The Batting Revolution of the 1920s.* New York: Beech Tree (Morrow). (288 pp., photos, index, $18.95 h) 0-688-06469-8

82. DiMaggio, Dom with Bill Gilbert. *Real Grass, Real Heroes, Baseball's Historic 1941 Season.* Introduction by Ted Williams. New York: Zebra Books. (Kensington Pub.) (240 pp., photos, $18.95 h) 0-8217-3032-0

83. Dinhoffer, Shelly Mehlman. *The Art of Baseball: The Great American Game in Painting, Sculpture, and Folk Art.* New York: Harmony Books (Crown Pubs.). (160 pp., photos, index, $40.00 h) 0-517-57567-1

84. Falkner, David. *Nine Sides of the Diamond: Baseball's Great Glove Men on the Fine Art of Defense.* New York: Times Books. (370 pp., photos, index, $18.95 h) 0-8129-1806-1

85. Fiffer, Steve. *Speed*. The World of Baseball Series. Alexandria, Va.: Re-definition, Inc. (185 pp., photos, $17.72 h) 0-924588-08-X

86. Fimrite, Ron and Bill Mandel and Bruce Jenkins. *Three Weeks in October*. Woodford Publishers, 4043 23rd St. San Francisco, Cal. 94114 (142 pp., photos, $45.00) 0-9426-2710-5

87. Fleming, G. H. *The Unforgettable Season (1908)*. Foreword by Lawrence Ritter. New York: Fireside Books. (332 pp., index, $9.95 p) 0-671-67660-1; reprint, Holt, Rinehart, Winston, 1981

88. Forker, Dom. *Sweet Seasons: Recollections of the 1955–1964 New York Yankees*. Dallas: Taylor Publishing. (220 pp., photos, index, appendix, $18.95 h) 0-87833-705-9

89. Forker, Dom. *The Men of Autumn: An Oral History of the 1949–1953 World Champion New York Yankees*. Foreword by Mel Allen. New York: Signet New American Library. (331 pp., photos, appendix, index, $4.95 p) 0-451-16659-0; reprint, Taylor, 1989

90. Gallagher, Mark and Neil. *Baseball's Great Dynasties: The Yankees*. New York: Gallery Books. (79 pp., photos, index, stats, $7.98 h) 0-8317-0656-2

91. Garagiola, Joe. *Baseball Is a Funny Game*. New York: Perennial (Harper & Row) (192 pp., $7.95 p) 0-06-091672-9; reprint, J. B. Lippincott, 1960; Bantam, 1960, 1962, 1980, 1985

92. Garber, Angus G. III. *The Baseball Companion*. New York: Mallard Press. (187 pp., photos, $29.98) 0-792-45291-7

93. Gold, Eddie and Art Ahrens. *The Chicago Cubs: The Renewal Era, 1985–1990*. Chicago: Bonus Books. (184 pp., photos, index, appendix, $15.95 h) 0-9293-8713-9

94. Gutman, Dan. *It Ain't Cheatenʼ If You Donʼt Get Caught: Scuffing, Corking, Spitting, Gunking, Razzing, and Other Fundamentals of Our National Pastime*. New York: Penguin Books (208 pp., photos, bibliography, $7.95 p) 0-14-011652-4

95. Halberstam, David. *The Summer of ʼ49*. New York: Avon Books. (336 pp., photos, index, $4.95 p) 0-380-71075-7; reprint, Morrow, 1989

96. Higgins, George V. *The Progress of the Seasons: Forty Years of Baseball in Our Town*. (Boston). Introduction by Daniel Okrent. New York: Spectator (Prentice-Hall) (228 pp., photos, index, $8.95 p) 0-13-728304-0; reprint, Henry Holt, 1989

97. Holl, James P. *The Canton Terriers: The Middle Atlantic League Years*. Daring Books, P.O. Box 20050-70, Canton, Ohio 44701 (includes stats, box scores, interviews)

98. Honig, Donald. *Baseball: The Illustrated History of America's Game*. New York: Crown Publishers. (340 pp., index, $45.00) 0-517-57295-8

99. Honig, Donald. *The Boston Red Sox: An Illustrated History.* New York: Prentice-Hall. (292 pp., index, appendix of season leaders, $24.95 h) 0-13-080326-X

100. Jedick, Peter. *League Park in Cleveland.* 1978. (photos, 24 pp.). Reprinted for the 1990 SABR convention, contact SABR P.O. Box 93183, Cleveland, Ohio 44101

101. Jennings, Kenneth M. *Balls and Strikes: The Money Game in Professional Baseball.* New York: Praeger (273 pp., index, bibliography, notes, $24.95 h) 0-275-93441-1

102. Johnson, Lloyd. *Dream Teams: Baseball's Greatest Players Decade by Decade.* New York: Gallery Books. (192 pp., photos, stats, $14,98 h) 0-8317-2499-4

103. Keplinger, Steve. *The Comeback Kids: A Fan Relives the Amazing Baltimore Orioles 1989 Season.* Publishers Place, 165 N. 100 E. Suite 2, Saint George, Utah 84770 (156 pp. $9.95 p) 0-939771-06-3

104. Krich, John. *El Beisbol: Travels through the Pan-American Pastime.* Introduction by Daniel Okrent. New York: Spectator (Prentice-Hall) (272 pp., $8.95 p) 0-13-247990-7; reprint, Atlantic Monthly Press, 1989

105. Luciano, Ron with David Fisher. *Baseball Lite: The Funniest Moments of the 1989 Season.* New York: Bantam Books (239 pp., photos, $3.95 p) 0-553-28447-9

106. McCombs, Wayne. *Let's Gooooo Tulsa: A History of Baseball in Tulsa.* from author, 5720 East 29th, Tulsa, Oklahoma 74114. (537 pp., photos, all-time roster, yearly standings, $20.00 & $2.50 p/h)

107. Mead, William. *Low and Outside.* World of Baseball Series. Arlington, Va.: Redefinition, Inc. (186 pp., photos, $17.72) 0-924588-07-1

108. Mead, William. *Two Spectacular Seasons: 1930, the Year the Hitters Ran Wild and 1968 the Year the Pitchers Took Revenge.* New York: Macmillan. (245 pp., photos, index, $18.95 h) 0-02-583731-1

109. Miller, James Edward. *The Baseball Business: Pursuing Pennants & Profits in Baltimore.* Chapel Hill: University of North Carolina Press (382 pp., photos, index, bibliography, notes, $24.95 h) 0-8078-1876-3

110. Names, Larry D. *Bury My Heart at Wrigley Field: The History of the Chicago Cubs.* Sportsbook Pub. Co., P.O. Box 102, Neshkoro, Wis. 54960 (260 pp., photos, $18.95 & $3.00 p/h) 0-9621684-0-8

111. Okrent, Daniel and Steve Wulf. *Baseball Anecdotes.* New York: Perennial (Harper & Row) (356 pp., index, $9.95 p) 0-06-097299-8; reprint, Oxford University Press, 1989

112. O'Neal, Bill. *The Pacific Coast League, 1903–1988.* Austin: Eakin Press. (344 pp., $14.95 p) 0-89015-776-6, order from PCL Office (602) 967-7679

113. Phillips, John. Capital Pub. Co., 8105 MacArthur Blvd., Cabin John, Maryland 20818

    The 1895 Cleveland Spiders. (90 pp., $17.50 p)

    114. *Bill Hinchman's Boner and the 1908 Naps.* (135 pp., $22.50 p)

    115. *The Crybaby Indians of 1940.* (88 pp., $16.50 p)

    116. *Odd Ball Games.* ($4.00 SABR members, $4.95 others)

    117. *Chief Sockalexis and the 1897 Cleveland Indians.* ($16.50 p)

    118. *A Cleveland Baseball Notebook.* ($7.50 p)

119. Pietrusza, David. *Baseball's Canadian–American League: A History of its Inception, Franchises, Participants, Locales, Statistics, Demise, & Legacy, 1936–1951.* Foreword by John Thorn. Jefferson, N.C.: McFarland (236 pp., photos, appendices, bibliography, index, $35.00 h) 0-89950-508-2

120. Reichler, Joseph and Jack Clary. *Baseball's Great Moments. Updated 1990 Edition.* New York: Galahad Books. (Rutledge) (256 pp., photos, $7.98 h) 0-88365-754-6

121. Reiss, Steven A. *City Games: The Evolution of American Urban Society and the Rise of Sports.* University of Illinois Press c/o CUP Services, P.O. Box 6525, Ithaca, NY 14851 (320 pp., photos, $29.95 h) 0-252-01573-8

122. Ritter, Lawrence S. *The Story of Baseball. Revised & Expanded Edition.* Foreword by Ted Williams. New York: Morrow. (210 pp., photos, index, $9.95 p) 0-688-09057-5; first printed, Morrow, 1983

123. Rogers, Phil. *Impossible Takes a Little Longer: The Texas Rangers from Pretenders to Contenders.* Dallas: Taylor Publishing Co. (196 pp., photos, index, $16.95 h) 0-87833-630-3

124. Rudd, Irving and Stan Fischler. *Sporting Life: The Duke and Jackie, Pee Wee, Razor Phil, Al, Mushky Jackson, and Me.* Foreword by Peter Golenbock. New York: St. Martin's Press. (288 pp., photos, index, $17.95 h) 0-312-0-4428-3, baseball, boxing, & horses

125. SABR, Jack Graney Chapter. *Baseball in Cleveland.* (40 pp., photos) distributed at the 20th SABR annual convention, July 1990, P.O. Box 93183, Cleveland, Ohio 44101

126. Salisbury, Luke. *The Answer is Baseball: A Book of Questions that Illuminates the Great Game.* Illustrations by Robert Paul Scudellari. New York: Vintage (Random House). (242 pp., $8.95 p) 0-679-72642-X; reprint, Times Books, 1989

127. Schoor, Gene. *The History of the World Series: The Complete Chronology of America's Greatest Sports Tradition.* New York: Morrow. (431 pp., photos, index, appendices, $27.95 h) 0-688-07995-4

128. Schott, Arthur. *Let's Go To Bat: Baseball Columns from the Clarion*

Herald, 1964–1965. from author, 459 Jewel Street, New Orleans, La. 70124, $7.00

129. Seymour, Harold. *Baseball: The People's Game.* New York: Oxford University Press. (639 pp., photos, index, bibliographical note, $24.95 h) 0-19-503890-8

130. Shaughnessy, Dan. *The Curse of the Bambino.* New York: E. P. Dutton. (207 pp., bibliography, $18.95 h) 0-525-24887-0

131. Shea, John and John Hickey. *Magic by the Bay: How the San Francisco Giants and the Oakland A's Captured the Baseball World.* Forewords by Roger Craig and Tony LaRussa. Illustrations by Thom Ross. Berkeley, Calif.: North Atlantic Books. (285 pp., photos, $12.95 p) 1-55643-086-8

132. *The Silver Season: 25 Years of Braves Baseball in Atlanta.* (64 pp., photos, $6.95 p & $2.00 p/h) from Sports Print, 226 Luckie St. N.W., Atlanta, Georgia 30303, 0-9626248-0-2 (Jackie Blackburn-Tyson, editor)

133. Simpson, Allan, editor. *The Baseball Draft: A 25 Year History, 1965–1989.* Durham, N.C.: Baseball America. (228 pp., photos, $19.95)

134. Smizik, Robert. *The Pittsburgh Pirates: An Illustrated History.* Gerald Astor, photo editor. New York: Walker & Company. (213 pp., $29.95 h) 0-8027-1102-2

135. Sugar, Bert Randolph. *Rain Delays: An Anecdotal History of Baseball Under One Umbrella.* Introduction by Joe Garagiola. New York: St. Martin's Press. (199 pp., $16.95 h) 0-312-04411-9

136. Sullivan, Neil J. *The Minors: The Struggles and the Triumph of Baseball's Poor Relation From 1876 to the Present.* New York: St. Martin's Press. (307 pp., photos, index, bibliography, notes, $19.95 h) 0-312-03864-X

137. Talley, Rick. *The Cubs of '69: Recollections of the Team that Should Have Been.* Chicago: Contemporary Books (354 pp., photos, index, appendix, $9.95 p) 0-8092-4156-0; reprint, Contemporary, 1989

138. Weiss, John, photographer and biographer. *The Face of Baseball.* essays by Wilfred Sheed. Thomasson-Grant, One Morton Drive, Suite 500, Charlottesville, VA 22901 (168 pp., index, $34.95 h) 0-934738-59-9

139. Whiting, Robert. *You Gotta Have Wa.* New York: Vintage Departures (Random House) (339 pp., photos, bibliography, list of foreign visits, 1908–1988, $10.95 p) 0-679-72947-X; reprint, Macmillan 1989, baseball in Japan

140. Will, George F. *Men at Work: The Craft of Baseball.* New York: Macmillan. (353 pp., photos, index, $19.95 h) 0-02-628470-7; Cal Ripken Jr., Tony LaRussa, Orel Hershiser, Tony Gwynn discuss their profession

141. Wright, Craig R. and Tom House. *The Diamond Appraised.* Foreword by Bill James. New York: Fireside. (409 pp., $9.95 p) 0-671-70719-1; reprint, Simon & Schuster, 1989

142. Zinsser, William. *Spring Training.* New York: Spectator (Prentice-Hall) (197 pp., photos, sources, index, $8.95 p) 0-13-837899-1; reprint, Harper & Row, 1989

SECTION V: HOBBY

143. Allison, Jon. *Baseball Contest 1990: Choose Your Own Team and Win $10,000, American League Players.* Cloverdale Press, Inc., 96 Morton St., NY, NY 10014 (188 pp., photos, $8.95 p) 0-316-08309-7

144. *American League Rotisserie League Baseball Handbook 1990. Second edition.* (120 pp., $19.95 & $3.00 p/h) from Reliable Rotisserie, P.O. Box 340, Thomaston, Ct 06787

145. Baker, Mark Allen. *The Baseball Autograph Handbook: Sports Collectors Digest Baseball Autograph Handbook: A Comprehensive Guide to Authentication and Valuation of Hall of Fame Autographs.* Iola, Wi.: Krause Pubs. (288 pp., index, bibliography, notes, $19.95 p) 0-87341-125-0

145a. *Baseball Card Dealer Directory 1990.* Westport, Conn.: Meckler (313 pp., $19.95 p) 0-88736-559-0

146. *Baseball's 100 Hottest Players Book and Baseball Cards.* Score. $12.95 0-88176-765-4

147. *Baseball Players Trivia Sticker Kit, 1990.* (64 pp., $12.95) 0-88176-739-5

148. Beckett, Dr. James. *Official Price Guide to Baseball Cards, 1991. 10th edition.* New York: House of Collectibles, 201 East 50th St., NY, NY 10022 (700 pp., $5.95 p) 0-876-37807-6

149. Beckett, Dr. James. *Sport Americana Baseball Card Price Guide, No. 12.* Edgewater Book Co., P.O. Box 40238, Cleveland, Ohio 44140 (704 pp., $14.95 p) 0-937424-46-3

150. Beckett, Dr. James. *Sport Americana Alphabetical Baseball Card Checklist #4.* Cleveland: Edgewater Book Co. ($9.95 p)

151. Benjamin, Christopher. *Most Valuable Baseball Cards.* New York: Perigee (Putnam & Sons) (64 pp., $10.95 p) 0-399-51592-5

152. Benson, John. *Rotisserie Baseball Analyst 1990.* Foreword by Don Zminda. Devyn Press, 3600 Chamberlain Lane, Suite 230, Louisville, Kentucky 40222 (320 pp., $17.95 p & $3.00 p/h) 0-910791-99-6

153. Berryman, Lee. *How to Win Statistical Baseball Leagues, 1990. Fifth Annual Edition.* from author, 8368 Glastonbury Ct., Annandale, Va. 22003 (209 pp., $14.95 p & $2.00 p/h)

154. Brecka, Jon, editor. *Sports Collectors Digest: Baseball Cards, Questions and Answers.* Iola, Wi.: Krause Pubs. (256 pp. $5.95 p) 0-87341-144-7

155. Florence, Gene M., Jr. *The Standard Baseball Card Price Guide. Second Edition.* Collector Books, P.O. Box 3009 Paducah, Ky 42001 (384 pp., $9.95 p) 0-89145-413-6; first edition published, 1989

156. Fritsch, Jeff and Dennis W. Eckes. *The Sport Americana Team Baseball Card Checklist #5*. Edgewater Book Co., Box 40238, Cleveland, Ohio 44140 (ca. 220 pp. $12.95 p) 0-937424-47-1

157. Gershman, Michael. *The Baseball Stadium Postcard Album (American League)*. Dallas: Taylor Publishing (31 postcards, $9.95 p) 0-87833-697-4

158. Gershman, Michael. *The Baseball Stadium Postcard Album (National League)*. Dallas: Taylor Publishing (31 postcards, $9.95 p) 0-87833-700-8

159. Gershman, Michael. *1990 Baseball Card Engagement Book*. Dallas: Taylor Publishing. (112 pp., photos, $11.95 p) 0-87833-672-9

160. Golenbock, Peter. *How to Win at Rotisserie Baseball, 1990 edition*. Introduction by Bryant Gumbel. New York: Carroll & Graf Pubs. (271 pp., $8.95 p) 0-88184-564-7; first edition, Vintage, 1987

161. Kiefer, Kit and Paul M. Green. *The Top 100 Best Baseball Cards to Own: Ranked and Rated for the Investor & Collector*. Chicago: Bonus Books. (303 pp., photos, $8.95 p) 0-933893-88-4

162. Kirk, Troy. *Collector's Guide to Baseball Cards*. Radnor, Pa.: Wallace-Homestead Book Co. 19089 (158 pp., index, appendices, photos, $12.95 p) 0-87069-533-9

163. Kronnick, Buck. *The Baseball Fan's Complete Guide to Collecting Autographs*. Betterway Pubs., P.O. Box 219, Crozet, Va 22932 (175 pp., $9.95 p) 1-55870-153-2, addresses & birth dates

164. Kurowski, Jeff, editor. *Sports Collector's Digest Baseball Card Price Guide, Fourth Edition*. Iola, Wi.: Krause Pubs. (736 pp., $13.95 p) 0-87341-131-5; other editions, 1987–1988–1989

165. Kurowski, Jeff, editor. *The Standard Catalog of Baseball Cards, Second Edition*. Iola, Wi.: Krause Pubs. (752 pp., index, rookie cards 1948–1990, terms, $29.95 p) 0-87341-138-2

166. Lemke, Bob, editor. *Sports Collector's Digest Baseball Card Pocket Price Guide*. New York: Warner Books (576 pp., $5.95 p) 0-446-36048-1

167. Mann, Steve and Ken Mallin. *Rotisserie and Fantasy League Guide: 1990*. St. Louis: The Sporting News (192 pp., $12.95 p) 0-89204-349-0

168. Myers, Larry S. *1990 Baseball Black Book: An Owners Manual*. from author P.O. Box 2313, West Sacramento, Ca. 95691 (86 pp., $12.95 & $1.50 p/h)

169. Owens, Tom, contributing author. *1990 Baseball Cards: 120 of the Hottest Players*. New York: Beekman House. (64 pp., $5.99 p) 0-517-01993-0

170. Owens, Tom. *Complete Book of 1990 Baseball Cards*. Publishers Int'l Ltd., 7373 N. Cicero Ave., Lincolnwood, Il. 60646 (320 pp., $14.99) 0-517-01997-3

171. Owens, Tom. *The Official Baseball Card Price Guide: 1990. Collector's Edition.* New York: Beekman House. (320 pp.) 0-517-03207-4

172. Patton, Alex. *Patton's 1990 Fantasy Baseball Price Guide.* New York: Fireside Books (268 pp., $8.95 p) 0-671-69605-X; first edition published in 1989

173. Patton, Phil, foreword. *Baseball Postcard Book: 30 Full Colored Cards to Keep or Send.* New York: Fawcett Columbine (31 pp., $7.95 p) 0-449-90487-3

174. Shapiro, Barry. *Baseball Contest 1990: Choose Your Own Team and Win $10,000; National League Players.* Cloverdale Press, 96 Morton St., NY, NY 10014 (175 pp., photos, $8.95 p) 0-316-08310-0

175. Slocum, Frank, and Red Foley, text. *The Complete Picture Collection: A 40 Year History of Topps Baseball Cards, 1951–1990.,* Introduction by Johnny Bench. Card history by Sy Berger. New York: Warner Books. (ca. 1,000 pp., index, $99.95 h) 0-446-51579-5

176. Smalling, Jack and Dennis W. Eckes. *Sport Americana Baseball Address List #6.* Cleveland: Edgewater Books ($12.95 p)

177. Waggoner, Glen and Robert Sklar, editors. *Rotisserie League Baseball: The Official Rule Book & Complete Guide to Player Values, Fourth Edition.* New York: Bantam Books (289 pp., $8.95 p) 0-553-34825-6; also published in 1984, 1987, & 1989

178. Welch, Wayne M. *The 1990 Fantasy Baseball Abstract.* New York: Perigee (Putnam's) (257 pp., $9.95 p) 0-399-51593-3

179. Wright, Jim and Jean Paul Emard. *Baseball Card Dealer Directory 1989.* Westport, Conn.: Meckler Books (200 pp. $19.95 p) 0-88736-375-x

SECTION VI: HUMOR AND TRIVIA

180. Bobrow, Jerry. *Bluff Your Way in Baseball.* Centennial Press, P.O. Box 80728, Lincoln, Ne 68501 (77 pp., photos, $3.95 p) 0-8220-2202-8

181. Bryson, Michael G. *The Twenty-four Inch Home Run and Other Outlandish, Incredible but True Events in Baseball History.* Chicago: Contemporary Books. (293 pp., photos, index, $9.95 p) 0-8092-4341-5

182. Davis, Al and Elliot Horne. *The All-Lover All-Star Team: And Fifty Other Improbable Baseball All-Star Lineups.* New York: Morrow (185 pp., $12.95 h) 0-688-09621-2

183. Mazer, Bill with Stan and Shirley Fischler. *Bill Mazer's Amazin' Baseball Book.* New York: Zebra Books (Kensington Pub. Co.), 475 Park Ave. S. 10016 (400 pp., photos, index, $19.95 h) 0-8217-2947-0

184. Nash, Bruce and Allan Zullo. *The Baseball Hall of Shame 4.* Bernie Ward, curator. New York: Pocket Books. (197 pp., photos, $7.95 p) 0-671-69172-4

185. Nemec, David. *The Most Extraordinary Baseball Quiz Book Ever.* New York: Signet New American Library (189 pp., $3.95 p) 0-451-16450-4

186. Schacht, Mike. *Baseball Profiles.* (50 players in silhouette 19th c. thru 1930s, $5.95 or $36/dozen) 925 Park Ave., NY, NY 10028

187. Sugar, Bert Randolph, editor. *Baseballistics: The Absolutely Postively without Question Greatest Book of Baseball Facts, Figures, & Astonishing Lists ever Compiled.* New York: St. Martin's Press (387 pp., $16.95 p) 0-312-03789-9

SECTION VII: INSTRUCTION, FITNESS, AND RULES

188. Adair, Robert Kemp. *The Physics of Baseball.* New York: Perennial (Harper & Row) (110 pp., 30 diagrams, index, $7.95 p) 0-06-096461-8, also $16.95 h, 0-06-055188-7

189. Alston, Walter and Don Weiskopf. *The Complete Baseball Handbook: Strategies & Techniques for Winning. Second Edition.* Championship Books, 2460 Kerper Blvd., Dubuque, Iowa 52001 (530 pp., photos, index, $19.95 h) 0-697-06819-6; first edition, Allyn & Bacon, 1972; revised & abridged editon, Allyn & Bacon, 1984

190. Boggs, Wade and David Brisson. *The Techniques of Modern Hitting.* New York: Perigee (Putnam's) (153 pp., photos, $12.95 p) 0-399-51595-X

191. Canseco, Jose and Dave McKay. *Strength Training for Baseball: Avoid Injuries and Improve your Stats by Increasing your Strength.* New York: Perigee (Putnam's) (159 pp., photos, $13.95 p) 0-399-51596-8

192. Jacobs, G. and J. R. McCrory. *Baseball Rules in Pictures. Revised & Updated Edition.* Illustrations by Michael Brown. Foreword by Ron Luciano. New York: Perigee (80 pp., $7.95 p) 0-399-51597-6; first edition published in 1985

193. Kruetzer, Peter and Ted Kerley. *Little League's Official How-to-Play Baseball Book.* Illustrated by Alexander Verbitsky. New York: Doubleday (209 pp., index, rules, $9.95 p) 0-385-24700-1; also $12.95 edition with baseball, 0-385-41278-9

194. McFarland, Joe. *Coaching Pitchers. Second Edition.* Champaign, Illinois: Leisure Press (131 pp., photos, $18.00 p) 0-88011-368-5; first edition, 1985

195. *NCAA 1990 Baseball Rules & Interpretations.* ($3.00 p) from NCAA Office, Mission, Kansas

196. *Official Baseball Rules: 1990 Edition.* St. Louis: The Sporting News (104 pp., $3.95 p) 0-89204-340-7

197. Rumble, Bradley, editor. *Official High School Baseball Rules. 1990 Edition.* National Federation of State High School Associations, 11724 Plaza Circle, P.O. Box 20626, Kansas City, Mo. 64195 (80 pp., index, $2.75 p)

198. Rumble, Bradley, editor. *Baseball Case Book, 1990 Edition*. Kansas City, Mo.: National Federation of State High School Associations. (65 pp., $2.75 p)

199. Waggoner, Glen with Kathleen Moloney and Hugh Howard. *Baseball by the Rules: Pine Tar, Spitballs, and Midgets: An Anecdotal Guide to America's Oldest and Most Complex Sport*. New York: Prentice-Hall (289 pp., photos, index, $8.95 p) 0-13-058561-0; reprint, Taylor Publishing, 1987

200. Watts, Robert G. and A. Terry Bahill. *Keep Your Eye on the Ball: The Science and Folklore of Baseball*. New York: Freeman & Co. (41 Madison Ave. 10010) (213 pp., index, notes, $18.95 h) 0-7167-2104-X

201. Wigge, Larry, editor. *Baseball's Knotty Problems*. Illustrated by Bill Wilson. St. Louis: The Sporting News (160 pp., rulebook, $6.95 p) 0-89204-344-X

202. Winfield, Dave with Eric Swenson, et al. *The Complete Baseball Player: How to Hit, Field, Catch, Pitch, Steal, Slide, Bunt, Pivot, and even Coach*. New York: Avon Books. (212 pp., photos, $9.95 p) 0-380-75830-X

203. Wolff, Rich. *Psychology of Winning Baseball. A Coach's Handbook*. New York: Prentice-Hall (181 pp., index, $9.95 p) 0-13734-138-5; published in hardcover in 1986 by Parker Publishers

SECTION VIII: JUVENILE WORKS

204. Alvarez, Mark. *The Official Baseball Hall of Fame Story of Jackie Robinson*. New York: Little Simon (96 pp., photos, $2.95 p) 0-671-69093-0; also $11.95 h, 0-671-69480-4

205. Appel, Marty. *Baseball Legends: Joe DiMaggio*. NY: Chelsea House. (64 pp., photos, $14.95 h) 0-7910-1183-6

206. Denenberg, Barry. *Stealing Home: The Story of Jackie Robinson*. NY: Scholastic Books (117 pp., photos, $2.95 p) 0-590-42560-9

207. Eckhouse, Morris. *Baseball Legends: Bob Feller*. NY: Chelsea House. (64 pp., photos, $14.95 h) 0-7910-1174-7

208. Eisenberg, Lisa. *The Story of Babe Ruth: Baseball's Greatest Legend*. NY: Dell-Yearling (92 pp., photos, $2.95 p) 0-440-40274-3

209. Emert, P. R. *Sports Heroes: Great Pitchers*. NY: Tom Doherty Associates (88 pp., photos, bibliography, $2.50 p) 0-812-59381-2

210. Emert, P. R. *Sports Heroes: Great Hitters*. NY: Tom Doherty Associates (84 pp., photos, bibliography, $2.50 p) 0-812-59379-0

211. Golenbock, Peter. *Teammates* (Jackie Robinson and Pee Wee Reese). Illustrated by Paul Bacon. San Diego: Gulliver Books (HBJ) (ca. 30 pp., photos, $15.95 h) 0-15-200603-6

212. Grabowski, John. *Baseball Legends: Willie Mays.* NY: Chelsea House. (64 pp., photos, $14.95 h) 0-7910-1183-6

213. Grabowski, John. *Baseball Legends: Jackie Robinson.* NY: Chelsea House. (64 pp., photos, $14.95 h) 0-7910-1188-7

214. Greene, Carol. *Jackie Robinson: Baseball's First Black Major Leaguer.* Chicago: Children's Press (47 pp., photos, index, $4.95 p) 0-516-44211-2

215. Hanks, Stephen. *Bo Jackson.* NY: St. Martin's Press (133 pp., photos, stats, $3.50 p) 0-312-92394-5

216. Kaplan, Jim and Dick Perez. *The Second Official Baseball Hall of Fame Book of Superstars.* NY: Little Simon (40 pp., $4.95 p) 0-671-69092-2; first edition, Little Simon, 1989

217. Kavanagh, Jack. *Baseball Legends. Grover Cleveland Alexander.* NY: Chelsea House (64 pp., photos, $14.95 h) 0-7910-1166-6

218. Macht, Norm. *Baseball Legends: Jimmy Foxx.* NY: Chelsea House. (64 pp., photos, $14.95 h) 0-7910-1175-5

219. Nash, Bruce and Allan Zullo. *Little Big Leaguers: Amazing Boyhood Stories of Today's Baseball Stars.* Compiled by Bernie Ward. NY: Simon & Schuster (95 pp., photos, $7.95 p) 0-671-69360-3

220. Sabin, Louis. *Willie Mays, Young Superstar,* Mahwah, NJ.: Troll Associates (48 pp., illustrated, $2.50 p) 0-8167-1776-1

221. Shannon, Mike. *Baseball Legends: Johnny Bench.* NY: Chelsea House. (64 pp., photos, $14.95 h) 0-7910-1168-2

222. Takasch, Jim. *Baseball Legends: Roy Campanella.* NY: Chelsea House. (64 pp., photos, $14.95 h) 0-7910-1170-4

223. Wheeler, Lonnie. *The Official Baseball Hall of Fame Story of Mickey Mantle.* NY: Little Simon (95 pp., photos, $2.95 p) 0-671-69094-9

224. White, Ellen Emerson. *Jim Abbott: Against All Odds.* NY: Scholastic Books (86 pp., photos, $2.75 p) 0-590-43503-5

225. Wolff, Rick. *Baseball Legends: Brooks Robinson.* NY: Chelsea House. (64 pp., photos, $14.95 h) 0-7910-1186-0

FICTION

226. Aaseng, Nathan. *Batter Up!* Elgin, Illinois: David C. Cook Pub. (137 pp.)

227. Barrett, Kirk. *The Flight of Fancy.* Roanoke Park Press, 4539 132nd Ave. S.E., Bellevue, Wa. 98006 (28 pp., $12.95) 0-9622496-0-2

228. Curtis, Gavin. *Grandma's Baseball.* New York: Crown Publishers. (29 pp., $12.95 h) 0-517-57389-X

229. Day, Alexandra. *Frank and Ernest Play Ball.* NY: Scholastic Books. (36 pp., illustrated, $12.95 h) 0-590-42548-X

230. Elish, Dan. *Jason and the Baseball Bear.* NY: Orchard Books (Franklin Watts) (147 pp., $13.95 h) 0-531-05868-9

231. Ellis, Lucy, creator (Kathilyn Proboz and Leah Jerome, authors) *The Girls Strike Back: The Making of the Pink Parrots.* NY: Sports Illustrated for Kids (119 pp. $3.50 p) 0-316-71967-6

232. Ellis, Lucy, creator (B. B. Calhoun, author). *All that Jazz: The Pink Parrots.* NY: Sports Illustrated for Kids. (120 pp., $3.50 p) 0-316-12445-1

233. Friend, David. *Baseball, Football, Daddy and Me.* Illustrated by Rick Brown. NY: Viking Penguin (29 pp., $12.95 p) 0-670-82420-8

234. Giff, Patricia Reilly, *Ronald Morgan Goes to Bat.* Illustrated by Susanna Natti. NY: Puffin (Penguin Books) (32 pp., $3.95 p) 0-14-050699–1; reprint, Viking/Penguin, 1988

235. Grosser, Morton. *The Fabulous Fifty.* New York: Atheneum (233 pp., $13.95 h) 0-689-31656-9

236. Hallowell, Tommy. *Duel on the Diamond.* New York: Viking Press. (122 pp., $2.95 p) 0-14-032910-2

237. Haynes, Mary. *The Great Pretenders.* New York: Bradbury Press (135 pp., $12.95 h) 0-02-743452-4

238. Hughes, Dean. *Angel Park All-Stars: Making the Team.* New York: Bullseye Books (Alfred A. Knopf), illustrated by Dennis Lyall (93 pp., $2.95 p) 0-679-80426-9

239. ———. *Angel Park All-Stars: Big Base Hit.* same info as above. (94 pp.) 0-679-80427-7

240. ———. *Angel Park All-Stars: Winning Streak.* same info as #238. (90 pp.) 0-679-80428-5

241. ———. *Angel Park All-Stars: What a Catch!* same info as #238. (84 pp.) 0-679-80429-3

242. ———. *Angel Park All-Stars: Rookie Star.* same info as #238. (80 pp.) 0-679-80430-7

243. ———. *Angel Park All-Stars: Pressure Play.* same info as #238. (84 pp.) 0-679-80431-5

244. ———. *Angel Park All-Stars: Line Drive.* same info as #238. (87 pp.) 0-679-80432-3

245. ———. *Angel Park All-Stars: Championship Game.* same info as #238. (94 pp.) 0-679-80433-1

246. Johnson, Neil. *Batter Up!* NY: Scholastic Books. (28 pp., $12.95 h) 0-590-42729-6

247. Kahaner, Ellen. *What's So Great About Fourth Grade?* Mahwah, NJ.: Troll Associates (92 pp., illustrated, $2.95 p) 0-8167-1703-6

248. Kessler, Leonard. *Old Turtle's Baseball Stories.* NY: Dell Pubs. (56 pp., illustrated by author, $2.95 p) 0-440-40277-8; reprint, Greenwillow Books, 1982

249. Kusugak, Michael A. *Baseball Bats for Christmas.* Toronto: Annick Press Ltd. (21 pp.)

250. Petersen, P. J. and Betsy James. *The Fireplug is First Base.* NY: Dutton Children's Books (60 pp., $10.95 h) 0-525-44587-0

251. Real, Rory and Bob Pelkowski. *A Baseball Dream.* Hauppauge, NY: Barron's Education Services (32 pp., illustrated, $3.95 p) 0-8120-4395-2

252. Slote, Alfred. *The Trading Game.* NY: J. B. Lippincott (200 pp., illustrated, $12.95 h) 0-397-32397-2

253. Soto, Gary. *Baseball in April and Other Stories.* San Diego: Harcourt, Brace, Jovanovich (111 pp., $13.95 h) 0-15-205720-X; only one of eleven stories is baseball-related

254. Stratemeyer, Edward (written as Franklin W. Dixon) *Foul Play: Hardy Boys Casefile No. 46.* New York: Pocket Books. (153 pp.)

255. Tunis, John R. *The Kid Comes Back.* New York: William Morrow (254 pp., $4.95 p) 0-688-09290-X; reprint, Morrow, 1946

256. Tunis, John R. *High Pockets.* New York: William Morrow (189 pp., $4.95 p) 0-688-09288-8; reprint, Morrow, 1948

257. Williams, Karen Lynn. *Baseball and Butterflies.* New York: Lothrop, Lee, & Shepard (79 pp., $12.95 h) 0-688-094899

GENERAL WORKS

258. Alexson, Bill. *Batting a Thousand.* NY: Thomas Nelson (108 pp., $5.95 p) 0-8407-3152-3

259. Aylesworth, Thomas G. *The Kid's World Almanac of Baseball.* Introduction by Orel Hershiser. Illustrations by John Lane. NY: Pharos Books (269 pp., index, $6.95 p) 0-88687-563-3

260. Carroll, Bob and Jim Trusilo. *Official Baseball Hall of Fame Sticker Book of Records.* NY: Little Simon (96 pp., $7.95 p) 0-671-69091-4

261. Foley, Red. *The Best Baseball Book Ever, 1990 Edition.* Illustrated by Jane Lieman. NY: Little Simon (96 pp., $7.95 p) 0-671-69482-0

262. Gutelle, Andrew. *Baseball's Best Five True Stories.* Illustrated by Cliff Spohn. NY: Step Four Book (Random House) (48 pp., photos, $2.95 p) 0-394-80983-1; (called shot, Joe D's hit streak, Jackie Robinson, Hank Aaron, Hall of Fame)

263. Hall, Katy and Lisa Eisenberg. *Baseball Bloopers*. Illustrated by Liz Callen. NY: Random House (96 pp., $2.95 p) 0-679-80335-1

264. Nash, Bruce and Allan Zullo. *The Baseball Hall of Shame: Young Fan's Edition*. New York: Archway (Pocket Books) (133 pp., $2.95 p) 0-671-69354-9

265. Sakurai, Jennifer M. *Baseball: The Rules of the Game for Children*. Illustrated by Jane Dieerksen. Los Angeles: Price, Stern, Sloan. (45 pp., $3.95 p) 0-8431-2430-X

266. Sullivan, George. *Baseball Kids*. NY: Cobblehill Books (Dutton) (93 pp., photos, index, glossary, $13.95 h) 0-525-65023-7

267. Teitelbaum, Michael. *Play Book! Baseball: You are the Manager, You Call the Shots*. Illustrated by Donna Nettis, NY: Sports Illustrated for Kids (89 pp., $4.95 p) 0-316-83624-9

268. Weber, Bruce. *Bruce Weber's Inside Baseball 1990*. New York: Scholastic Books (108 pp., photos, $2.25 p) 0-590-43463-2

SECTION IX: REFERENCE, STATISTICS, ANNUAL WORKS

269. *American League Statistical Report 1990*. $13.00 from Bottom of the 9th Statistics, P.O. Box 450643, Westlake, Ohio 44145

270. American Sports Publishing Company (Baseball America), P.O. Box 2089, Durham, N.C. 27702-9990
    Baseball Almanac 1990 (312 pp., photos, $7.95 p) 0-671-69614-9

271. *Baseball Directory 1990* (192 pp., $7.95 p) 0-671-69615-7

272. *Radio, T.V. & Cable Directory* ($4.95 p)

273. Graczyk, Wayne, compiler. *Japanese Professional Baseball Handbook 1990* ($12.95 p)

274. Baseball Blue Book, Inc., P.O. Box 40847, St. Petersburg, FL 33743, Larry Halstead, president
    Baseball Blue Book, 1990. 82nd year. (ca 300 pp., $37.00 p)

275. *Minor League Digest, 1990*. 30th year. (165 pp., $37.00 spiral)

276. *Major League Year and Notebook*. since 1912 (ca. 100 pp., $26.00)

277–283. *Organizational Record Books* (lifetime stats on each member of the organization) $6.95 each, for Braves, Chisox, Cubs, Expos, Twins, Mets, and Blue Jays only

284. *The Baseball Notebook: American League Players*. $8.95 from Hittin'-n-Runnin' Sports, 122 S. Main St., Woodstock, VA 22664

285. Carter, Craig, editor. *Daguerreotypes: The Complete Major and Minor League Records of Baseball's Immortals. Eighth Edition*. St. Louis: The

Sporting News (320 pp., photos, index, $12.95 p) 0-89204-352-0; 1st edition, 1934, 7th edition, 1981

286. Cohen, Eliot, Peter Palmer, and John Thorn. *The 1990 Baseball Annual* New York: Warner Books (328 pp., $12.95 p) 0-446-38577-8

287. Coleman, Ken with Dan Valenti. *Grapefruit League Roadtrip: A Guide to Spring Training in Florida. Third Edition.* Foreword by Peter Gammons. Lexington, Mass.: Stephen Greene (166 pp., $8.95 p) 0-8289-0774-9; also published in 1988 and 1989

288. Dewan, John, and Don Zminda and Stats, Inc. *The Stats Baseball Scoreboard.* Illustrations by John Grimwade. NY: Ballantine (326 pp., $9.95 p) 0-345-36434-1

289. Dewan, John, editor. *The Scouting Report 1990: The Most In-Depth Analysis of the Strengths and Weaknesses of Every Active Major League Baseball Player.* NY: Perennial (681 pp., photos, index, $15.95 p) 0-06-096447-2

290. Dittmar, Joseph J. *Baseball's Benchmark Boxscores: Summaries of the Record-Setting Games.* Jefferson, N.C.: McFarland (240 pp., photos, boxscores, charts, index, $27.50 h) 0-89950-488-4

291. Garrity, John. *The Traveler's Guide to Baseball Spring Training 1991 Edition.* KC/NY: Andrews & McMeel (177 pp., photos, $9.95 p) 0-8362-7982-4

292. Gimbel, Mike. *Mike Gimbel's Baseball Player and Team Rankings.* From Boerum Street Press, 131 Boerum St., Brooklyn, NY 11206 (240 pp., $8.95 and $2.00 p/h)

293. Greenberg, Steve. *Minor League Road Trip: A Guide to America's 170 Minor League Teams.* Foreword by Bill Lee. Lexington, Mass.: Stephen Greene Press (150 pp., $9.95 p) 0-8289-0771-4

294. Hanke, Brock. *The 1990 Baseball Sabermetric.* Mad Aztec Press, 1215 Willow View Drive, Kirkwood, Mo 63122 (301 pp., $15.95) 0-9625846-3

295. Hollander, Zander, editor. *The 1990 Complete Handbook of Baseball, 20th Edition.* NY: Signet New American Library (400 pp., photos, $5.95 p) 0-451-16449-0, annually since 1971

296. Holmes, Tot. *Dodgers Blue Book, 13th Edition.* Holmes Pub. Co., P.O. Box 11, Gothenberg, NE 69138

297. Holmes, Tot. *Dodger Baby Blue Casebook, 4th Edition.* ($5.00 and $1.50 p/h) see address above

Horton Publishing Company, P.O. Box 29234, St. Louis, MO 63126

298–303. *Reach Baseball Guides, 1896–1901* (reprints) 1896–1898 $20.00 each; 1899–1901 $25.00 each

304–306. *Spalding Baseball Guides, 1902–1904* (reprints) $35.00 each; other reprints published in previous years also available

307. James, Bill. *The Baseball Book: 1990*. New York: Villard (343 pp., photos, $12.95 p) 0-679-72411-7

308. James, Bill. *Bill James Introduces Stats 1990 Major League Handbook*. Stats, Inc., 7250 N. Cicero, Lincolnwood, IL 60646 (285 pp., $17.95 p) 0-9625581-0-9

309. James, Bill. *Stats 1991 Major League Handbook*. see address above. (311 pp., $17.95 p) 0-9625581-1-7

310. Kaplan, Jim, editor. *The SABR Baseball Research Journal. No. 19*. SABR: P.O. Box 93183, Cleveland, Ohio 44101 (96 pp., photos, $8.00) 0-910137-43-9

311. Laird, A.W. *Ranking Baseball's Elite: An Analysis Derived from Player Statistics, 1893–1987*. Foreword by Pee Wee Reese. Jefferson, N.C.: McFarland (238 pp., photos, appendices, index, bibliography, $24.95 h) 0-89950-397-3

312. Landry, Roger. *Hot Prospects: The Total Guide to 1990's Minor League and Rookie Talent*. New York: Warner Books (197 pp., photos, $12.95 p) 0-446-39129-8

313. Levine, Peter, editor. *Baseball History 3*. Westport, Conn.: Meckler (162 pp., photos, $39.50 h) 0-88736-577-9

314. Lipsey, Richard, editor. *Baseball Market Place, 1990: The Offcial Directory of the American Baseball Coaches Association*. Princeton, NJ: Sportsguide, Inc. (319 pp., photos, $9.95 p)

315. Maclean, Norman, editor. *Who's Who in Baseball, 75th Edition*. New York: Who's Who in Baseball Magazine Co. (1115 Broadway—10010) (279 pp., photos, $4.95 p) since 1912

316. *Media Guides/Record Books*, published annually by each major league team and many minor leagues and teams. Contact individual teams or leagues.

317. Mercurio, John A. *Record Profiles of Baseball's Hall of Famers: All the Records Set by Baseball's Greatest Players*. NY: Perennial (470 pp., photos, bibliography, $16.95 p) 0-06-096448-0

318. Neft, David and Richard Cohen. *The Sports Encyclopedia: Baseball, 10th Edition*. NY: St. Martin's Press (638 pp., $17.95 p) 0-312-03938-7; 1st ed. 1974, 9th ed. 1989

319. Neft, David and Richard Cohen. *The World Series: A Complete Play-by-Play of Every Game, 1903–1989, 4th Edition*. NY: St. Martin's Press (443 pp., $16.95 p) 0-312-03960-3; also 1976, 1979, 1986 editions

320. Nufer, Doug. *1990 Guide to Northwest Minor League Baseball*. Sammamish Press, P.O. Box 895, Issaquah, WA 98027 (160 pp., $9.95)

321. *The Official Major League Baseball Scorebook 1990.* NY: Collier Books ($9.95 p) 0-02-029435-2

322. Phillips, John. *A Century of Hope: Cleveland Baseball Transactions, 1892–1989.* Capital Pub. Co., 8105 MacArthur Blvd., Cabin John, MD 20818 ($21.50 p)

323. Regenstein, Elliot and Tony Formo, publishers. *1990 Left Field Baseball Extravaganza.* (237 pp., $12.00 p) from Left Field, 301 Muriel Street, Ithaca, New York, 14850

324. Shandler, Ron. *The Baseball Forecaster: 1990 Annual Review, 5th Edition.* from Shandler Enterprises, P.O. Box 1001-L, Merrimack, New Hampshire 03054 (116 pp., $19.95 p)

325. Shatzkin, Mike and Jim Charlton, editors. *The Ballplayers: Baseball's Ultimate Biographical Reference.* John Thorn and Peter Palmer, photograph editors. NY: William Morrow (1230 pp., photos, $39.95 h) 0-87795-984-6

326. Siwoff, Seymour and Steve, Peter, and Tom Hirdt. *The 1990 Elias Baseball Analyst.* NY: Macmillan (437 pp., $14.95 p) 0-02-028712-7

327. Sparks, Bob, editor. *National Association of Professional Baseball Leagues: Orange Book.* NAPBL Promotion Corp., Publisher. (60 pp.) includes minor leagues statistics

Sporting News Publications, P.O. Box 44, St. Louis, MO. 63166

328. Carter, Craig and Larry Wigge, editors. *The National League Box-Score Book.* (1989 games) (147 pp., $9.95 p) 0-89204-347-4

329. ———. *The American League Box-Score Book,* (1989 games) (156 pp., $9.95 p) 0-89204-346-6)

330. Carter, Craig, editor. *The Complete Baseball Record Book: 1990.* (352 pp., photos, index, $12.95 p) 0-89204-338-5

331. *National League Green Book.* (104 pp., photos, $9.95 p) 0-89204-342-3

332. *American League Red Book.* (104 pp., photos, $9.95 p) 0-89204-341-5

333. Rains, Rob. *1990 Top 150 Minor League Prospects.* (168 pp., photos, $9.95 p) 0-89204-335-0

334. Seaver, Tom, with Rick Hummel and Bob Nightengale. *Tom Seaver's Scouting Notebook, 1990.* (429 pp., photos, index, $14.95 p) 0-89204-339-3

335. Shakespeare, Ed. *The Sporting News Guide for Kids, 1990.* (95 pp., photos, $5.95 p) 0-89204-348-2; (adults will find this guide helpful, also)

336. Siegel, Barry, editor. *The Baseball Register, 1990.* (576 pp., photos, $10.95 p) 0-89204-336-9, annually since 1940

337. Sloan, Dave, editor. *The Baseball Guide, 1990.* (536 pp., photos, $10.95 p) 0-89204-337-7, annually since 1942

338. Thorn, John and Pete Palmer, editors. *Total Baseball: 1990 Update.* New York: Warner Books (188 pp., $14.95 h) 0-446-51576-0

339. Thorn, John and Bob Carroll, editors. *The Whole Baseball Catalogue: The Ultimate Guide to the Baseball Marketplace.* NY: Fireside (369 pp., photos, index, $17.95 p) 0-671-68347-0

340. Tiemann, Robert, editor. *The National Pastime, No. 10.* SABR: P.O. Box 93183, Cleveland, Ohio 44101 (88 pp., photos, $8.00 p) 0-910137-40-4

341. Valenti, Dan. *Cactus League Road Trip: A Guide to Spring Training in Arizona.* Foreword by Roger Craig. Lexington, Mass.: Stephen Greene Press (130 pp., $8.95 p) 0-8289-0759-5

342. Van Overloop, Mark E. *Baseball's Greatest Total Hitters.* (188 pp., tables, charts, bibliography, $9.95 p and $2.00 p/h) from On The Mark Publications, Box 133, Washingtonville, New York 10992; best seasons and careers (power & average) of batters over the last 70 years.

343. Wayman, Joseph. *Grandstand Baseball Annual: 1990, Volume 6.* (127 pp., $7.95 p) 0-895-5501; from author, P.O. Box 4203, Downey, Calif 90241; vol. 1 (1985)–vol. 5 (1989) available

344. Welch, Bill with Jeff Moses. *Baseball Analysis and Reporting System: American League Report.* Slawson Communications, Box 50, Chillicothe, MO 64601 (396 pp., index, $17.95 p) 0-929633-03-2

345. ———. *Baseball Analysis and Reporting System: National League Report.* see address above. (340 pp., index, $17.95 p) 0-929633-04-0

346. ———. *The Tenth Man.* see address above. (492 pp., $14.95 p) 0-929633-00-8

347. Wolff, Rick, editorial director. *The Baseball Encyclopedia, Eighth Edition.* NY: Macmillan (2781 pp., $49.95 h) 0-02-579040-4; includes Negro League stats and fielding stats for the first time; 1st ed., 1969, 7th ed., 1988

348. Wood, Robert. *1990 Baseball Woodview: A Sabermetric Look.* (97 pp., $7.95 p) from author, 2101 California St. #224, Mountain View, Calif. 94040

349. Yearbooks, published annually by each major league team and some minor league teams and leagues. Contact individual teams and leagues. Two special yearbooks, however, are worth noting:

Guilfoile, Bill, editor. *The National Baseball Hall of Fame and Museum Yearbook: 1991 (51st edition)* from HOF Bookstore, Box 590, Cooperstown, NY 13326, $8.00 p

350. *Canadian Baseball Hall of Fame Yearbook.* Box 4008, Station A, Toronto, Ontario, Canada M5W 2R1

Baseball Publications: January–April 1991

SECTION I: ANTHOLOGIES

001. Angell, Roger. *Once More Around the Park: A Baseball Reader.* NY: Ballantine. (351 pp., $18.95 h) 0-345-36737-5

002. Bjarkman, Peter C., editor, *Baseball and the Game of Life: Stories for the Thinking Fan.* NY: Vintage (Random House) (212 pp., appendices, $10.00 p) 0-679-73141-5; reprint, Birch Brook Press, 1990

003. Einstein, Charles, editor. *The New Baseball Reader: More Favorites from the Fireside Books of Baseball.* NY: Viking (459 pp., $24.95 h) 0-670-83504-8

004. Gallen, David, editor. *The Baseball Chronicles.* Introduction by Mark Harris. Afterword by Peter Golenbock. NY: Carroll & Graf. (388 pp., photos, $21.95 h) 0-88184-694-5

005. Riley, Dan, editor. *The Red Sox Reader, Revised Edition.* Boston: Houghton-Mifflin. (289 pp., photos, $9.95 p) 0-395-58776-X; reprint, Ventura Arts, 1987.

006. Riley, Dan and Miro Weinberger, editors. *The Yankees Reader.* Boston: Houghton-Mifflin. (256 pp., photos, $9.95 p) 0-395-5877-8

007. Riley, Dan and David Fulk, editors. *The Cubs Reader, Revised Edition.* Boston: Houghton-Mifflin. (240 pp., photos, $9.95 p) 0-395-58779-4; reprint, Ventura Arts, 1990.

SECTION II: BIOGRAPHIES AND PERSONAL ACCOUNTS

008. Aaron, Hank and Lonnie Wheeler. *I Had a Hammer: The Hank Aaron Story.* NY: Harper-Collins. (333 pp., photos, $21.95 h) 0-06-016321-6

009. Cromartie, Warren, with Robert Whiting. *Slugging it Out in Japan: An American Major Leaguer in the Tokyo Outfield.* Tokyo: Kodansha International. (277 pp., photos, $19.95 h) 4-770-01423-6

010. Drysdale, Don, with Bob Verdi. *Once a Bum, Always a Dodger: My Life in Baseball From Brooklyn to Los Angeles.* NY: St. Martin's Press. (327 pp., photos, index, $4.95 p) 0-312-92462-3; reprint, St. Martin's, 1990

011. Fedo, Michael. *One Shining Season: Profiles of Baseball's One-Year Wonders.* Introduction by Ira Berkow. NY: Pharos Books. (169 pp., index, $16.95 h) 0-88687-608-7; 11 bios, from Willard Marshall to Wes Parker

012. Feller, Bob, with Bill Gilbert. *Now Pitching, Bob Feller: A Baseball*

Memoir. NY: Harper-Perennial. (231 pp., photos, index, $8.95 p) 0-06-097373-0; reprint, Birch Lane Press, 1990

013. Golenbock, Peter. *The Forever Boys: The Bittersweet World of Major League Baseball as Seen Through the Eyes of the Men Who Played One More Time.* NY: Birch Lane Press (391 pp., photos, index, $19.95 h) 1-55972-034-4; story of the St. Petersburg Pelicans of the Senior League.

014. Holway, John B. *Josh and Satch: The Life and Times of Josh Gibson and Satchel Paige.* Westport, Conn.: Meckler (238 pp., photos, $35.00 h) 0-88736-333-4

015. Holway, John B. *Black Diamonds: Life in the Negro Leagues from the Men Who Lived It.* NY: Stadium Books (dis. by Talman Co. Inc.) (189 pp., photos, index, $12.95 p) 0-9625132-3-7; reprint, Meckler, 1989

016. Honig, Donald. *The Greatest Catchers of All Time.* Dubuque, Iowa: William C. Brown (118 pp., photos, index, lifetime records, $18.95 h) 0-697-12806-7

017. John, Tommy, with Dan Valenti. *T.J.: My 26 Years in Baseball.* NY: Bantam Books (305 pp., photos, stats., $19.95 h) 0-553-07184-X

018. Johnson, Dick (editor) and Glenn Stout (text) et. al. *Ted Williams: A Portrait in Words and Pictures.* NY: Walker & Co. (225 pp., index, bibliography, stats, appendix, $24.95 h) 0-8027-1140-5

019. Lally, Dick. *Louisville Slugger Presents the Chicago Cubs.* NY: Bonanza Books (Random House) (ca. 65 pp., photos, $7.00 h) 0-517-05791-3

020. Mantle, Mickey, and Phil Pepe. *My Favorite Summer 1956.* NY: Doubleday (248 pp., photos, homerun log, $18.95 h) 0-385-41261-4

021. Maranville, Walter "Rabbit". *Run, Rabbit, Run: The Hilarious and Mostly True Tales of Rabbit Maranville.* Introduction by Harold Seymour, Ph.D. Afterword by Bob Carroll. SABR: P.O. Box 93183, Cleveland, Ohio 44101 (96 pp., photos, index, career stats, $9.95 p) 0-910137-44-7

022. Mayer, Ronald A. *Perfect! Biographies and Lifetime Statistics of 14 Pitchers of "Perfect" Baseball Games, with Game Summaries and Boxscores.* Jefferson, N.C.: McFarland (240 pp., photos, tables, notes, index, $25.95 h) 0-89950-571-6

023. Murdock, Eugene. *Baseball Players and Their Times: Oral Histories of the Game, 1920–1940.* Westport, Conn.: Meckler (300 pp., photos, $37.50 h) 0-88736-235-4

024. Pallone, Dave, with Alan Steinberg. *Behind the Mask: My Double Life in Baseball.* NY: Signet New American Library (348 pp. photos, $5.99 p) 0-451-17029-6; reprint, Viking, 1990.

025. Seidel, Michael. *Ted Williams: A Baseball Life.* Chicago: Contemporary Books (400 pp., photos, notes, stats, index, $19.95 h) 0-8092-4254-0

026. Thrift, Syd and Barry Shapiro. *The Game According to Syd: The Theories and Teachings of Baseball's Leading Innovator.* NY: Fireside (304 p., index $9.95 p) 0-671-73365-6; reprint, Simon & Schuster, 1990

027. Wills, Maury and Mike Celizic. *On the Run: The Never Dull and Often Shocking Life of Maury Wills.* NY: Carroll & Graf. (334 pp., photos, $19.95 h) 0-88184-640-6

028. Yastrezemski, Carl and Gerald Eskenazi. *Yaz: Baseball, The Wall, and Me.* NY: Warner (303 pp., photos, stats, $4.95 p) 0-446-36103-8; reprint, Doubleday, 1990

SECTION III: FICTION AND POETRY

029. Brock, Darryl. *If I Never Get Back.* NY: Ballantine. (470 pp., $5.95 p) 0-345-37055-4; reprint, Crown, 1990

030. Evers, Crabbe (pseudonym of William Brashler & Reinder Van Til). *Murder in Wrigley Field.* NY: Bantam (ca. 270 pp., $3.95 p) 0-553-28915-2

031. Fehler, Gene. *Center Field Grasses: Poems from Baseball.* Jefferson, N.C.: McFarland (192 pp., $15.95) 0-89950-604-6

032. Gordon, Allison. *The Dead Pull Hitter.* NY: Onyx Books (256 pp., $3.99 p) 0-451-40240-5; reprint, St. Martin's Press, 1988

033. Lyle, Sparky and David Fisher. *The Year I Owned the Yankees: A Baseball Fantasy.* NY: Bantam (313 pp., $4.95 p) 0-553-28692-7; reprint, Bantam, 1990

034. Norman, Rick. *Fielder's Choice.* Little Rock, Arkansas: August House. (194 pp., $17.95 h) 0-87483-172-5

035. Shaara, Michael. *For Love of the Game.* NY: Carroll & Graf (152 pp., $16.95 h) 0-88184-695-3

SECTION IV: HISTORIES AND GENERAL WORKS

036. Alexander, Charles C. *Our Game: An American Baseball History.* NY: Henry Holt (388 pp., photos, index, bibliographic essay, $25.00 h) 0-8050-1594-9

037. Bankes, James. *The Pittsburgh Crawfords: The Lives and Times of Black Baseball's Most Exciting Team.* Dubuque, Iowa: William C. Brown (173 pp., photos, index, appendix, $15.95 p) 0-697-12889-X

038. Blake, Mike. *The Minor Leagues: A Celebration of the Little Show.* NY: Wynwood Press (400 pp., photos, index, bibliography, list of cities and leagues, 1877–1990, $19.95 h) 0-922066-60-4

039. Bjarkman, Peter, editor. *Encyclopedia of Major League Baseball Team Histories, Volume I: American League.* Westport, Conn.: Meckler (600 pp., photos, $65.00 h) 0-88736-373-3

040. Bjarkman, Peter, editor. *Encyclopedia of Major League Baseball Team*

Histories, Volume II: National League. Westport, Conn.: Meckler (600 pp., photos, $65.00 h) 0-88736-374-1

041. Cosell, Howard, with Shelby Whitfield. *What's Wrong with Sports.* Foreword by Al Davis. NY: Simon & Schuster. (349 pp., index, $21.95 h) 0-671-70840-6

042. Clifton, Merritt. *Disorganized Baseball Volume I. (Quebec Provincial League, 1894–1970)* expanded and revised version of 1982 book, from author, 456 Monroe Turnpike, Monroe, Conn. 06468 $6.00

043. Clifton, Merritt, with Jim Langlois and Ed Brooks. *Disorganized Baseball Volume II (Vermont Northern League, 1887–1952)* $6.00; see address above.

044. *Cooperstown Symposium on Baseball and the American Culture (1989).* Westport, Conn.: Meckler with State University of New York, College at Oneonta (363 pp., photos, $49.50 h) 0-88736-719-4

045. Creamer, Robert W. *Baseball in '41: A Celebration of the Best Baseball Season Ever in the Year America Went to War.* NY: Viking (330 pp., photos, index, $19.95 h) 0-670-83374-6

046. Curran, William. *Big Sticks: The Phenomenal Decade of Ruth, Gehrig, Cobb, and Hornsby.* NY: Harper-Perennial (288 pp., photos, index, $8.95 p) 0-06-097365-X; reprint Morrow, 1990, as *Big Sticks: The Batting Revolution of the 1920s*

047. Dickerson, Gary E. *The Cinema of Baseball: Images of America, 1929–1989.* Westport, Conn.: Meckler (178 pp., photos, $37.50) 0-88736-710-0

048. DiClerico, James M. and Barry J. Pavelec. *The Jersey Game: The History of Modern Baseball from its Birth to the Big Leagues in the Garden State.* New Brunswick, N.J.: Rutgers University Press. (224 pp., photos, $18.95 h) 0-8135-1652-8

049. Godin, Roger A. *The 1922 St. Louis Browns: Best of the American League's Worst.* Jefferson, N.C.: McFarland (192 pp., photos, appendices, bibliography, index, $24.95 h) 0-89950-591-0

050. Goldstein, Richard. *Superstars and Screwballs: 100 Years of Brooklyn Baseball.* NY: Dutton (383 pp., photos, index, sources, $21.95 h) 0-525-24958-3

051. Hetrick, J. Thomas. *Misfits! The Cleveland Spiders in 1899: A Day by Day Narrative of Baseball Futility.* Jefferson, N.C.: McFarland (240 pp., photos, references, appendices, bibliography, index, $25.95) 0-89950-608-9

052. Honig, Donald. *The St. Louis Cardinals: An Illustrated History.* NY: Prentice-Hall (244 pp., index, appendices, $24.95 h) 0-13-840026-1

053. Honig, Donald. *The Chicago Cubs: An Illustrated History.* NY: Prentice-Hall (258 pp., index, appendices, $24.95 h) 0-13-131327-4

054. Klein, Alan M. *Sugarball: The American Game, The Dominican Dream.*

New Haven, Conn.: Yale University Press (179 pp., photos, notes, index, $19.95 h) 0-300-04873-4

055. Koppett, Leonard. *The New Thinking Fan's Guide to Baseball.* NY: Fireside (381 pp., $10.95 p) 0-671-73205-6; a revision of his 1967 work: *A Thinking Man's Guide to Baseball,* published by Dutton

056. Kuklick, Bruce. *To Every Thing a Season: Shibe Park and Urban Philadelphia 1909–1976.* Princeton, N.J.: Princeton University Press (237 pp., photos, source notes, index, $19.95 h) 0-691-04788-X

057. Lamb, David. *Stolen Season: A Journey through America and Baseball's Minor Leagues.* NY: Random House (283 pp., photos, list of towns with teams today by state, $20.00 h) 0-394-57608-X

058. Lansche, Jerry. *Glory Fades Away: The Nineteenth Century World Series Rediscovered.* Foreword by John Thorn. Dallas: Taylor Publishing (328 pp., photos, index, references, boxscores, $19.95 h) 0-87833-726-1

059. Linn, Ed. *The Great Rivalry: The Yankees and the Red Sox 1901–1990.* NY: Ticknor & Fields (359 pp., photos, index, appendix, $19.95 h) 0-89919-917-8

060. Lowenfish, Lee and Tony Lupien. *The Imperfect Diamond: The Story of Baseball's Reserve System and the Men Who Fought to Change It. Revised Edition.* NY: DaCapo Press. (301 pp., photos, index, bibliographical notes, $14.95 p) 0-306-80430-1; reprint, Stein & Day, 1980

061. Mullarkey, Karen, editorial director. *Baseball in America: From Sandlots to Stadiums. A Portrait of our National Passion by 50 of our Leading Photographers.* San Francisco: Collins (223 pp., $45.00 h) 0-00-215731-4

062. Pietrusza, David. *Major Leagues: The Formation, Sometimes Absorption, and Mostly Inevitable Demise of 18 Professional Baseball Organizations, 1871 to the Present.* Jefferson, N.C.: McFarland (368 pp., photos, tables, appendices, bibliography, index, $35.00 h) 0-89950-590-2

063. Robinson, George and Charles Salzberg. *On a Clear Day They Could See Seventh Place: Baseball's Worst Teams.* NY: Dell (288 pp., photos, stats, $8.95 p) 0-440-50345-0

064. Robinson, Ray. *The Home Run Heard 'Round the World: The Dramatic Story of the 1951 Giants–Dodgers Pennant Race.* NY: Harper-Collins (244 pp., photos, $19.95 h) 0-06-016477-8

065. Ruck, Rob. *The Tropic of Baseball: Baseball in the Dominican Republic.* Westport, Conn.: Meckler (photos, $35.00 h) 0-88736-707-0

066. Shaughnessy, Dan. *The Curse of the Bambino.* NY: Penguin (220 pp., bibliography, $8.95 p) 0-14-015262-8: reprint, Dutton, 1990

067. Stark, Benton. *The Year They Called Off the World Series: A True Story.*

Garden City Park, NY: Avery Publishing Group (236 pp., photos, index, bibliography, $17.95 h) 0-89529-480-X

068. Vlasich, James A. *A Legend for the Legendary: The Origin of the Baseball Hall of Fame*. Preface by David Q. Voigt. Bowling Green University (Ohio) Popular Press (266 pp., photos, notes, index, bibliography, $20.95 p, $41.95 h)

069. Whitford, David. *Extra Innings: A Season in the Senior League*. NY: Edward Burlingame Books (imprint of Harper-Collins) (255 pp., $19.95 h) 0-06-016459-X

070. Will, George. *Men at Work: The Craft of Baseball*. NY: Harper-Perennial (353 pp., photos, index, $9.95 p) 0-06-097372-2; reprint, Macmillan, 1990

071. Zagaris, Michael (photography and captions), with John Hickey (profiles). *The Oakland A's*. San Francisco: Chronicle Books (88 pp., $12.95 p) 0-87701-892-8; concentrates on 1988–1990 seasons

SECTION V: HOBBY

072. *American League Rotisserie Handbook '91*. third annual edition. ($16.95 and $3.00 p/h) from Reliable Rotisserie, P.O. Box 340, Thomaston, Conn. 06787

073. Beckett, Dr. James. *The Sport Americana Baseball Card Price Guide #13*. Edgewater Book Co., P.O. Box 40238, Cleveland, Ohio 44140 (816 pp., photos, $14.95 p) 0-937424-51-X

074. Beckett, Dr. James. *The Official 1992 Price Guide to Baseball Cards. 11th edition*. NY: House of Collectibles (ca. 800 pp., $5.95 p) 0-876-37850-5

075. Boyd, Brendan C. and Fred C. Harris. *The Great American Baseball Card Flipping, Trading, and Bubble Gum Book*. NY: Ticknor & Fields (151 pp., $10.95 p) 0-395-58668-2; this is a reprint of their book of the same title published by Little, Brown in 1973; new introduction.

076. Golenbock, Peter. *How to Win at Rotisserie Baseball: 1991 Edition*. NY: Carroll & Graf (354 pp., $9.95 p) 0-88184-651-1; 1987 and 1990 editions also

077. Gutman, Bill, with Dave Weiner and Jonathan Markson. *Micro League Baseball: Official Field Guide and Disk*. NY: Bantam (486 pp., photos, index, $27.95 p) 0-553-35344-6

078. Kurowski, Jeff, editor. *Sports Collector's Digest Baseball Card Price Guide. Fifth Edition*. Iola, Wisconsin: Krause Publishers (736 pp., $13.95 p) 0-87341-155-2

079. Kurowski, Jeff, editor. *Sports Collector's Digest Baseball Card Pocket Price Guide 1991 Edition*. NY: Warner Books (575 pp., photos, $5.95 p) 0-446-36171-2

080. Meyers, Larry S. *Baseball Black Book 1991: The Winning Edge for Serious Rotisserie/Fantasy Owners. Fourth Edition*. Prima Publishers (dist. by St. Martin's) (211 pp., $12.95 p) 1-55958-086-0

081. Michael, Bob. *Bob Michael's Fourth Annual Fantasy Baseball Guide*. P.O. Box 111509, Miami, Florida 33111 (200 pp., $12.95 and $2.50 p/h)

082. Obojski, Robert. *Baseball Memorabilia*. NY: Sterling (160 pp., photos, index, $16.95 h) 0-8069-7290-4

083. Owens, Tom, contributing writer. *The Complete Book of 1991 Baseball Cards*. Publishers Int'l Ltd., 7373 N. Cicero Ave., Lincolnwood, Illinois 60646 (320 pp., $14.99 h) 0-517-05673-9)

084. Owens, Tom, contributing writer. *Consumer's Guide's Official Baseball Card Price Guide, 1991 Illustrated Collector's Edition*. Publishers Int'l Ltd. (see #083) (576 pp., photos, $5.99 p) 0-451-16985-9

085. Patton, Alex. *Patton's 1991 Fantasy Baseball Price Guide*. NY: Fireside (314 pp., $9.95 p) 0-671-69626-2

086. Waggoner, Glen and Robert Sklar, editors. *Rotisserie League Baseball: The Official Rule Book and Draft Day Guide. Fifth Edition*. NY: Bantam Books (328 pp., $12.95 p) 0-553-35247-4; also published in 1984, 1987, 1989, and 1990

087. Welch, Wayne M. *The Fantasy Baseball Abstract 1991*. NY: Perigee (Putnam's) (249 pp., $11.95 p) 0-399-51661-1

SECTION VI: HUMOR AND TRIVIA

088. Blake, Mike. *The Incomplete Book of Baseball Superstitions, Rituals, and Oddities*. NY: Wynwood Press. (204 pp., index, bibliography, $8.95 p) 0-922066-59-8

089. Forker, Dom. *Big League Baseball Puzzlers*. Illustrated by Sanford Hoffman. NY: Sterling (128 pp., index, $4.95 p) 0-8069-7337-4

090. Gross, S. and Jim Charlton, editors. *Play Ball: An All-Star Lineup of Baseball Cartoons*. NY: Harper-Perennial (ca. 100 pp., $8.95 p) 0-06-096598-3

091. Mazer, Bill, with Stan and Shirley Fischler. *Bill Mazer's Amazin' Baseball Book: 150 Years of Baseball Tales and Trivia*. NY: Zebra Books (Kensington Pub. Group) (400 pp., photos, index. $8.95 p) 0-8217-3361-3; reprint, Kensington, 1990

092. Nemec, David. *The Baseball Challenge Quiz Book*. NY: Signet New American Library (191 pp., $4.99 p) 0-451-16943-3

093. Schmittberger, R. Wayne. *Test Your Baseball Literacy*. NY: John Wiley & Sons (234 pp., index, bibliography, $9.95 p) 0-471-53622-9

SECTION VII: INSTRUCTION, FITNESS, AND RULES

094. Carroll, Bob. *The Major League Way to Play Baseball*. NY: Little Simon (88 pp., photos, $5.95 p) 0-671-70441-9; aimed at juveniles

095. Dorfman, H.A. and Karl Kuehl. *The Mental Game of Baseball: A Guide to Peak Performance*. South Bend: Diamond Communications (337 pp., appendix, $14.95 p) 0-912083-32-8; reprint, Diamond Communications, 1989

096. Feldman, Jay. *Hitting*. NY: Little Simon (88 pp., photos, $5.95 p) 0-671-70442-7; aimed at juveniles

097. Figone, Al (Humbolt State University) *Teaching the Mental Aspects of Baseball: A Coach's Handbook*. Dubuque, Iowa: William C. Brown (227 pp., photos, index, $15.95 p) 0-697-12767-2

098. *Official Baseball Rules: 1991 Edition*. St. Louis: The Sporting News. (104 pp., $3.95 p) 0-89204-385-7

099. Pecci, Stephen. *Building a Better Hitter*. Foreword by George Foster. Dubuque, Iowa: William C. Brown (112 pp., photos, $10.95 p) 0-697-11404-X

100. Ryan, Nolan, with Tom House and Jim Rosenthal. *Nolan Ryan's Pitcher's Bible: The Ultimate Guide to Power, Precision, and Long-Term Performance*. Foreword by A. Eugene Coleman. NY: Fireside (175 pp., photos, career stats, $10.95 p) 0-671-70581-4

101. Schlossberg, Dan. *Pitching*. NY: Little Simon (86 pp., photos, $5.95 p) 0-671-70443-5; aimed at juveniles

SECTION VIII: JUVENILE WORKS

FICTION

102. Montgomery, Robert. *The Show!* Mahwah, N.J.: Troll Associates (171 pp., illustrated, $2.95 p) 0-8167-1985-3

103. ———. *Hitting Streak*. Troll Associates (171 pp., $2.95 p) 0-8167-1983-7

104. ———. *Triple Play*. Troll Associates (170 pp., $2.95 p) 0-8167-1991-8

105. ———. *Home Run!* Troll Associates (170 pp. $2.95 p) 0-8167-1987-X

106. ———. *MVP*. Troll Associates (167 pp., $2.95 p) 0-8167-1993-4

107. ———. *Grand Slam*. Troll Associates (169 pp., $2.95 p) 0-8167-1989-6

108. Rosenblum, Richard. *Brooklyn Dodger Days*. NY: Atheneum (32 pp.) boys venture to Ebbets Field in 1946

109. Slote, Alfred. *Finding Buck McHenry*. NY: Harper (256 pp.) a team needs a coach and school janitor might be former Negro League great

BIOGRAPHIES

110. Cohen, Eliot, editor. *My Greatest Day in Baseball: Baseball Stars of Today and Yesterday Tell Their Exciting Stories*. NY: Little Simon (150 pp., photos, $3.95 p) 0-671-70440-0

111. Gutman, Bill. *Bo Jackson: A Biography.* NY: Archway (Pocket Books) (ca. 130 pp., photos, stats, $2.95 p) 0-671-73363-X

112. Lally, Dick. *Baseball's Best Hit Men.* Photographs by Tom DiPace. NY: Little Simon (24 pp., bios., 18 stickers, $3.95 p) 0-671-73637-X

113. ———. *Home Run Kings.* Photos by Tom DiPace. NY: Little Simon (24 pp., bios, 18 stickers, $3.95 p) 0-671-73636-1

114. ———. *Record Breakers.* Photos by Tom DiPace. NY: Little Simon (24 pp., bios, 18 stickers, $3.95 p) 0-671-73634-5

115. ———. *Aces of the Mound.* Photos by Tom DiPace. NY: Little Simon (24 pp., bios, 18 stickers, $3.95 p) 0-671-73635-3

116. Nash, Bruce and Allan Zullo. *More Little Big Leaguers: Amazing Boyhood Stories of Today's Baseball Stars.* Tom Muldoon, compiler. NY: Little Simon (96 pp., photos, 45 cards, $7.95 p) 0-671-73394-X

117. O'Conner, Jim. *Roberto Clemente: All-Star Hero.* Illustrated by Stephen Marchesi. NY: Dell-Yearling. (107 pp., $2.95 p) 0-440-40425-8

118. Raber, Thomas R. *Bo Jackson: Pro Sports Superstar.* Minneapolis: Lerner (64 pp., photos, stats, $3.95 p) 0-8225-9585-0 (actually a 1990 book)

119. Rolfe, John. *Jim Abbott.* NY: Sports Illustrated for Kids (124 pp., photos, glossary, $4.95 p) 0-316-75459-5

120. Rolfe, John. *Bo Jackson.* NY: Sports Illustrated for Kids (124 pp., photos, $4.95 p) 0-316-75457-9

121. White, Ellen Emerson. *Bo Jackson: Playing the Games.* NY: Scholastic (86 pp., photos, $2.95 p) 0-590-44075-6 (December 1990)

GENERAL WORKS

122. Foley, Red. *Red Foley's Best Baseball Book Ever.* Illustrated by Jane Lieman. NY: Little Simon (96 pp., 130 stickers, $7.95 p) 0-671-72723-0; also published in 1987, 1988, 1989, and 1990

123. Hollander, Zander, editor. *The Baseball Book: The Illustrated Encyclopedia of Baseball from A to Z. Revised Edition.* NY: Random House (184 pp., index, $9.95 p) 0-679-81055-2; reprint, Random House, 1982

124. Nash, Bruce and Allan Zullo. *The Baseball Hall of Shame: Young Fan's Edition Volume 2.* Bernie Ward, curator. NY: Archway (Pocket Books) (130 pp., photos, $2.95 p) 0-671-73533-0; first edition, Archway, 1990

125. Obojski, Robert. *Baseball Bloopers and Diamond Oddities.* NY: Sterling (128 pp., photos, index, $4.95 p) 0-8069-6981-4; reprint of 1989 work called *Baseball Bloopers and Other Curious Incidents*

126. Weiner, Eric. *The Kid's Complete Baseball Catalogue.* NY: Julian Messner (254 pp., photos, index, $12.95 p) 0-671-70197-5

SECTION IX: REFERENCE, STATISTICS, ANNUAL WORKS

Baseball America (American Sports Publishing), P.O. Box 2089, Durham, NC 27702

127. *Baseball America's 1991 Almanac* (Allan Simpson, editor) (313 pp., photos, stats., $9.95 p) 0-671-73369-9

128. *Baseball America's 1991 Directory* (192 pp., $8.95 p) 0-671-73368-0

129. Charlton, James, editor. *The Baseball Chronology: The Complete History of the Most Important Events in the Game of Baseball.* NY: Macmillan (608 pp., $35.00 h) 0-02-523971-6

130. Dewan, John, Don Zminda and Stats, Inc. *Stats 1991 Baseball Scoreboard.* Foreword by Peter Gammons. Illustrations by John Grimwade. NY: Ballantine (ca. 330 pp., $12.95 and $2.00 p/h) 0-9625581-2-5

131. Dewan, John, Don Zminda and Stats, Inc. *The Scouting Report 1991: The Most In-Depth Analysis of the Strengths and Weaknesses of Every Active Major League Baseball Player.* NY: Perennial (677 pp., photos, index, $15.95 p) 0-06-273002-9

132. Dickinson, Dan and Kieran. *Major League Stadiums: A Vacation-Planning Reference to the 26 Baseball Parks.* Jefferson, NC: McFarland (380 pp., photos, $24.95) 0-89950-610-0

133. Dickson, Paul, editor. *Baseball's Greatest Quotations.* NY: Edward Burlingame (524 pp., photos, index, bibliography, $29.95 h) 0-06-270001-4

134. Dickson, Paul, editor and compiler. *The Dickson Baseball Dictionary: 5000 Terms Used by Players, the Press, and People Who Love the Game.* NY: Avon (438 pp., photos, bibliography, $14.95 p) 0-380-71335-7; reprint, Facts on File, 1989

135. Gimbel, Mike. *Mike Gimbel's Baseball Player and Team Ratings. 1991 Edition.* from Boerum Street Press, Suite 400, 131 Boerum Street, Brooklyn, NY 11206 ($10.95 and $2.50 p/h)

136. Hanke, Brock. *The 1991 Baseball Sabermetric.* (320 pp., $15.95 p) 0-9625846-4-9; from Mad Aztec Press, 1215 Willow View Drive, Kirkwood, MO 63122

137. Hollander, Zander, editor. *The 1991 Complete Handbook of Baseball. 21st edition.* NY: Signet New American Library (415 pp., photos, schedules, rosters, stats, $5.99 p) 0-451-16922-0; annually since 1971

138–141. *Reach Baseball Guides* Reprints of 1883 ($15.00) and 1902–1904 ($35.00 each) Horton Publishing Company, P.O. Box 29234, St. Louis, MO 63126

142. *Sporting News Baseball Register,* 1940 (228 pp.) $50.00 Horton Publishing Company, P.O. Box 29234, St. Louis, MO 63126

143. James, Bill. *The Baseball Book 1991*. NY: Villard Books (391 pp., $15.00 p) 0-679-73530-5

144. Maclean, Norman, editor. *1991 Who's Who in Baseball*. (288 pp., photos, stats, $4.95 p) lifetime records of major leaguers, 76th year, since 1912

145. Major League Baseball Properties and Editors of the Baseball Encyclopedia. *The Official Major League Baseball 1991 Stat Book* (includes 1991 Baseball Encyclopedia Update) NY: Collier (465 pp., $13.95 p) 0-02-063381-5

146. McCue, Andy. *Baseball by the Books: A History and Complete Bibliography of Baseball Fiction*. Dubuque, Iowa: William C. Brown (164 pp., photos, notes, appendices, $19.95 h) 0-697-12764-8

147. Nathan, David H. *Baseball Quotations: The Wit and Wisecracks of Players, Managers, Owners, Umpires, Announcers, Writers, and Fans on the Great American Pastime*. Jefferson, NC: McFarland (192 pp., indices, $24.95) 0-89950-562-7

148. Neft, David S. and Richard M. Cohen. *The Sports Encyclopedia: Baseball: 11th Edition*. NY: St. Martin's Press (649 pp., $18.95 p) 0-312-05519-6; first edition, 1974 and 10th edition, 1990

149. *The Official Major League Baseball Scorebook 1991*. NY: Collier (n.p. stats, $10.95 spiral) 0-02-063384-X

150. Owens, Tom, David Nemec, Pete Palmer, et al. *The 1991 Baseball Almanac*. Publishers Int'l Ltd.: Lincolnwood, Illinois (672 pp., $6.95 p)

151. Palmer, Pete and John Thorn, editors. *The Baseball Record Book: The Game's Great Records and the Stories Behind Them*. NY: Little Simon (90 pp., photos, $5.95 p) 0-671-70444-3; aimed at juveniles

152. Siwoff, Seymour with Steve, Tom, and Peter Hirdt. *The 1991 Elias Baseball Analyst*. NY: Fireside (437 pp., $14.95 p) 0-671-73325-7

Sporting News Publications

153. Carter, Craig and Larry Wigge, editors. *American League Box Score Book (1990)* (158 pp., $10.95 p and $19.95 h) Sporting News Publications, P.O. Box 44, St. Louis, MO 63166.

154. ———, editors. *National League Box Score Book (1990)* (150 pp., $10.95 p and $19.95 h) Sporting News Publications, P. O. Box 44, St. Louis, MO 63166

155. *American League Red Book. 62nd Year*. (104 pp., $10.95 p) Sporting News Publications, P.O. Box 44, St. Louis, MO 63166

156. *National League Green Book* (104 pp., $10.95 p) Sporting News Publications, P.O. Box 44, St. Louis, MO 63166

157. Carter, Craig, editor. *The Complete Baseball Record Book. 1991*

Edition. (344 pp., photos, index, $14.95 p) 0-89204-384-9 Sporting News Publications, P.O. Box 44, St. Louis, MO 63166

158. Hoppel, Joe and Craig Carter, editors. *The Series: An Illustrated History of Baseball's Postseason Showcase 1903–1990.* (ca. 350 pp., photos, $12.95 p) 0-89204 Sporting News Publications, P.O. Box 44, St. Louis, MO 63166

159. Siegel, Barry, editor. *The Sporting News Baseball Register 1991* (568 pp., $11.95 p) 0-89204-383-0; annually since 1940 Sporting News Publications, P.O. Box 44, St. Louis, MO 63166

160. Sloan, Dave, editor. *The Sporting News Baseball Guide 1991.* (536 pp., photos, index, $11.95 p) 0-89204-382-2; annually since 1942 Sporting News Publications, P.O. Box 44, St. Louis, MO 63166

161. Thorn, John, Pete Palmer, and David Reuther, editors. *Total Baseball. Second Edition.* NY: Warner Books (2629 pp., $49.95 h) 0-446-51620-1; first edition, Warner, 1989

BOOK REVIEWS

INTRODUCTION

In this year's annual, Larry Ritter observed:

> Baseball books are getting more and more interesting. In the distant past, they were written mainly for younger teenagers and were concerned primarily with the benefits of clean living and the heroics of ninth-inning rallies. But the times, as folk-rock singer Bob Zimmerman once predicted, they certainly are a-changin'.

The context of Larry's comment was his review of *Behind the Mask: My Double Life in Baseball,* a book Ritter succinctly summarized as "a chronicle of what life is like in the big leagues for a strikebreaking homosexual umpire with a short fuse and a ton of suppressed rage."

Baseball books certainly have come a long way from Christy Mathewson's *Pitching in a Pinch,* which "enslaved" the young Roger Kahn, who eventually helped change the face of baseball literature with his very adult masterpiece, *The Boys of Summer.* Of course, even earlier, reviewer Ritter had, himself, produced the classic of baseball oral history, *The Glory of Their Times,* a book postadolescent fans could feel secure in recommending to friends who didn't know the difference between a box score and a batters' box.

Overall, the books reviewed this year amply justify Ritter's current optimistic assessment of the evolution of baseball literature. On the one hand, readers will be able to see how such pioneer works as *The Boys of Summer* and *The Glory of Their Times* have continued to inspire interesting variations on the genres they helped create. On the other hand, the recent crop of baseball books displays some fascinating new trends. For example, the first four books reviewed all deal with baseball outside North America: in the Dominican Republic, Japan, and Poland. Two other works use sophisticated modern scientific concepts and techniques to analyze the amazing complexities of throwing, hitting, and catching a baseball, while a third views the game as a modern craft form.

Readers can draw their own conclusions as to what such trends might mean. However, it is indisputable that no matter how many good baseball books appear, there always seems to be something more worth writing about our national pastime, and, fortunately for us, some of America's most interesting and talented writers still find themselves hopelessly seduced by the game.

Fred Roberts
Michigan State University

Klein, Alan M. *Sugarball: The American Game, The Dominican Dream*. New Haven: Yale University Press, 1991.

Ruck, Rob. *The Tropic of Baseball: Baseball in the Dominican Republic*. Westport, Connecticut: Meckler Publishing, 1991. 205 pp. $35.00.

As all baseball fans know, the Dominican Republic [DR] has sent more players to the major leagues per capita than any nation in the world, including the United States. And, most fans recognize the Dominican sugar-factory town of San Pedro de Macorís as the City of Shortstops because it is the hometown of a succession of all-star performers at the number 6 spot. The notable success of Latin American stars, especially Dominicans, has created fan interest in Latin ballplayers, their backgrounds, and their countries' baseball, as well as curiosity about the cultural differences between baseball in the "Bigs" and baseball in Latin America. Above all, fans want to know why the Dominican Republic has become the mother of ballplayers, especially shortstops. Two recent (1991) books, *Sugarball* by Alan Klein and *The Tropic of Baseball* by Rob Ruck, provide answers to these questions.

Ruck offers a history of the game in the Dominican Republic from its Cuban origins in 1891, through its early years challenging U.S. occupation teams (1916–1924), and includes the era of Caribbean rivalry, the Trujillo episode, and the years of cooperation with the major leagues from 1956 to the present. He makes this accounting come alive, integrating interviews and folk stories with traditional sources about great games and great players. This recounting is punctuated, as it should be, with sketches of such legends as Tetelo Vargas, the DR's greatest star before the integration of the majors; Martin Dihigo, the Cuban who played in Santo Domingo (and everywhere else the game was played) and is enshrined in the halls of fame in Cuba, Mexico, and the United States; and Juan Marichal, who personifies the island's impact on baseball. Ruck carefully retells the story of the legendary 1937 season, when Dominican club owners sold, mortgaged, and pawned everything they could to bring ballplayers from across the Caribbean and from the Negro Leagues. Arguably, the best baseball in the world in 1937 was played in the DR, where so many stars had come from the Pittsburgh Crawfords that the team had to drop out of the Negro League. The Ciudad Trujillo Dragons fielded a team that included Josh Gibson, Cool Papa Bell, and Satchel Paige and eventually won the championship. The season broke the DR's professional teams, and Dominican baseball lapsed back into semipro and amateur standing until 1951. But what a season—it remains etched in the memories of DR fans.

Ruck combines the techniques and talents of an historian and a journalist (not really so far apart), to provide a well-researched and readable narrative that rests on thoughtful analysis. He searched behind the common knowledge to see what was going on, to ask who and why. As a result, Ruck raised questions about who the families were in sugar cane towns who provided so many sons to baseball. He uncovered the fascinating story of immigrants from the Anglo-Caribbean, especially the Virgin Islands, called Cocolos, who came to cut cane. These were tight-knit, strong-disciplined families, who had a heritage of mutual assistance—and cricket. In the second generation, the families moved slightly up the immigrant ladder and adopted baseball. Today their sons, still schooled in family unity and discipline, have gone on to the major leagues.

Ruck also asked simple but interesting questions, such as who was the legendary Padre José—the apostle of baseball in the sugar-mill towns? Ruck tracked him to provincial Ontario, where Father Joseph Ainslie confessed that he had no interest in baseball; he merely promoted the game to take advantage of an existing interest among the Dominicans and then used the sport to bring the people together and to teach cooperation and mutual assistance that could be applied to other aspects of their lives.

For the most part, Ruck offers an excellent book. Some, however, will be slightly put off by Ruck's occasional lapse into a kind of gonzo journalism, reporting his experiences with the weather, the fans, and the stadium. This is not a travel account, so we don't know enough about Ruck or his journey to be prepared for this style; as a result, it is mildly annoying, especially when he could be telling us more about the fascinating history of DR baseball and its legends. But this is only quibbling.

Alan Klein has written a complementary volume to the Ruck book. Overall, Klein provides information not available anywhere else. There are flaws in the book. There are some copyediting lapses by his press. He presents his general discussion in the threadbare dependency model and in the theoretical claptrap that results from declaring that Dominican baseball represents an example of the resistance to hegemony discussed in James Scott's marvelous book, *The Weapons of the Weak*. Assertion and jargon are not the same as analysis. The reader might easily bog down in the theoretic quagmire, if he or she worried too much, to pick an example, about Klein's efforts to prove that resistance to United States baseball hegemony had a class character. Klein documents this assertion by showing that 12 more lower-class fans (established by occupation) than middle-class fans out of 164 would buy baseball caps with Dominican team names rather than caps with major league team emblems. Well, don't worry and don't expect any statistical apparatus, such as indications of reliability. Klein has interesting things to say, and readers should go quickly to them.

The rise of the baseball academy in the Dominican Republic provides an arresting story of recruitment, training, and education of ballplayers. The Blue Jays established the first academy, but the touchstone for major league efforts in the Dominican Republic is the Dodger facility called Campo Las Palmas. Klein is at his best describing the experience of young recruits: trying out for the academy, becoming rookies, and receiving instruction, above all, in baseball, but also in personal hygiene, social interaction, and English. The academy's instructors attempt to do everything possible to insure that a player with talent and dedication reaches his fullest potential with the Dodger organization. Klein provides an excellent account of the academy experience and was even able, for a brief time, to modify the English classes to offer more practical instruction.

Moreover, Klein gives the reader an arresting sketch of the center of baseball in the Dominican Republic, Quisqueya Stadium in the nation's capital. He evokes the feeling that tropical nights, rum, and merengue are as necessary for baseball in the DR as high humidity, a Bull City burrito, and a cold Bud are in

Durham, North Carolina. There is a special character to Dominican baseball, and he captures it in this chapter.

Both authors decry the changes in the Dominican winter league: Dominican major leaguers with multimillion-dollar contracts increasingly cannot, or will not, play at home; U.S. major leaguers come in fewer numbers and do not stay through the season; fans, with less disposable income and facing higher ticket prices, remain at home. Free agency for Dominican league players will not solve the problem; nor will including the Dominican Republic's players in the major league draft (as the Puerto Ricans are) save the winter league. On the other hand, the arrival of Japanese scouts on the island may presage Japanese investment in the Dominican league that will save it. Who knows? Meanwhile, readers interested in the DR can turn to these two interesting, worthwhile books.

William H. Beezley
Texas Christian University

Whiting, Robert. *You Gotta Have Wa: When Two Cultures Collide on the Baseball Diamond*. New York: Macmillan, 1989. 339 pp. $17.95.

Until quite recently, Western followers of Japanese baseball who relied solely on the American media for information were hard put to keep up with events; an occasional, brief AP dispatch on the Japan Series and a story or two on the feats of American players in Japan—Bob Horner, Warren Cromartie, Cecil Fielder— were about all that was available. Fortunately, that has changed now. *Baseball America* carries a regular column by Wayne Graczyk, longtime baseball writer for the *Japan Times* and the *Tokyo Weekender,* and distributes Graczyk's annual *Fan Handbook and Media Guide,* previously virtually unavailable in this country. David Falkner's 1984 biography of Japan's legendary slugger, *Sadaharu Oh: A Zen Way of Baseball,* is much more than just another "as told to" book. It offers fascinating insights into Japanese culture and ideology as well as the game itself. Jean and Joe Stanka's 1987 *Coping with Clouters, Culture and Crisis* is a first-rate wife's-eye view of the difficulties of adjustment faced by American players and their families in Japan.

The primary interpreter of Japanese baseball for American audiences, however, remains Robert Whiting. Whiting's 1977 *The Chrysanthemum and the Bat: Baseball Samurai Style* was the first systematic attempt to depict the nuances of the Japanese game within its sociocultural context, and, although the concentration on American players was a bit heavy for this reviewer's tastes, in general the work was highly successful. Now, twelve years later, the same author has produced a worthy sequel, *You Gotta Have Wa.* ("Wa" means harmony, a quality much prized in Japan, on the diamond and in everyday life.)

Readers of the earlier book should not be put off by the first few chapters of *You Gotta Have Wa.* My initial reaction was that Whiting seemed to have little new to say, and was merely rehashing points he had already made with the addition of some fresh anecdotal material. That first impression was wrong, however; there is much here that is new, and Whiting's entertaining style makes even the familiar stories enjoyable to read.

One minor drawback of both of Whiting's works is a lack of internal cohesion; each chapter seems to follow its predecessor more or less at random, in no particular logical order. This poses no great problem to the casual reader, since both books are uniformly interesting, but it does create difficulties for the reviewer who would like to comment about either work as a whole. Given the space constraints of a short review, I will focus on two chapters of *You Gotta Have Wa* that have no counterparts in the first book.

Chapter eleven, "The Schoolboys of Summer," is a fascinating analysis of the annual national high school baseball tournament at Koshien stadium near Osaka. A reader who has never spent a sultry August in Japan cannot imagine the level of interest generated by this two-week extravaganza involving forty-nine prefectual champions. Games are telecast continuously every day from 9:00 A.M. to 6:00 P.M., and seemingly every TV set in the country is tuned in to them. Those without access to television—cab drivers, for example—are glued to the radio coverage. A tremendous amount of local pride is invested in the performance of each prefectural team. The closest American parallel might be the March madness of the NCAA basketball tournament, except that many U.S. states are unrepresented in that, and some diehard basketball fans are left with no one to root for. If you can imagine something like the Indiana state high school tournament contested on a national level (think of the film *Hoosiers*), you will have some idea of the intensity of interest in Koshien.

As Whiting puts it, "To many Japanese, Koshien is more than an athletic contest; it is a celebration of the purity and spirit of Japanese youth." Symbolism is everywhere, from the opening ceremony, with forty-nine teams marching onto the field behind massed flags to the blare of a military band to the stereotyped, orchestrated cheers of the official rooting sections, completely indistinguishable from one another in their drab school uniforms; from the ritual postgame bows of the two antagonists, lined up on the first and third base lines, followed by a further obeisance by the winners to their loyal fans, to the tear-streaked faces of the losers as they frantically scrape small samples of the sacred Koshien soil into plastic bags, to be cherished for the rest of their lives. All of this is masterfully captured by Whiting. The Koshien tournament is the essence of Japanese baseball, and this is, by far, the best account of it ever written in English.

In chapter nine, Whiting examines a rare but growing phenomenon on the Japanese diamond: the deliberate nonconformist who rebels against rigid discipline and team harmony. Whiting primarily focuses on pitcher Suguru Egawa and infielder Hiromitsu Ochiai. The Ochiai case is particularly interesting. A gifted natural hitter, Ochiai quit his high school team no fewer than seven times because he could not tolerate the Spartan practices. At Toyo University he lasted less than a year, refusing to perform the menial tasks expected of all freshman players, such as washing the underwear of older teammates. After six years of industrial ball, he finally turned pro with the Lotte Orions in 1978 at age twenty-six. He won his first batting title in 1981 with a .326 average, and followed that with three triple crown years, in 1983 (.325, 32 HR, 99 RBI), in 1985 (.367, 52, 146), and in 1986 (.360, 50, 116). Throughout this time, he continued to scoff at the incredibly arduous traditional Japanese training regime: ". . . while his teammates went through long and hard pregame workouts that left them soaked with sweat, Ochiai would lounge on the sidelines."

After that 1986 season, Lotte fired its easygoing manager and replaced him with a martinet who refused to tolerate Ochiai's individualism. As a result, in spite of back-to-back triple crowns, the maverick slugger was traded over the winter to the Chunichi Dragons. He has continued to sparkle in a Chunichi uniform, but remains a figure of controversy. Chided by Sadaharu Oh for his relaxed approach to training, Ochiai retorted that ". . . if *doryoku* (effort) was Oh's motto, then his would be, 'Enjoy yourself and get rich.'"

There are, of course, numerous American counterparts of Ochiai; Jose Canseco and Dick Allen spring immediately to mind, or, in an earlier era, even Babe Ruth. But Japan is not the United States; it is a society in which conformity is taken for granted, where the most familiar proverb is "the nail that sticks up gets hammered down."

Still, Ochiai and Egawa and the other *shinjin-rui* (new breed) ballplayers discussed by Whiting in this chapter may be harbingers of things to come. In the ubiquitous Japanese *karaoke* bar, where customers take turns singing solo vocals of popular songs to taped instrumental accompaniments, three American songs are invariably available: "You Are My Sunshine," "Country Roads," and "My Way." I attribute no particular sociological significance to the presence of "You Are My Sunshine"; it is simple and easy to sing. The popularity of John Denver's "Country Roads," however, reflects a pervasive bucolic nostalgia in a thoroughly, but very recently, urbanized society. Every Tokyo businessman in his immaculate blue suit is only a generation or two removed from the rice field. "My Way" is the most interesting of the three—a virtual anthem to individualism. Although it is a song which very few Americans know well enough to sing in public, it is belted out nightly in hundreds of *karaoke* bars by thousands of ultra-conformist Japanese. One can only conclude that locked up inside every Japanese conformist is a nonconformist trying to get out, and that the exploits of Ochiai, Egawa, and a handful of other antiestablishment ballplayers, on and off the field, provide vicarious satisfaction to these closet individualists. Again, Whiting has identified a highly significant social phenomenon and elucidated it brilliantly through the medium of baseball.

This is not merely an excellent book on Japanese baseball—probably the best we have in English—it is also an outstanding analysis of Japan in general. I have used it as a text for a course on Japanese society, and several students commented that even though they had no interest in the sport, they learned a lot about Japan from reading the book. It is not without flaws—it could be better organized, there is a bit too much material on the American player in Japan—but, all in all, it is a first-rate piece of work. Perhaps the time is ripe for a comprehensive English-language history of baseball in Japan. If so, no one is better equipped to write it than Robert Whiting.

Stephen I. Thompson
University of Oklahoma

Gildner, Gary. *The Warsaw Sparks.* Iowa City: University of Iowa Press, 1990. 239 pp. hardcover $25; paperback $12.50.

On first glance, Gary Gildner's *The Warsaw Sparks* might appear to be of marginal interest to the avid, or even average, reader of baseball literature. This autobiographical memoir deals with the 1988 season that Gildner, then a Fulbright professor at the University of Warsaw, coached and managed the Warsaw Sparks in an eight-team league in Poland (a league that has existed formally only since 1985). Judging from Gildner's descriptions of the often erratic and uneven quality of play, the Sparks were, at best, an amateur team playing in an industrial league that was still in its infancy. The previous season the Sparks had not won a league game, and the best the Sparks seemed able to hope for was to be made "presentable." But one should never underestimate the power of a gifted poet (Gildner published five volumes of poetry from 1969 to 1984) who is a shrewd cultural observer and a lover of the sport of baseball as a game. Gildner fashions this seemingly unpromising material into a remarkably compelling narrative that takes baseball back to its true origins, to its pleasures and satisfactions as well as its frustrations, and to its universal meanings and rewards.

After Gildner received his call to manage the team, he encountered the constant frustrations of trying to train and develop players who knew little about the sport but who made up for what they lacked in experience with enthusiasm and tenacity. Determined to "turn these guys into a real baseball team," Gildner tried to mold them into a team of chatter, intense concentration, and consistency. However, as he came to realize, he was going against the grain of Polish national character as well as against the Polish outlook that confusion and disorganization are to be expected and accepted as part of life in a nation where a socialistic system has created much inertia and cynicism. The game that Mark Twain had described as "the very symbol, the outward and visible expression of the drive and push and rush and struggle of the raging, tearing, booming nineteenth century" has to be adjusted to the realities and customs of a foreign country where things operate differently. While Gildner's players benefit from his competitive intensity and his constant urging for more practice, they also demonstrate their own more casual approach or intractable idiosyncrasies, such as one player's tendency to sulk or go into a dark funk immediately after he has failed to make a play, or other players' inconsistent commitment to the team. Even the league rules are perplexing to Gildner. In a brilliant piece of invective, Gildner rails thus against the "knock down" rule that stops a game after a ten-run spread: "And piss on that God damn knock down rule. How could the Poles, who prided themselves on going against the odds—spending sixty years on horseback getting the Swedes off their backs, rising up with a ragtail army against the Nazis squatting on their faces—how in the hell could they stop a baseball game like Little Leaguers after only a ten-run spread? Didn't they know it wasn't over until it was *all* over?"

While Gildner never surrenders his competitive approach to baseball and his role as manager/coach of the Sparks, he does learn to adjust to the vagaries of Polish life and character as these determine the approach of his players to the game. His team does win games, avenging shutout embarrassments from the previous season and winning against teams they lost to in the first half of the season. When he begins to relax, Gildner and his team become absorbed in the game and isolated from all the conditionalities of Polish life. They experience the simple beauty of the game, its potential for making a team feel happiness and togetherness, and its emotional ebb and flow. For the Sparks, the most satisfying period of time is when they travel to Chelmzä for a summer-holiday series of practices and fourteen inter-squad games where the teams changed their major league names (starting with the Tigers vs. the Yankees) for every game. Without the pressures of long travel and uncertain lodging arrangements or the different peculiarities of the fields, which they have experienced in the first half of their league season, the two Sparks squads play a series of close, well-played games, as well as an exhibition game for fifty of the townspeople. It is a belated spring training camp that pulls the team together in a true communal situation. One is reminded here of the early origins of the game of baseball before leagues were organized and when the sport was still a curiosity to people, and a novelty even to the players. All problems during the team's stay in Chelmzä were resolved, including an unfortunate fight between two team members, and their stay was climaxed with a team banquet filled with "long toasts, really, to baseball and Poland and ourselves."

This memoir is about the education of Gary Gildner in Polish culture and life, and his reeducation in the meanings and rewards of baseball. At age forty-nine, Gildner's active career in baseball is long in the past of his Little League and American Legion participation, but, through his role as coach/manager of the Sparks, he rediscovers what the game can mean and what it can do for those who believe in it. In the tumult and heady confusion of Polish society in 1988, with strikes and tense antigovernment demonstrations, baseball provides a means of transcending the social condition. After the interlude of summer training camp, Gildner rushes through the second half of the Sparks season; and, eventually, even he betrays his loyal team members, who are expecting him to show up in Silesia for a big international baseball tournament in which he would coach one of the Polish national teams. He opts for romance rather than baseball. But they understand without a hint of accusation or disappointment, and the team finishes its season with three straight wins at home, beating the two top teams in the league.

All in all, this proves to be a remarkably satisfying season for Gildner, as baseball has served to bring him to a closer understanding of the Polish people and their particular condition and remarkably resilient and philosophical outlook. The experience also enables Gildner to examine and appreciate his own Polish heritage and background, especially his Catholic upbringing and his maternal grandfather, Stefan Szostak. His grandfather was an avid reader of Joseph Conrad, as well as a silent, almost inscrutable, man who spoke only Polish. Gary Gildner's father married into this Polish family. Gildner's 1987–1988 sojourn in Poland causes him to cross the territory of his own family life and youth, where two cultures interacted and created the life he knew in northern lower Michigan. While baseball serves as the focus for his narrative, many crosscurrents run through this book, creating a rich and densely textured memoir in which past and present overlap and fuse.

In many ways, this is a book about loss (the loss of a grandfather and father, the loss of youth, the loss of a past). But all these losses are somehow compensated for by their vivid recovery in memory, and by other rewards of the present (friendship and true camaraderie, the daughter and a woman friend who show up to be with Gildner in Poland, and the gaining of an understanding of another culture and its truly remarkable people). Having spent a year as a Fulbright lecturer in Poland from 1976–1977, I can truly understand Gildner's experiences with the people and with the peculiarities of Polish life. I have been to most of the places in Poland he describes so vividly and accurately, and the book brought back a rush of memories and impressions. In the end, I came to the same appreciation of the strength and patience of the Polish people and their remarkable ability to remain resilient in the face of almost constant frustration and difficulties.

Those looking for a book about baseball in its simplest and purest form will find *The Warsaw Sparks* a revelation and a delight. In an era of instantly-produced autobiographies of baseball stars or autobiographical records of single seasons, Gildner's memoir stands out, sparkling in its execution and its remarkable range of perceptions and understanding of the sport and of its resources for the human spirit. Baseball, after all, is a human text created by people, situations, the context of culture, and the structure and ritual of the game. Its greatest legends are the individuals who loved the game and served as its ambassadors, and Gildner and his Sparks meet one such legend when Stan Musial comes to Warsaw. Son of a coal miner from Silesia and Pennsylvania, Musial graciously answers questions, autographs picture cards, and says he's happy to see Poles interested in baseball. After reading this book, one knows that Gary Gildner, too, deeply loves this game and that he served as one of its ambassadors in his role as coach/manager of the Warsaw Sparks. And he gained more from the game and his involvement in it, and with the individuals of this team, than he could ever have hoped for.

Douglas A. Noverr
Michigan State University

Seymour, Harold. *Baseball: The People's Game* (Volume III). New York: Oxford University Press, 1990. xi & 639 pp.

Seymour is the well-known author of the first scholarly—i.e., reliable—history of professional baseball. Volume three of his book *Baseball* has long since been promised to carry his original narrative past World War Two, where the first two volumes ended. The story initially proposed for volume three, however, is now to appear in volume four. The third volume, here reviewed, represents a new, and in many ways exciting, departure for sports history. Instead of a book on the majors in the postwar period, Seymour has written an account of all "non-organized" baseball from the middle of the nineteenth century to the 1940s.

He begins with boys and their game. Along the way, this lengthy book takes up college and semipro endeavor; baseball in the military and in prisons; the sport as played by women and blacks; and softball. The treatment is detailed and encyclopedic. Many readers will relish the skillful, empirical compendium that displays Seymour's unparalleled knowledge of the game. On the other hand, I missed any sustained analysis of the material Seymour presents, the *point* of the collection of these baseball facts. For example, I found the minutiae of prison baseball absorbing, but was bored by the recounting of long-forgotten college games.

This volume of *Baseball* thus illustrates, I think, some of the weaknesses of the kind of baseball history that Seymour has done so much to create. Yet the author also hints at a more compelling way of studying American sport. The standard baseball histories of the professionals have followed Seymour in focusing on the recovery of the records of games, pennant races, individual achievements, and so on. These studies have fascinated many people because major league baseball itself has engaged such a considerable number of Americans over the last 100 years. Baseball in prisons, however, has not been of great importance to people and, consequently, interest in its development cannot be expected to be high. And we might expect that in another 100 years the standard lore of even major league baseball might be less significant to many individuals—just as baseball stars of the 1870s are of less concern than those of the 1940s and 1950s. The trouble is that much baseball history is antiquarian—of moment only to those devoted to the game; the history has not been connected to anything outside the game.

At the same time, Seymour intimates the potential of a different sort of baseball history. To show that his volume is not about the majors, Seymour subtitles it "The People's Game." Moreover, he has a useful extended metaphor to indicate the topics he covers: he sees the institution of baseball as a house—a sort of pyramidal structure—whose basement is founded on the love of children. Professional sport is only the top story (or penthouse), and, as paramount as it is, it exists only because it is supported by what is underneath it. This metaphor—particularly its idea of the boys in the cellar whose affection sustains the majors—gets at a more exciting perspective on the sport. We might, in the future, want to consider why, in our history, baseball came to have the power it has. Why did it mean so much to so many? Why did it nourish so many communities? How did it manage to insinuate itself into the hearts of Americans? Volume three of Seymour's *Baseball* provides much of the data to begin to answer questions like these.

Bruce Kuklick
University of Pennsylvania

Bess, Philip. *City Baseball Magic: Plain Talk and Uncommon Sense about Cities and Baseball Parks* Minneapolis: Minneapolis Review of Baseball, 1989;

second edition—Madison: William C. Brown Publishers, 1991. 48 pp. paperback $5.95.

Kuklick, Bruce. *To Every Thing a Season: Shibe Park and Urban Philadelphia, 1909–1976*. Princeton: Princeton University Press, 1991. 237 pp. $19.95.

Mythology grants baseball pastoral origins, furnishing such birthplaces as a Cooperstown pasture and Hoboken's Elysian Fields. Reality is not as bucolic; the Cooperstown tale has long been discredited, and we now know that structured games took place in Brooklyn before Hoboken's famed opener. Whatever it may have become in recent years, baseball was a city sport for much of its history. To frame its action and serve its spectators, baseball evolved a stadium form as distinctly American as a concurrent building type, the skyscraper. For almost a century, ballparks were integral with the industrial age's urban patterns, before being rendered physically and socially isolated objects through suburbanization and automotive hegemony.

There has been little serious writing on ballparks, and almost none on their design and role in the city. Now, two substantive new works help fill those gaps. Philip Bess's pamphlet is a manifesto on the design of stadiums and cities, as well as an explicit marketing tool for his stadium design services. Bruce Kuklick's book is a social history of a single important park.

Architect Bess formerly studied philosophy and theology, disciplines that sometimes impose solemnly on his discussion. His otherwise provocative essay charts the devolution of the ballpark since World War II, and proposes an alternative aimed at producing a more interesting game, more intimate viewing conditions for fans, and better integration of the stadium with its surroundings. Along the way, he gives reasons for the success of pre-1930 ballparks, punctures the opportunistic rhetoric of current stadium designers, fills us in on postmodernist city planning theory, and offers some cautionary economic analysis.

The heart of the book is Bess's Armour Field project (a.k.a. the SABR Urban Ballpark), a hypothetical design that received financial support from the Graham Foundation, the National Endowment for the Arts, and the Society for American Baseball Research's Ballparks Committee. Devised in 1988 as an alternative to the new Comiskey Park, it meant to show how a modern ballpark could embody certain vanished civic and sporting values. To this end, Bess designed an urban neighborhood with a baseball stadium and a city park as its centerpieces, and with most parking placed in garages. Armour Field is framed by real streets fronted by shops, offices, and housing. Residents can see the game from their upper windows, and fans can view the city from their seats. A Polo Grounds-like layout of short foul lines and deep power alleys makes for an "unfair" and lively game of 290-foot homers and 420-foot outs. Since structural columns block some seats, the upper deck can, theoretically, be closer to the field. Outside, the brick-clad stands look like a cross between Cleveland's Municipal Stadium and Chicago's vintage industrial architecture.

Armour Park would doubtless have been better for the south side than the new Comiskey, and probably would have been better for baseball, as well. Its design is especially commendable for its comprehensive treatment of an entire city district, but the park itself has flaws. Despite positing intimacy over unobstructed views, its average seating proximity to the plate and the bases is no better (and may be a bit worse) than at the impersonal new Comiskey Park. Many outfield seats face center field rather than home. Simplistic cost estimating methods are used to uphold the belief that Armour Park would be cheaper to build than Comiskey. Most drawings of the park aren't suited to reproduction, and are thus frustratingly murky and unrevealing.

This ambitious essay is also hampered by an inadequate format. The *Minneapolis Review of Baseball's* small pages originally dictated tiny type, and many of the four dozen illustrations which were so well-suited to advance Bess's arguments were too small to make their point properly. In the second edition, these flaws were retained and, on many pages, the type was damaged to boot. *City Baseball Magic* deserves to be published as a real book, with larger pages, more readable type, decently sized urban maps, and cleanly drawn plans of either Armour Park or a later and more evolved design paradigm. But even without these niceties, the pamphlet's core message still comes through: Ballparks of distinct character and architectural merit, compatibly set in functioning city neighborhoods, need not only be products of the past.

Bruce Kuklick's felicitous title makes me wish that the fan who haunts sports events bearing a "John 3:16" sign will turn up at Veterans Stadium with an "Ecclesiastes 3:1" placard, touting this book about the Vet's great predecessor. Written by a historian at the University of Pennsylvania, its focus is less on Shibe Park itself than on its interaction with its North Philadelphia neighborhood and neighbors. In lucid and graceful prose (whose quality, alas, is not matched by the book's photos and diagrams), Kuklick surveys the park's antecedents; its siting next to a hospital for contagious diseases; its birth as baseball's first "fireproof," and possibly most ornate, venue; the waxing and waning fortunes of the Athletics and later the Phillies; several implemented and unrealized expansions and remodelings; its dubious renaming as Connie Mack Stadium; and, finally, its drawn-out demise.

Shibe's abandonment resulted from neighborhood decay compounded by municipal apathy and ineptitude. Once a source of secondary (and sometimes primary) employment and small-scale entrepreneurial opportunity, and tightly linked with the local social fabric, it later became a foreign object in an increasingly impoverished and unsafe part of town.

Kuklick draws on written and cartographic records and on the memories of Philadelphians whose lives were touched by Shibe. The latter process can spawn incredible tales, such as a fan's claim that Ted Williams once hit a foul ball that eventually landed more than 500 feet *beyond* the right field fence. (A golf ball, perhaps?) But more often, these accounts give life to the saga of North Philly's most significant public building. They affirm a flourishing urban ecology where local boys could make the team (or at least find work as vendors), established players roomed in the neighborhood, and residents of Twentieth Street sold admission to rooftop stands and upstairs windows, much as denizens of Chicago's Wrigleyville do even to this day. The Philadelphia practice was halted in 1935 when the Depression-squeezed A's built their famous spite fence, raising the right-field wall from 12 feet to 50 feet and thereby creating bad blood that lasted at least into the 1950s.

After that, another kind of bad blood developed as the once Irish and Italian neighborhood gave way to the expanding North Philly ghetto. In a community neglected by a city government that favored downtown renewal, blacks resented the presence of a team and spectators whom they deemed racist; conversely, the overwhelmingly white fans experienced their trips to the park as forays into hostile territory. In 1964, the same year the Phizz Kids blew a "sure" pennant, four days of rioting and looting swept North Philly. Six years later, it was the fans' turn to riot; they ruined the Phillies' last game by destroying seats, tearing up sod, and carting off turnstiles and urinals. The damaged park stood empty for six more years, sapped by further vandalism, arson, time, and invasive vegetation. This eyesore was razed just before the city's tourist-oriented bicentennial summer, a link the author overlooks.

The book closes on a poignant note that addresses not just a ballpark but also, by extension, the human condition: "Meaning and the items that bear it are fragile. . . . There used to be a ball field at Twenty-first and Lehigh, but Shibe Park had its time, and then its time was over. In some more time it will be forgotten. It is good to remember it as long as we can, but we cannot expect to remember it forever."

Ballparks die, their memories die, and we all die. Yet there is a form of immortality that comes from memories being passed down through generations. It is a fine irony that this book will do much to soften its own conclusion; thanks to Kuklick's effort, Shibe Park will be remembered that much longer.

John Pastier
Los Angeles, California

Will, George F. *Men at Work: The Craft of Baseball.* New York: Macmillan Publishing Company, 1990.

George Will packed lightly for his foray into the Land of Baseball, leaving with only two satchels; but they would both be needed. One was brimming with his lifelong love of the game; the other was neatly piled with Will's lifelong relationship to intellectual matters (his father was a philosophy professor who also loved the game). The result was a book that is smart and close to the game.

Baseball, Will argues, is Cartesian. It is best understood when it is broken down into constituent pieces, mastered (i.e., studied carefully), then reassembled. Will goes about this task by breaking the sport down into four fundamental functions: managing, pitching, hitting, and fielding. Each of these elemental processes is epitomized by a true craftsman.

The manager for the postindustrial age is the Oakland A's Tony La Russa. His penchant for data gathering and analysis is well known, as is his studiousness. Will shows him to be every bit as serious and compulsive as one would expect. In strategy sessions, replete with a professional and motivated coaching staff (e.g., Dave Duncan, Rene Lachemann), massive amounts of quantitative and qualitative material are scrutinized closely in an effort to find some little edge. With La Russa, baseball has truly become a game of "tendencies" based on voluminous data. But, since he sees the game as high percentage, i.e., failure, he is also strategizing for the best possible risk. The contradictory union of risk and certainty of data analysis has bred the speed and power that La Russa has successfully put together on the Oakland team.

Orel Hershiser, the Dodger pitching standout, is Will's selection for pitcher. With one of pitching's most sacred records under his belt (59 consecutive scoreless innings pitched), Hershiser is considered one of baseball's smartest pitchers. He has developed deliveries that prevent the speediest runners from getting a jump on him, handled batters intending to bunt, and upset the timing of the best of hitters. But this chapter is also rich in the history of pitching. Will presents interesting insights into the historic battle between hitters and pitchers (e.g., the famous year 1968 when pitchers dominated as they had never done before, or the more recent impact of the split-finger fastball).

San Diego's Tony Gwynn is Will's choice for best hitter. Here, again, we have a player who has become completely dependent upon modern technology to perfect his craft. Gwynn, who collects and studies all of his at-bats, reviews his work meticulously in order to perfect the little things. Will details Gwynn's success at coming out of a slump by viewing hours of footage and finally noting a small but significant error in his mechanics. To arrive at this observation Gwynn actually counted the frames that elapsed between the release of the ball by the pitcher and his initiation of the swing. This chapter also contains fascinating discussions of issues related to batting. The controversy around aluminum bats is one intriguing example. His discussion of baserunning is another.

In documenting the success of the 1989 Baltimore Orioles, Will makes the case for the importance of defense, and his selection for the most impressive man at the position is Cal Ripkin, Jr. Considered the smartest defensive player by his peers, Ripkin, like all the others mentioned in this book, pays attention to details. He must know, for instance, how his pitchers will pitch a certain batter in order to position himself. Then he must know where in the count the batter and pitcher are, since that will determine the response of each. A history of the position of shortstop is also provided, and, as with all of these mini-histories, Will has the ability to choose the most important issues from among the multitude that accumulate around a game like baseball.

I am particularly interested in the way Will chose to go about examining the sport. To choose the metaphor of work was, considering Will's conservative-Republican background, an odd move. The discussion of baseball as craft and work is more likely to come from the other side of the political spectrum. Yet, his discussions are provocative and show considerable insight. Will's examination of the sport, while couched in work metaphors that reside in the past (i.e., baseball as a lengthy apprenticeship and as craft), is simultaneously situated in a post-industrial America in which success comes from mastery of technology, and in which the game is, in part, reduced to statistically-based decisions. At one point, Will even goes so far as to refer to Marx's relation between base and superstructure (in discussing the different impacts of wood and aluminum bats on the game). One has to wonder whether, now that Communism has failed in the East, it is at last safe for neo-conservatives to toy with it in their discussions. Watch out, George, you might be opening yourself up to charges by some self-righteous Right Winger of being a Communist sympathizer when the Cold War resumes at some point.

In selecting individuals as paradigmatic, one leaves oneself open to criticism. Social/cultural selection, for instance. In this book the issue of race is handled fairly judiciously by the inclusion of Gwynn. There is even a section discussing race and the attribution of traits (i.e., calling African-American athletes "naturals"—Will is critical of this). If there was a consciousness to Will's selection of representatives from differing backgrounds (and one assumes so as he went on at some length about race), then the absence of a Latino in this book stands out quite clearly.

In all, however, this book has an intelligence, depth, and clarity of purpose that makes it a standout.

Alan M. Klein
Northeastern University

Watts, Robert G. and Terry A. Bahill. *Keep Your Eye on the Ball: The Science and Folklore of Baseball.* New York: W. H. Freeman & Co., 1990. 213 pp. $18.95.

Adair, Robert K. *The Physics of Baseball.* New York: Harper & Row, Publishers, 1990. 110 pp. $16.95 hardcover; $7.95 paperback.

Baseball is a game that cherishes its pretechnological roots. The basic equipment is made of such low-tech materials as wood, leather, and woolen yarn. Players use rosin, pine tar, and dirt to improve their grip on bats and balls. And where else on the American scene is the use of chewing tobacco as widespread? Could anyone imagine Michael Jordan or Joe Montana ejecting blobs of tobacco juice while resting on the bench? Belying its nineteenth-century origins in the urban centers of the northeast and midwest, baseball still seems to conjure up images of a game played by a bunch of farmboys.

In this tradition-bound game, there is a decidedly antiscientific and indeed, anti-intellectual atmosphere. Only about 25% of professional baseball players have attended college; baseball teams strongly encourage prospects to go directly to the minor leagues out of high school. The athletes themselves live in a state of terminal adolescence, relying entirely on their managers and coaches for technical advice. Not surprisingly, baseball probably has resisted the offerings of modern science and technology more than any other sport. The use of artificial turf represents the only major encroachment, and the radar gun is gradually becoming an essential part of scouting and coaching. Nonetheless, other sports make far greater use of scientifically-based advances in physical fitness, training and performance techniques, and equipment design.

Against this background, what purpose is served by writing a book about the physics of baseball? It is difficult enough to convince the practitioners of the game that the laws of physics have any relevance to what they do. Despite this, there are a number of myths to be challenged and controversies to be examined. Does a curveball really curve? Can a fastball rise? Are aluminum bats really that much better than wooden ones? Does corking a bat give the batter a significant advantage?

The answers to these and other questions can be found in the two books under consideration here: Watts and Bahill's *Keep Your Eye on the Ball* and Adair's *The Physics of Baseball*. In both of these books, the power of analytical physics is brought to bear on the basic interactions of the game: the delivery of a pitched ball; its journey to the plate; the collision with the bat; the trajectory of the ball after it has been struck. Both books are written for the scientifically and mathematically literate; a basic knowledge of introductory physics and algebra is taken for granted, and the ability to read and comprehend graphs is a necessity.

In comparing the two books, I found Watts and Bahill to be much the better of the two. The authors are both professors of engineering who, with their graduate students, have conducted laboratory research on various aspects of baseball, and who have each published several papers on their findings in physics and engineering journals. Much of their book is based on this research, and their expertise is clearly reflected in their thorough and fully realized expositions of the subject matter. Adair's credentials are somewhat less direct. A distinguished nuclear physicist at Yale University, he was a good friend of the late Bart Giamatti, and wrote the book initially as a technical report for Giamatti's benefit (in return for the honor of being appointed "Physicist to the National League"). Subsequently, at Giamatti's suggestion, Adair decided to publish the report as a book for the general public. While he is obviously a knowledgeable baseball fan of long standing, Adair is a relative newcomer to the physics of baseball, and his unfamiliarity with the existing research occasionally shows through. Most of his calculations and graphs are based on his own unpublished measurements and mathematical models, giving rise to occasional conflicts with the accepted theory. *The Physics of Baseball* is a rather brief, incomplete, but generally interesting work. On the other hand, *Keep Your Eye on the Ball* sometimes goes too far in the other direction of too much detail, and several pages will be intelligible, and of interest, only to other researchers in the field. Basically, everything in Adair is covered in Watts and Bahill in more detail, and the latter also includes some interesting material on the visual acuity of baseball players—in particular, their ability to track a moving object. Regrettably, neither book emphasizes what I consider to be the most significant fact that arises from a study of the physics of baseball—namely, the incredible level of skill required for major leaguers to pitch and hit a baseball with the consistency that we fans demand of them.

Despite the differences in style and depth, both books arrive at the same general conclusions. Yes, a curveball *does* curve. For years, the baseball media have tried to sell the myth that physicists consider the curveball to be an optical illusion, implicitly (and sometimes explicitly) intimating that physicists are all ivory-tower types who don't know one end of a bat from another. In fact, no physicist has ever claimed that a curveball is anything but real, and theories of why a spinning ball curves in flight have been proposed as far back as the seventeenth century. The rising fastball, on the other hand, turns out to be either an optical illusion or a matter of semantics, depending on your point of view. Physical analysis shows that a baseball thrown with a backspin experiences an upward force that only *partly* counteracts the downward pull of gravity; hence the ball cannot physically rise (i.e., go up, away from the ground) on its way to the batter. However, the pitch does "rise" in a relative sense, in that it does not fall as much as it would if thrown at the same speed with little or no spin. And it may very well be that, to the batter's eye, it appears to rise by contrast. Besides, if a fastball really did rise, what would happen to it if it were not stopped by the catcher—would it wind up in the mezzanine?

By and large, these are not books for athletes or coaches; learning the theory behind the curveball is not going to help you throw or hit one. It helps to be born with exceptionally good hand–eye coordination and quick reflexes; with good coaching and lots of practice, one may develop into an outstanding ballplayer. Otherwise, all the physics in the world will not help you get around on a 90-mile-an-hour fastball. Rather, these books are really for the intellectually curious sports fan who has an appreciation for the insights provided by the scientific method. Either book would also serve as a nice gift for youngsters who are showing some interest in science. While they will not understand everything there is to read, they will at least come away with the idea that physics isn't always the dull and abstract subject it is sometimes made out to be.

Peter J. Brancazio
Brooklyn College

Jennings, Kenneth M. *Balls and Strikes: The Money Game in Professional Baseball.* New York: Praeger, 1990. 273 pp. $24.95.

In *Balls and Strikes: The Money Game in Professional Baseball,* Kenneth Jennings reviews baseball's tangled history of industrial relations. His perspective is shaped by twenty years experience in the field and his current position as a professor at the University of North Florida.

The book is divided into three parts. The first reviews the history of collective bargaining in major league baseball. The second discusses the major participants, including commissioners, the media, agents, players, and owners. The final part of the book examines some contentious issues such as race, alcohol and drugs, and player discipline.

The principal appeal of the book is to a fan who would like a general descriptive introduction to the white-collar aspects of baseball. Jennings has relied on published material to give the reader a wide-ranging survey of the people and issues that have comprised this rich facet of the game. He mentions briefly the nineteenth-century labor wars, moves quickly to the Marvin Miller era, and covers in some detail the disputes between players and owners that have occupied baseball for the past twenty-five years.

Vignettes are offered about major league owners, managers, and players, but Jennings draws as readily from academic journals as from "jock lit." If the reader is eager to learn more, the generous use of footnotes points the direction. The anecdotes carry the discussion along, making the book accessible to most fans.

The final part of the book examines statistically some of the current issues about salaries and performance. The data are rather straightforward, as is their analysis. The author provides an undemanding entry into the quantitative side of collective bargaining in baseball.

For readers who are already familiar with front-office baseball, the book is less satisfying. Jennings is content to assemble the established record without much in the way of critical comment. His expertise in industrial relations should enable him to give us interesting ideas about this side of baseball, but he does not.

The book has no discernible major themes nor even any clear conclusions. The preface begins with the observation that "Player–management relationships in baseball are dynamic multidimensional phenomena." We either knew that already, or we can see it from the material that Jennings provides. He could have helped us understand more about the phenomena that he describes: again, he does not.

The organization of the book makes it difficult even to infer what Jennings thinks is significant about baseball's industrial relations. A chapter titled "Player Pressures and Problems" mentions Donnie Moore's suicide, corked bats, a bullfrog in Gene Michael's athletic supporter, race, and drugs.

The book breezes along through these and other topics, pausing when Jennings examines a particular labor dispute or financial claim. The casual fan may find the book interesting and entertaining, and the rest of us can hope that Jennings will take a narrower focus next time out, and tell us what he thinks about the front-office games.

Neil Sullivan
Baruch College

Forker, Dom. *Sweet Seasons: Recollections of the 1955–64 New York Yankees.* Dallas, Texas: Taylor Publishing Company, 1990. 220 pp. $18.95.

Madden, Bill and Moss Klein. *Damned Yankees: A No-Holds-Barred Account of Life with "Boss" Steinbrenner.* New York: Warner Books, 1990. 292 pp.

Read in tandem, these two books of markedly different genres constitute a poignant history of the rise and fall of baseball's premier franchise over the past 35 years—save for the pivotal decade (1965–76) of CBS mismanagement and the abortive rebirth under George Steinbrenner. The volumes are especially valuable to baseball historians precisely because neither is a traditional historical account of the Yankees as a business institution or a chronicle of the team's competitive achievements. Instead, we have a firsthand, intimate look at the personalities that determined the club's on- and off-field fortunes. Too often, scholars treat the components of the sports industry as bureaucratic entities, whereas these delightful, albeit disturbing, books remind us that sports franchises are but the composite of the people who comprise them at any given time.

A sequel to *The Men of Autumn* (1989), *Sweet Seasons* completes Dom Forker's "oral history" of the Bronx Bombers from 1949 to 1964. The format and execution of the volumes are the same—edited interviews with 55 players, enhanced by informative introductions to each interview, appendices containing statistical career profiles, and a mini-album of outstanding photographs. The strengths and weaknesses of the volumes are the same. The in-person taped interviews invariably are better than those conducted by telephone; the brevity of the interviews produces more banal chitchat than substantive reflection; the decision to interview only players seriously distorts the historical record; and the failure to press interviewees on sensitive topics such as racism and front-office relations both limits the value of the books as "oral history" and perpetuates a nostalgic, naive view of baseball's past. As compensation for such shortcomings, Forker, a veteran sportswriter, obtained valuable remembrances from role-players as well as superstars, succeeded in portraying his subjects as men as well as athletes, and captured the aura of seasons past. An inveterate Yankee fan, as is this reviewer, Forker admirably avoided taking an hagiographic approach to his subject. If the overall tone of the interviews is upbeat and the reminiscences focus narrowly on diamond happenings, what else should one expect from those who, for almost a generation, dominated baseball's autumn classic and enjoyed the sweetest seasons in the game's history?

The Men of Autumn and *Sweet Seasons* must be read and regarded as a set, but *Sweet Seasons* differs from the earlier volume in several important respects. Most significantly, it has all the flaws of a "rush job." Forker admits he wrote the book "in just eight weeks." The introductions are rather perfunctory, and the interviews are both considerably shorter and more superficial than those in *Men of Autumn*. Many (most?) of the interviews were obtained hastily during the 1989 Old Timers' Day at Yankee Stadium, and fare poorly when compared with those conducted under less distracting circumstances. The responses in other interviews, especially those conducted by telephone, are disappointing— as long distance interviews invariably are—because the subjects were unprepared, uncomfortable, or resentful of the imposition on their time. On the other hand, the interviews, collectively, are more valuable to the historian than those in the previous volume. Changes in managers and team success invariably led some interviewees to go beyond reminiscing about games and teammates. Comparative assessments of the managerial styles and talents of Casey Stengel, Ralph Houk, Yogi Berra, and Johnny Keane are revealing, as are comments about the reasons for the dynasty's demise, such as problems with the farm system and unwise decisions about coaching and administrative personnel. And while Forker left Joe DiMaggio out of *Men of Autumn* for want of an interview, he wrote "biographical sketches" for *Sweet Seasons* to compensate for those who declined interviews (Mickey Mantle and Yogi Berra) or had died (Elston Howard and Roger Maris).

While Forker has preserved for historians the recollections of players past, Bill Madden and Moss Klein, Yankees-beat reporters for the *New York Daily News* and *Newark Star-Ledger*, respectively, have combined to produce an invaluable firsthand, behind-the-scenes chronicle of the personnel and operation of the New York club from 1977 through 1989. Their analysis is clear: After the Yankees regained the heights of success with World Series victories in 1977 and 1978, "chaos, confusion, and craziness pervaded a once mighty and proud New York Yankee franchise and doomed it (damned it, if you will) to a decade of frustrating also-ran finishes."

The book's primary contribution is recording private, inside information of critical importance to historians that otherwise would be lost. Also valuable are the informed opinions of expert students of the game and their perceptive assessments of the personalities of key players in the tragicomedy, ranging from George Steinbrenner and Billy Martin to Bob Lemon and Reggie Jackson. (There is no reason to identify the low points of the story. They are well known and too painful to bear repeating.) As a bonus, their candid portrayal of the trials and tribulations of covering the Yankees during those calamitous years is the most revealing account of the world of the baseball-beat writer yet published.

The most damning indictment of the Yankee players and management is in the reading. That is to say, a sprightly written account of zany characters and bizarre happenings soon becomes so predictable as to become first monotonous and then boring. Like viewers of a poor Grade B movie, readers of *Damned Yankees* quickly come to anticipate what will happen and how it will happen pages in advance of the authors. There simply are no surprises or alternatives. That, perhaps, is the real tragedy of the Steinbrenner Yankees. Given the cast of characters, the saga of the team's demise simply could not have unfolded in any other way. Even the eventual denouement of both the franchise and its principal actors was predictable.

The New York Yankees have long been America's most loved and most loathed baseball franchise. Strangely, Yankee fans and foes alike will enjoy these two books. All will enjoy Forker's nostalgic trip to baseball of yesteryear and will learn much from Madden's and Klein's exposé of the contemporary baseball industry. (Indeed, even the most ardent Yankee-hater will likely feel sympathy for the team and its supporters because the plight of the New Yorkers, admittedly expressed to the extreme, is disconcertingly symptomatic of the state of the modern baseball franchise.) For very different reasons, this brace of books that record, more than interpret, the game's past are important contributions to baseball history.

Larry R. Gerlach
University of Utah

Sokolove, Michael Y. *Hustle: The Myth, Life and Lies of Pete Rose*. New York: Simon and Schuster, 1990. 304 pp. $19.95.

Michael Sokolove covered Pete Rose as baseball writer for the *Cincinnati Post*. But Sokolove is more than just a sportswriter, having won the Overseas Press

Club citation for his coverage of the U.S. Marine engagement in Lebanon in 1983. In a sense, Sokolove is covering another conflict, one between Pete Rose and organized baseball, particularly the commissioner's office during the abbreviated tenure of the late Bart Giamatti.

Although Sokolove admires Pete Rose the ballplayer for his hustle on the field, he finds very little that is admirable in his character. It is, of course, a major challenge to any writer to find new angles in the Rose story. But, through painstaking research and hundreds of interviews conducted with writers, players, managers, lawyers, baseball officials, and some unsavory police characters, Sokolove manages to do just that.

His profile of Rose is that of a veteran gambler who often refused to pay Cincinnati bookies. Eventually, his hometown bookmakers would no longer accept his bets and he turned to other, more unsavory characters, who eventually destroyed him. At least some of these bookies had mob connections, and this, clearly, was reason enough for baseball to ban Rose for life, whether he bet on baseball games or not.

Testimony from the likes of Paul Janszen, Tommy Gioiosa, Ron Peters, and some other unsavory characters helped to end Rose's baseball career and pave the way for a subsequent federal income tax evasion conviction and jail term.

Sokolove argues that rules were, from Rose's perspective, made to be broken. They applied to others, not to him. He believes that Rose carefully cultivated writers and sportscasters over the years and that they, club owners, and general managers anxious to put "asses in the seats," tolerated a great deal and often looked the other way. Both Bill Giles of Philadelphia and Bill Bergesch of Cincinnati are named in this respect.

One of the more serious charges made by Sokolove is that baseball itself, under Commissioner Bowie Kuhn, did not choose to pursue leads vigorously, despite existing evidence that Rose had been associating with sleazy gamblers for years. The author concludes that Rose associated with these gamblers for his entire 26-year career.

Sokolove portrays American baseball hero Rose as a self-centered adolescent who never grew up. He quotes Tom House, a Texas Ranger pitching coach who also holds a Ph.D. in psychology: "All professional athletes are in a state of terminal adolescence."

Rose's only admirable quality, Sokolove suggests, was his work ethic toward his job: baseball. He did give his employer and the fans their money's worth. Otherwise, he was not loyal to friends and couldn't maintain long-term relationships with teammates. He was an adulterer who violated even the morally-lax players' rule: don't mess around at home, only on the road. He neglected his children and had little respect for the truth.

Sokolove is hard on Rose, some might say unnecessarily so. Why beat a "dead horse"? But the author suggests that Charlie Hustle, now out of jail, may be "hustling" again, to regain support for an eventual spot in the game's Hall of Fame. Sokolove finds little evidence of real contrition or rehabilitation on Rose's part.

The author believes that baseball fans should learn from the sorry saga of Peter Rose, even if Rose has not. "We should," he says, "expect great athletes to be just as flawed as the rest of society—probably more flawed. We should honor and admire great athletes for what they do, not what they are," he concludes.

Perhaps surprisingly, after several hundred pages of detailing Rose's sins, character flaws, and general lack of redeeming virtues, Sokolove concludes that Pete still belongs in the Hall of Fame. Although no convicted felon has yet entered Cooperstown, Sokolove suggests that some already there were drunkards, adulterers, child molesters, and gamblers who were lucky enough to have Judge Kenesaw Mountain Landis look the other way. Landis, despite his reputation for toughness, could do that when it suited baseball's interest, Sokolove concludes.

John Molloy
Michigan State University

Robinson, Ray. *Iron Horse*. New York, London: W.W. Norton & Company, 1990. 300 pp. $22.50.

A self-professed admirer of Lou Gehrig since his school days when he attempted to interview the famed Yankee, Ray Robinson has, not surprisingly, written a laudatory biography of his hero. Although it contains little that is new about Gehrig, it does include a number of incidents and observations which reveal some of the Iron Horse's less admirable traits.

Extraordinarily self-conscious and inarticulate as a young player, Gehrig put off many of his teammates with his personality and his penurious habits. And although he clearly earned his fellow Yankees' respect as he matured as a player and as a man, Gehrig's persona of perfection, of rectitude, grated on many of them. Although he was solicitous of many of his teammates, especially the younger ones, a number of others resented his long silences and inability to communicate. "He said 'hello' when he showed up at spring training and 'goodbye' at the end of the season," one of his teammates commented. Aloof and introverted, "Loner Lou" did not take well to kidding. Moreover, he was hard on those who took their responsibilities as players less seriously than he did.

The press also posed problems for Lou, whose self-consciousness and essentially private nature led him to shy away from reporters. To many, Gehrig's photogenic smile was a shield for his insecurity. The author suggests that Gehrig's inability ever to master the art of small talk caused him much pain in his relationships with sportswriters. Once, when he learned that a person who had become violently ill after consuming a hot dog at Yankee Stadium was a writer, Gehrig snapped, "Good, they should have given the guy rat poison!"

Ray Robinson maintains that Gehrig "seemed to assign to himself the role of preserving, certifying, and codifying all rules of Yankee behavior. As well, he was the protector of what he perceived to be the Yankee image." Gehrig certainly stood in sharp contrast to his flamboyantly popular teammate Babe Ruth, who was the quintessential rule-breaker, the bigger-than-life figure who

176

led an often reckless life. And while Ruth carried on without penalty or public scorn, the serious Gehrig often looked rigid and self-righteous in comparison.

The book details the highlights of Lou Gehrig's record of playing in 2,130 consecutive games from June 1, 1925, to April 30, 1939, paying full attention to the personal qualities of courage, selflessness, and sense of duty which enabled him to set a record which may never be broken. A physical examination performed on the Iron Horse in the early 1930s revealed that he had suffered seventeen fractures of his hands, all of which had healed by themselves.

With one possible exception (the fact that the possessive and strong-willed Mom Gehrig made several road trips with the Yankees in the late 1920s), Robinson relates little that does not appear elsewhere about Lou's relationship with the two most important women in his life, his mother and his wife. The same can be said about his long-time teammate, Babe Ruth. The author, however, does well with Gehrig's final days as a player and the events between his farewell appearance at Yankee Stadium on July 4, 1939 and his death on June 2, 1941.

Although Robinson's book is generally well written, an occasional glaring cliché and unusual adjectives—"a seething ground ball"—detract. His frequently used device of describing a tangential American event or personality at the beginning of chapters, however, is forced and often annoying, doing little to illuminate Gehrig's personality or times. As a whole, the book is pleasant reading, and serves once again to remind the reader of Lou Gehrig's remarkable and inspiring career.

William G. Nicholson
Watertown, Connecticut

DiMaggio, Dom with Bill Gilbert. *Real Grass, Real Heroes: Baseball's Historic 1941 Season.* Zebra Books, 1990. 240 pp. $18.95.

Seidel, Michael. *Streak: Joe DiMaggio and the Summer of '41.* The Penguin Sports Library, 1989. 219 pp. $7.95.

American innocence is forever in danger of permanent eviction from the American psyche. If we Americans did not lose our collective sense of innocence at Valley Forge, then surely we lost it at Gettysburg. But innocence, American-style, apparently is a forever-renewable resource. In the two decades following Verdun and Versailles, American innocence was retired, recycled, and reborn. Then came Pearl Harbor. . . .

But before there was the seventh of December there was the entire summer of 1941. It was the last summer that America would be at peace until, well, until the next onset of the end of American innocence that accompanied the journey of the *Enola Gay.* The summer of 1941 was a summer of harrowing anticipation and narrowing concentration. It was a summer for worrying—and escaping.

And what better way to escape frightening realities and to preserve that uniquely American sense of innocence than to spend the summer of '41 at the ballpark? In Michael Seidel's retrospective journal, *Streak: Joe DiMaggio and the Summer of '41*, events between and beyond the foul lines are interwoven into a single tapestry of an America still at play, even as it was an America on the eve of war. In the process, heroes in nonmilitary uniforms helped assure that American innocence would be preserved for brief stretches of time on patches of "real grass."

In particular, by the end of the summer of 1941, two men in baseball uniforms methodically were adding luster to their names and providing riveting diversions to millions of Americans. One, Ted Williams, was a man-child composed of equal parts single-minded passion and indiscriminate venom; the other, Joe DiMaggio, was an immigrant's son with extraordinary innate grace.

This was for baseball fans, above all, the summer of the Joe DiMaggio streak, the summer that gave the number 56 meaning, purpose, and proportion that it continues to possess for anyone who has ever wondered when and where Joe DiMaggio might have been going, going, gone. And yet Joe D. ended his season with a batting average which stood at a mere .357, placing him a whopping 49 points beneath the last .400 hitter in major league baseball. In fact, DiMaggio didn't even finish second to Williams in 1941. Cecil Travis of the Washington Senators wedged himself barely between them at .359.

Still, this will forever be remembered as Joe DiMaggio's year. More accurately, it was DiMaggio's two months between May 15 and July 17—with an epilogue over the course of a sixteen-game mini-streak which followed Game 57. *The* streak began innocently enough. After going 0–3 against Cleveland on May 14, DiMaggio singled in the first inning of a game with the White Sox at Yankee Stadium. It would be his only hit of the day, and it drove in the only run in a 13–1 loss. Nothing memorable here. In fact, the day might have remained memorable only because it happened to be Jimmy Dykes's final day as a player, thus ending the White Sox infielder's twenty-two-year career and triggering Jimmy Dykes Day at the stadium.

Actually in late May, 1941, DiMaggio was working his way out of a frustrating slump, and his team was still looking up at the first-place Indians. According to Seidel, the Yankees were a "grim crew" when DiMaggio began his rendezvous with destiny. Their largely rookie pitching staff had been making a habit of blowing early leads. DiMaggio had dropped 200 points from his batting average during the previous three weeks. Moreover, the Yanks were five-and-a-half games out of first and "falling."

In another part of the world, Rudolf Hess had fallen, too. On May 10, the deputy Führer had descended by parachute into Scotland, en route to a dubious streak of his own, as an inmate in Spandau Prison. In the short term, the Yankees proved to be more fortunate. Thanks in no small measure to DiMaggio, the team managed to reverse its free-fall and win yet another pennant in a romp.

But we are getting too far ahead of our story. Just when did the DiMaggio "streak" become recognizable? In *Real Grass, Real Heroes*, Dom DiMaggio and Bill Gilbert point to June 2 and Game 19. Joe singled and doubled off Bob Feller in a 7–5 loss to the Indians. This broke a Feller streak of three straight shutouts and 31 scoreless innings. Meanwhile, *The New York Times* began to notice another string: "DiMaggio, incidentally, has hit safely in nineteen straight games." Still, Joe DiMaggio was not the baseball—or even the Yankee—story of the day. On June 2, 1941, Lou Gehrig died.

It was the story of another Yankee first baseman with a modest streak of his own which leads Seidel to lobby for May 28 and Game 13 as the day that the baseball public became conscious of the streak. Columnist Dan Daniel was traveling with the team and following the sudden emergence of first-year player Johnny Sturm, who would play only this single year before suffering a career-ending injury in World War II. Why was Daniel interested? Because young Sturm was on a tear of his own. And Dan Daniel knew a story when he saw one. And Michael Seidel recognized a source when he interviewed him. "One can still hear pride and a kind of quizzical resentment in Sturm's voice that make otherwise obscure games come alive. DiMaggio himself told me he had largely forgotten the earlier games . . . which Sturm remembers."

According to Sturm, "all the writers were keeping tabs. They noticed as soon as I started. But DiMaggio already had a head start and no one sensed it—not even him. Pretty soon I stopped and Joe kept going." But before he stopped, Dan Daniel noticed. Game 13 "saw all three hitting streaks on the Yankees continued. DiMaggio hit in his 13th consecutive contest, Sturm in his 11th, and Crosetti in his 10th."

This may sound as though Daniel had been charting his trio for days. In truth, he hadn't. Dan Daniel's real interest was in the rookie Sturm. But he did begin to notice DiMaggio. Soon the entire country would.

Fellow players began to pay attention as well. But brother Dominic DiMaggio remembers that most players kept at least part of one eye on the news from the draft board. In June, the Selective Service announced that the initial limit of 900,000 men would soon be lifted. But for brother Joe, things continued to be good, in fact very good—until Game 38. The place was Yankee Stadium. The opponents were the lowly St. Louis Browns. And George Sisler's modern-day record of 41 straight games was within DiMaggio's sight. In the fourth inning, the hitless DiMaggio bounced a grounder to Browns shortstop John Berardino (now Dr. Steve Hardy of *General Hospital* fame), "who muffed it for an obvious error" (in Seidel's view). Official scorer Dan Daniel agreed, much to the displeasure of a small, but vocal, crowd of 8,692. To complete the cycle, Dom DiMaggio sides with the historian and the scorer: it was a "gutsy call." And almost the end of brother Joe's "streak."

With the Yankees ahead 3–1 in the 8th (and with DiMaggio still hitless), Tommy Henrich walked to the plate with a runner on and one out. Then he made an abrupt U-turn to the dugout for a chat with manager McCarthy. The result of their brief exchange was, in Seidel's view, the "first strategic move of the streak calculated solely for DiMaggio's benefit." Fearful of a double play, McCarthy agreed to let Henrich bunt, even though this was an "odd bit" of baseball strategy with a two-run advantage at this stage of the game. Brother Dominic agrees: "You don't bunt with a two-run lead in the 8th inning. But then, when do you ever have a teammate trying to make baseball history right behind you in the batting order?" Given a final reprieve by a successful Henrich bunt, DiMaggio lined the first pitch for a double. Sisler was still in his sights.

Yankee pitcher Marius Russo, who took a no-hitter into the 7th inning, told

Seidel that it was this game that first made him aware "how riveting DiMaggio's streak was for player and fan alike. Here he was throwing a no-hitter, and not a soul in the ballpark gave a damn." By the time June drew to a close, few fans anywhere gave a damn that Ted Williams was hitting a gaudy .412. More precisely, Williams was hitting .441 (to Joe's .380) over the comparable stretch of what had become a 38-game streak.

In fact, not even the theft of DiMaggio's favorite bat mattered. During a June 29 double-header at Griffith Stadium, DiMaggio surpassed Sisler with a long double in the first inning of the first game and a clean single in his final at-bat of game two. The latter was achieved with a borrowed Henrich bat, Joe's piece of wood having been swiped between games.

Historian Seidel and memoirist Dom DiMaggio agree that this was obviously a moment for Joe DiMaggio to treasure. The Sisler mark meant more to him than did the 44-game skein of Wee Willie Keeler. "Everybody" knew about Keeler, recalls brother Dom. But who had heard of his streak? Certainly, neither DiMaggio had. Besides, the rules of that era tainted all batting marks, because no strike was charged when a foul ball was hit. "Everybody?" Not brother Joe. If Seidel is correct, he had only learned of Keeler's existence a few days earlier. And the Keeler streak? "Hell," said Dom to Seidel, "I thought they made it up."

As fate would have it, Joe tied Wee Willie in the second game of a double-header against the Red Sox. In the first game, another, as yet unmatched, Yankee streak ended: 25 consecutive games in which a New York Yankee had homered—until the wrong DiMaggio (Dom) hit the game's only four-bagger in Game 43 of "the streak."

After Joe DiMaggio passed Keeler, the streak "entered a less intense, though no less wondrous phase." No less wondrous was Ted Williams's dramatic ninth inning home run which gave the American League a 6–5 All-Star Game victory in Detroit. Upstaging his Yankee rival was already a Williams specialty.

Perhaps it was a new realization of that rivalry which drove DiMaggio on. In the eleven games after breaking Keeler's record, Joe went 24 for 44. Which takes us to game 56 in Cleveland's old League Park. DiMaggio rapped out three hits, leaving him at .375 for the season. Williams, meanwhile, had slipped to .395. Catching him was not yet out of the question. But the more immediate DiMaggio objective was to better his own 61-game hitting streak, established in 1933 when he played for his hometown San Francisco Seals.

Neither goal would be achieved, with immediate thanks to Ken Keltner and ultimate thanks to Ted Williams. According to Dominic, Keltner "was the one who had the most to do with stopping Joe." Not one, but two, DiMaggio shots down the line were backhanded by Keltner, whose momentum carried him beyond the third base chalk lines. "When he straightened up to make his throws, he was behind the bag and both of his feet were still in foul territory. Both his throws were strikes to Oscar Grimes at first base." To Seidel, it was simply acrobatic "skullduggery."

Why was Keltner playing DiMaggio so close to the line? He told Seidel that he was thinking less about the streak than about this series being the last serious chance to challenge the Yankees in a pennant race that was soon to disappear. The decision was purely tactical: both Indian pitchers, Jim Bagby and Al Smith, were left-handed; DiMaggio often drove balls down the line when a southpaw was on the mound—and he seldom bunted.

Ken Keltner has gained a measure of fame as a footnote to the DiMaggio story. But Bob Feller told Seidel that Keltner was "simply the best (third baseman) in the American League." The single most intriguing Seidel source, Johnny Sturm, called him a "hell of a ballplayer." But Dominic DiMaggio notes that the Indian third baseman "wasn't thrilled" by such compliments at the time. A two-run Indian rally in the bottom of the ninth was not enough to overcome the Yanks, who held on for a 4–3 win.

But the streak was history. Eight years later, Dom DiMaggio set the Red Sox record by hitting safely in 34 consecutive games. Vic Raschi of the Yankees stopped him. "And who made the catch on my last time up? Joe."

Dom DiMaggio has written an affectionate, candid, and occasionally bittersweet memoir about an era of baseball history which he wants to believe is not to be duplicated. Not only were the grass and the heroes more "real," but so was the owners' stinginess. Joe's reward for his 1941 season was a wartime contract calling for a $5,000 pay cut. Dominic is mum on his own salary negotiations, but he is quick to note that he, too, had a good year in 1941, hitting .283 in his second full season and finishing third in runs scored, behind Ted Williams and Joe DiMaggio.

In fact, in their separate ways, Dominic DiMaggio and Michael Seidel both assume that the heroes of that era were more "real." Why? Perhaps because the times seemingly were less complicated. Maybe so, although neither book is simply an exercise in nostalgia. True, both books include running lists of popular movies and songs from the summer of 1941. But were the times all that less complicated? They may seem so in retrospect, but, at the time, they surely were not. Impending war—and the ongoing baseball wars—complicated life— even for a comic-book-reading Joe D. Innocence is always a retrospective state of mind. And the apparent end of American innocence is never obvious to those Americans who happened to be at play—or work—in the midst of its subsequently reported demise.

John C. ("Chuck") Chalberg
Normandale Community College

Pallone, Dave with Alan Steinberg. *Behind the Mask: My Double Life in Baseball.* New York: Viking Penguin, 1990. 331 pp. hardcover $18.95; paperback (Signet Books, 1991) $5.99.

Baseball books are getting more and more interesting. In the distant past, they were written mainly for younger teenagers and were concerned primarily with the benefits of clean living and the heroics of ninth-inning rallies. But the times, as folk-rock singer Bob Zimmerman once predicted, they certainly are a-changin'.

For example, former National League arbiter Dave Pallone, assisted by Alan Steinberg, has written a chronicle of what life is like in the big leagues for a strikebreaking homosexual umpire with a short fuse and a ton of barely suppressed rage. About the only surprise is that he lasted ten years in the majors before the inevitable explosion occurred that abruptly terminated his career.

Dave Pallone became a big league umpire in 1979 when he accepted an offer to become a "permanent replacement" for the regular umpires who, at the start of that season, went on strike for better wages and working conditions. When the walkout was settled, in May, eight of the replacement umpires were retained: Derryl Cousins, Dallas Parks, John Shulock, and Fred Spenn by the American League; and Fred Brocklander, Steve Fields, Lanny Harris, and Pallone by the National League.

Subsequently, the eight newcomers were ostracized by virtually all the union umpires and treated like social outcasts. On at least one occasion, one of the newcomers arrived in the umpires' dressing room to find the names of the three old-timers taped over their lockers, while SCAB appeared above his. Pallone's equipment was sometimes shredded, and his fellow umpires let him fend for himself, on the field as well as off. The shunning continues to this day; and although it is not the only reason, it must have contributed to the fact that of the eight who started as replacements in 1979, only Derryl Cousins and John Shulock remain on the job today.

In addition to entering the scene as a strikebreaker, Pallone had another strike against him, so to speak, in the macho world of professional baseball: his homosexual social urges kept getting in the way of his professional common sense. His attempts to stay in the closet were halfhearted, at best; and once he began to frequent gay bars in various cities around the league it was only a matter of time before his secret became public knowledge. Given the hostility many fans feel toward umpires in general, the antagonism his fellow umpires felt toward him in particular, and the public spotlight in which he did his job, his attraction to gay bars can only be seen as subconsciously self-destructive with respect to his professional career.

One of the best things about the book is its brutal honesty, particularly with respect to the author himself and his fellow umpires. Hardly any of them, least of all Pallone, come across as people one would want to spend much time with. The tight little circumscribed world of umpiring, with its rigid pecking order and don't-question-me attitudes, is hardly calculated to attract open-minded seekers after truth and wisdom, not to mention alternative life-styles.

Along with Lee Gutkind's *The Best Seat in Baseball, But You Have to Stand* (1975) and Larry Gerlach's *The Men in Blue* (1980), Pallone's book ranks as one of the most insightful ever published on the subject of umpires and umpiring.

Behind the Mask has another fascination as well: How Dave Pallone ever thought someone so quick-tempered and emotionally needy could carry on a covert countercultural life-style and simultaneously be a major league umpire, of all things, makes the book an engrossing case study in miscalculation and self-delusion.

Lawrence S.Ritter
New York University

O'Neal, Bill. *The Texas League, 1888–1987: A Century of Baseball.* Austin, Texas: Eakin Press, 1987. 389 pp. $12.95.

O'Neal, Bill. *The Pacific Coast League, 1903–1988.* Austin, Texas: Eakin Press, 1990. 364 pp. $14.95.

Bill O'Neal, a history professor at Panola Junior College in Texas, has produced two well-researched, solidly written, and reasonably priced minor league histories.

The Texas League history was written in commemoration of that circuit's 1987 centennial. Texas has long been a hotbed of minor league baseball. In fact, more cities in Texas have had minor league franchises than those in any other state. In many respects, the Texas League seems to have followed a fairly typical path. Unable to complete many of its early seasons, the league gained stability in the beginning years of the twentieth century. It ebbed and flowed through wars, depression, and major league expansion. The league possessed a typical mixture of future immortals on their way up (e.g., Tris Speaker, Hank Greenberg), local stars, and role-players. Particularly interesting are the hard-drinking Fort Worth Panthers, who won six consecutive pennants in the early 1920s and are considered one of the best-ever minor league teams. For many years, the Texas League champion squared off against its Southern Association counterpart in the popular Dixie Series.

Only the most avid fan can absorb one hundred pennant races in one sitting. O'Neal wisely breaks up what could easily become a numbing narrative with sidebars and asides. He takes an apparent delight in describing the league's numerous eccentrics; perhaps, it's that legendary Texas individualism. My favorite involves Snipe Conley, a Dallas spitballer in the early 1920s. It seems that the Wichita team, notorious for its pranks, surreptitiously applied creosote to the game balls. By the end of the game, the hapless Conley's burning lips were so swollen that he was unable to talk. We also learn details of the league champion treated to a night in the local red-light district by grateful fans, the player traded for a dozen doughnuts, endless practical jokes, and every promotional gimmick ever tried.

Most of the book is more mundane, of course. O'Neal carefully charts pennant races, new ballparks, league champions, and so forth. He does so in a curious format. O'Neal begins with a chronological narrative which takes up less than half the book. He then has separate chapters on all of the 38 cities that have hosted teams in the league, plus additional chapters on such varied topics as ballparks, media, and nicknames. The result is as much encyclopedia as history. Although this approach makes finding specific information fairly easy, it leads to considerable redundancy. The book is enhanced by a player and city index, a comprehensive statistical appendix, and a good selection of pictures.

It's easy to see why O'Neal would want to follow his Texas League history with a study of the Pacific Coast League, probably the most interesting of all minor leagues. Geographical isolation, benign weather, and steady attendance allowed the PCL to follow its own path. In some years a PCL team would play more than 200 games, leading to some truly astonishing statistics. For example, in 1929, Ike Boone batted .407, with 323 hits, 55 home runs, and 218 runs batted in. Players such as Boone, Buzz Arlett, Ox Eckhardt, Smead Jolley, and Frank Shellenback became longtime PCL superstars, while other locals such as Joe DiMaggio and Ted Williams went on to other things. Until the late 1950s, the league was characterized by unusual franchise stability and player continuity. Its ranks have included such glamorous cities as Los Angeles, Hollywood (complete with movie star stockholders), San Francisco, Las Vegas, and Honolulu (Hawaii franchise). In the 1950s, the league made an unsuccessful bid for status as a third major league.

These halcyon days ended when the Dodgers and Giants moved into the neighborhood. Forced to scramble for survival, the PCL ended up in some unlikely places—including Indianapolis, Oklahoma City, and Tulsa. The league eventually stabilized and regained its stature as an elite minor league.

O'Neal's PCL history has the same format as his Texas League history, along with the same attention to detail. It does contain one glaring mistake. O'Neal identifies Jackie Robinson as "the first black in the big leagues." Surely, the pioneering efforts of Moses Fleetwood Walker and other nineteenth-century black major leaguers have been documented sufficiently by now to warrant their inclusion in baseball's collective history.

O'Neal's two books are not written for a scholarly audience and, therefore, are not footnoted. Both contain useful bibliographies, however. Given the author's obvious research skills and academic training, many readers may wish for more detail on such questions as racial integration or the development of farm systems. Yet it would be unfair to criticize O'Neal for not writing books he never intended to write. Within their given parameters, both histories are comprehensive, entertaining, and highly useful.

Jim Sumner
North Carolina Division of
Archives and History

184

CONTRIBUTORS

Richard W. Arpi is currently an archivist for the St. Paul Companies and the Minnesota Historical Society, both in St. Paul Minnesota. A Twins fan, Richard is also doing research on the Northern League.

Jesse Berrett is a graduate student in the history program at the University of California, Berkeley. He has been a devout Red Sox fan since 1978.

Robert Cole is a professor of English and director of journalism at Trenton State College. His stories and articles on baseball have appeared in *Baseball Research Journal,* the *National Pastime* and *Best Sports Stories.*

Joel Franks' article on Charley Sweeney appeared in the winter 1987 issue of *Baseball History.* Joel teaches history and cultural pluralism at San Jose State University.

John B. Holway is the author of a number of studies of black baseball, including *Black Diamonds, Josh and Satch,* and the award-winning *Blackball Stars.*

W.P. Kinsella's award-winning baseball fiction is well known to enthusiasts. A collection of his stories, including some that have appeared previously in these pages, is forthcoming.

Bill Meissner is the director of the Creative Writing Program at St. Cloud State University in Minnesota. His short stories have appeared in numerous literary magazines and newspapers. In 1989 he was awarded the Loft-McKnight Award of Distinction in Fiction. His book of baseball fiction and poetry, *Hitting Into the Wind,* will be published in '93 by W.C. Brown Publishers.

James E. Overmyer is a member of the Society for American Baseball Research's Negro League Committee. He is writing a book on Effa and Abe Manley, the owners of the Newark Eagles of the Negro National League.

Stephen I. Thompson, associate professor of anthropology at the University of Oklahoma, makes his second appearance in *Baseball History.* His current research is on Japanese popular culture, with particular emphasis on American country music in Japan.

AAV-3534

43.9

1-31-92